JOURNAL FOR THE STUDY OF THE OLD TESTAMENT
SUPPLEMENT SERIES
240

Sheffield Academic Press

A Biblical Itinerary

In Search of Method, Form and Content
Essays in Honor of George W. Coats

edited by
Eugene E. Carpenter

Journal for the Study of the Old Testament
Supplement Series 240

Published by Sheffield Academic Press Ltd
Mansion House
19 Kingfield Road
Sheffield S11 9AS
England

Printed on acid-free paper in Great Britain
by Bookcraft Ltd
Midsomer Norton, Bath

British Library Cataloguing in Publication Data

A catalogue record for this book is available
from the British Library

ISBN 1-85075-653-8

CONTENTS

PREFACE

This book of essays in honor of George Wesley Coats, Jr was occasioned by his early retirement, because of illness, from Lexington Theological Seminary. When I was asked to prepare a festschrift volume for Dr Coats I gladly accepted the offer. He has become a close friend and Old Testament colleague over the past nine years.

Each of the persons who have contributed articles for this volume has done so for various reasons: inspiration they received from Dr Coats to enter Old Testament studies, friendship that proved mutually supportive, scholarship challenges from Dr Coats's diligent pursuit of academic excellence in Old Testament studies, collegial relationships that developed in university days—but all have willingly taken part as a token of appreciation for his contributions to the development of Old Testament studies and his influence upon their lives.

The first two articles deal with a central concern of Dr Coats's scholarship—Moses (Rendtorff, Clark). Dr Coats's last book dealt with this theme (*Moses: Heroic Man, Man of God: The Moses Traditions in the Old Testament* [JSOTSup, 57; Sheffield: JSOT Press, 1989]). Most of the contributions in this volume deal with various hermeneutical approaches to the study of the Old Testament (Van Seters, Butler, Roffey, Stone, Carpenter, Blenkinsopp, Crenshaw), especially contemporary literary and structural approaches. The remaining essays deal with (1) the shift from historical-critical methods to literary/other approaches (Tucker), (2) the promise of reintroducing a life-changing approach to the Old Testament 'as story' into mainline churches and, finally (3) a consideration of the goal of all of these efforts—the production of Old Testament theology using all of the viable methodologies (Knierim).

Eugene E. Carpenter
Bethel College
Mishawaka, Indiana

ABBREVIATIONS

BASOR	*Bulletin of the American Schools of Oriental Research*
BKAT	Biblischer Kommentar: Altes Testament
B R	*Biblical Research*
BZAW	Beihefte zur *ZAW*
CBQ	*Catholic Biblical Quarterly*
ConBOT	Coniectanea biblica, Old Testament
EBib	Etudes bibliques
FOTL	The Forms of the Old Testament Literature
HAR	*Hebrew Annual Review*
IDBSup	*IDB*, Supplementary Volume
Int	*Interpretation*
JBL	*Journal of Biblical Literature*
JNES	*Journal of Near Eastern Studies*
JSOT	*Journal for the Study of the Old Testament*
JSOTSup	*Journal for the Study of the Old Testament*, Supplement Series
NCB	New Century Bible
NICOT	New International Commentary on the Old Testament
OBO	Orbis biblicus et orientalis
OTL	Old Testament Library
OTM	Oxford Theological Monograph
OTS	Oudtestamentische Studiën
R B	*Revue biblique*
SANT	Studien zum Alten und Neuen Testament
SBLDS	SBL Dissertation Series
SBS	Stuttgarter Bibelstudien
SBT	Studies in Biblical Theology
SJOT	*Scandinavian Journal of the Old Testament*
S T	*Studia theologica*
TS	*Theological Studies*
UF	*Ugarit-Forschungen*
VT	*Vetus Testamentum*
VTSup	*Vetus Testamentum*, Supplements
WBC	Word Biblical Commentary
ZAW	*Zeitschrift für die alttestamentliche Wissenschaft*

LIST OF CONTRIBUTORS

Joseph Blenkinsopp
Department of Theology, University of Notre Dame, USA

Trent C. Butler
Managing Editor, Broadman–Holman, Nashville, TN, USA

Eugene C. Carpenter
Bethel College, Mishawaka, IN, USA

Malcolm Clark
Department of Religious Studies, Butler University, Carmel, IN, USA

Rolf P. Knierim
School of Theology, Claremont, CA, USA

Rolf Rendtorff
University of Heidelburg, Germany

John W. Roffey
St Barnabas Theological College, Belair, Australia

Lawson Stone
Asbury Theological Seminary, Wilmore, KY, USA

Gene M. Tucker
Candler School of Theology, Emory University, Atlanta, GA, USA

John Van Seters
Department of Religious Studies, University of North Carolina, Chapel Hill, NC, USA

SOME REFLECTIONS ON THE CANONICAL MOSES:
MOSES AND ABRAHAM

Rolf Rendtorff

The figure of Moses was one the major topics of George Coats's scholarly work. Conversely, he was one of the great interpreters of this
central biblical figure. Consequently, while working in the field of Pentateuchal traditions and theology I made constant use of George's ideas
and interpretations of the Mosaic traditions.

Dr Coats analysed the traditions about Moses, the 'Heroic Man, Man
of God' as he memorably called him, with great skill, while showing a
sensitivity for the present form of the canonical texts into which the
different traditions had been worked and shaped. I want to go a step
further in the last mentioned direction. It is a very complex image of
Moses that is presented by the Pentateuchal texts, but the question is
whether the different traditions and aspects are simply put beside one
another to form a coherent whole. Furthermore, how does the image of
Moses in the Pentateuch relate to certain aspects of the image of Moses
found outside the Pentateuch?

I will try to imagine how the *readers* or *listeners* received and
understood the biblical texts in their final form. This is a kind of canonical reading because my interest is focused on the text in its given,
canonical form. Yet I want to concentrate first of all on exegetical
questions such as the structure of the text and the intertextual relations
of certain narrative elements, while leaving aside certain specific theological or even Christian theological aspects that sometimes are related
to the term 'canonical'. Those theological questions are not unimportant. But I believe that there are so many interesting and important
exegetical questions to be asked in the framework of a canonical reading
that I want to concentrate on them.

Within the limited framework of this essay I can present only a few
examples of this kind of canonical reading, and I will deal mainly with

the first chapters of the Moses story; hence the title: 'Some Reflections on the Canonical Moses'. As the subtitle indicates, it is mainly one aspect that will come to the fore: the relation of the image of Moses to the image of Abraham.

1. I begin with some observations about the way Moses is introduced into the story. It is often said that Exodus 1 is just a kind of introduction to the birth of Moses. This is only half the truth. In the birth story (Exod. 2) no allusion is found to the preceding story of the midwives. And more importantly, the birth story itself contains no hint about Moses' future nor about the relations Moses maintained with his origins. Of course, the circumstances of Moses' birth and the way he came to the pharaonic court is a very peculiar story, so that the reader expects something extraordinary. However, no information is given to the reader about what will follow as is the case in comparable birth stories such as those of Samuel (1 Sam. 1–2) or of Samson (Judg. 13) where it is clearly announced that something extraordinary will happen to this child. This is not the case with Moses. And nothing is said with regard to Moses' relationships to his people. His mother served only as his wet-nurse and could not have told him very much about his background, and even less about the religion and history of his own Hebrew people. In ch. 2, in Midian, Moses is regarded by the Midianites as an Egyptian (Exod. 2.19). So this part of the story does not give any hint to a future role Moses might play in the history of his people.

The brief two-part story in Exod. 2.11-22 is ambivalent in this respect. It is stated that after many years, when Moses had grown up, he went out one day 'to his brethren' (v. 11). We are not told how Moses knew about his relationship to the Hebrew slave labourers. Most commentators mention this lack, but no one gives an explanation for it.[1] It seems to me that this is one of the points where we have to read the story on two levels. The reader knows certain things that are not explicitly told. But here the situation is particularly ambivalent because it is not quite clear where Moses belongs. The commentators seem to be too quick to jump over this ambivalence. Childs, for example, says, 'Moses goes out to look with sympathy on the toil of his kinsmen', and

1.   B.S. Childs (*Exodus: A Commentary* [OTL; London: SCM Press, 1974], p. 30) writes, 'No words in the story are wasted...'; similarly T.E. Fretheim (*Exodus* [Interpretation; Louisville, KY: John Knox, 1991], p. 41): 'The narrator wastes no time...'

'the concern focuses on Moses' purposeful seeking out his kinsmen'.[2] But the text does not say anything like this. It does not say *why* Moses went out. It just says, 'He went out, and he saw' (v. 11). Also Moses' identification with the Israelites is quite vague. On the one hand the text speaks of 'his brethren' (v. 11). But, on the other hand, Moses could only behave as he did because he was not identified with the Israelite slave labourers, but obviously looked like a member of the Egyptian higher society. On the second day (2.13) even his kinsmen did not accept the role Moses claimed. Moses seemingly remains in limbo, neither clearly a Hebrew nor an Egyptian.

The narrator desires to make two points: (1) to demonstrate Moses' feelings of justice and his readiness to act on behalf of the underdog, and (2) to report the conflict that finally led to Moses' flight. There is a further interesting remark. On the second day the one at fault (רשע) between the two Hebrews asked Moses, 'Who made you a ruler and judge over us?' (v. 14). At this point it is just a rhetorical question that has to be answered by 'No one did.' But later on we learn that God did exactly that: he made Moses a judge over his people (18.13-27). Here again we have to read this story on different levels. The reader knows more than the persons acting, but should not confuse these two levels.

On the narrative level Moses fails and then has to flee. When he arrives in Midian the story comes to a reasonable conclusion. He marries and settles there. Of course, in Midian at the well the story gives still another example of Moses' acting on behalf of the underdog, in this case the daughters of the Midianite priest. But it is important to pay attention to the actual language of the story: 'He consented to stay', ויואל לשבת (v. 21), not just as a visitor but as a *ger*, a permanent resident, so to speak, with wife and children. We could compare this expression with the story of the Levite in Judges 17. The Levite left his home town Betlehem 'to live wherever he could find a place'. When Micah sought to have him stay with him and to become his priest the story says, 'He consented to stay' ויואל לשבת (v. 11). And again the story comes to an end.

I want to emphasize that these two brief stories in Exodus 2 are not only an introduction to what follows, but that they cover an independent chapter in the story the book of Exodus tells us. This first

2.   Childs, *Exodus*, p. 30.

chapter was a failure, and it ends without any prospect of a better
future. To understand this is important for two main reasons. One is
that Exodus 3 may now begin exactly at this point. Moses is a semi-
Egyptian shepherd in the service of a certain Midianite, and nothing
else. (I will come back to that.)

The other reason lies in the importance of the last three verses of
ch. 2. Earlier commentators were satisfied to identify these verses as
'P' and then more or less to ignore them. More recent commentators
have begun to understand the importance of this vital piece of text. This
is the case with Brevard Childs's commentary of 1974 and even more
explicitly with Terence Fretheim's of 1991—he spends three pages of
his commentary on these three verses. In my view the most important
element in this paragraph are the words, 'And God remembered his
covenant with Abraham, Isaac and Jacob' (v. 24). These words show
clearly that these verses are to be understood as an integral part of an
overarching theological concept of the Pentateuch. That God will
remember his covenant is one of the crucial elements in his first establishing of a covenant with Noah. God promises that he will remember
his covenant every time there is a situation that looks as if a new flood
could be on the way. At that time he will remember the covenant, 'and
the waters shall never again become a flood to destroy all flesh' (Gen.
9.14-16). To remember is a crucial part of God's covenant.

This is what happens in Exod. 2.23-25. God had established his
covenant with Abraham and the other patriarchs. Now it looks as if
Abraham's descendants will continue to suffer under Egyptian oppression without any hope. At this point God remembers (זכר) his
covenant. From Genesis 9 we know that this does not at all mean that
he had forgotten his covenant previously (cf. 8.1). It does mean that
now the point has come when God, by reason of his covenant, is going
to act on behalf of his people. For the moment none of the Israelites—
or Hebrews, as they are called in the story—knows about God's
remembering, Moses included. But the reader knows and understands
that now God is about to act.

We will follow this line for a moment. In Exod. 6.5 it is repeated that
God remembered his covenant. But then God says this to Moses within
the framework of a highly sophisticated theological speech. We have to
read these texts in Exodus 2 and 6 in continuation. First God decided
to act, but then he—or, of course, the author of the text—explains this
to Moses and to the reader in its theological context.

Let me offer here a brief remark on synchronic and diachronic reading. It is obvious that these texts are only comprehensible as elements of a theological composition of the Pentateuch as a whole and not as an independent source. All the priestly key texts are closely related to their non-priestly context. This is clearly the case with Exod. 6.2-8. This text plays a crucial part in the priestly composition of the Pentateuch. We have to read it in relation to Genesis 17. In Genesis 17 the covenant with Abraham was established; now in Exodus 6 God will draw the consequences of his promise given to Abraham and will rescue his people. But there are some more important relations between the two texts. One is with regard to the so-called covenant formula, the *Bundesformel*. This formula appears first in Genesis 17 where God says to Abraham, 'I will establish my covenant between me and you, and your offspring after you... *to be God to you and to your offspring after you*' (v. 7). This is, so to speak, the first half of the covenant formula: to be God to you. This formula is here presented as the very essence of the covenant: *I will establish my covenant—to be God to you*. Now, in Exodus 6 there appears the two-part formula: 'I will take you as my people, and I will be your God'. Only since the beginning of Exod. 1.1-7 does Israel exist as people. The word עַם, referring to Israel, appears first in Exod. 1.9 when the Pharaoh speaks about עַם בְּנֵי יִשְׂרָאֵל. Now God confirms what he has promised to Abraham, at the same time expanding it to the whole people that arose from Abraham's offspring.[3]

This shows a very important connection between Abraham and Moses. This relation also appears in the changing of the formula of God's self-representation. In Genesis 17 he represents himself by 'I am El shaddai' (v. 1); now in Exodus 6 he says 'I am the LORD', explaining explicitly that he did not yet speak that way to Abraham, and then repeating this formula several times within this paragraph (vv. 2, 6, 8; cf. 7). Hence the author indicates that Moses is the real successor of Abraham, but in a totally different role. Now the people of Israel exist and Moses stands between God and the people. But before pursuing the similarities and differences between Abraham and Moses, I have to go back to where we left Moses, as he was herding the flock of his Midianite father-in-law.

2. At this point Moses is not prepared in any way to receive a

3. Cf. R. Rendtorff, *Die 'Bundesformel': Eine exegetisch-theologische Untersuchung* (SBS, 160; Stuttgart, 1995).

divine call.[4] He is a shepherd, and when he comes across an unusual natural phenomenon, he is amazed. He hears a divine voice, but has no specific idea what kind of god might speak to him. Hiding his face, he is afraid to look at 'the deity' (הָאֱלֹהִים). The narrator is eager to emphasize that Moses *did not know* who the god was who spoke to him. Also, later in this chapter, when Moses speaks to God the narrator always notes that he speaks to הָאֱלֹהִים (vv. 11, 13).[5] Therefore, in the context of this chapter it is quite consistent for Moses to ask for the name of the god who is speaking to him. It is interesting to compare this story to the call of Jeremiah, for example. When God speaks to Jeremiah he answers אֲהָהּ אֲדֹנָי יהוה (Jer. 1.6), which indicates that Jeremiah knows who is speaking to him. Moses does not. Thus, one side of the story.

The other side is quite different. God appears to Moses as he did to the patriarchs. The same verb is used, וַיֵּרָא (v. 2), as is used when God appears to the patriarchs, beginning in Gen. 12.7 and then several more times. Here again, Moses is described as the successor of the patriarchs. God calls Moses by name, using the name twice as he had done with Abraham (Gen. 22.11) and Jacob (46.2), and Moses answers הִנֵּנִי as they did. Then God introduces himself, saying, 'I am the God of your father'—in the singular, adding the names of the three patriarchs. But then the difference becomes visible. God does not speak about the future of Moses himself, but of that of his people. God says 'my people', and it is the first time in the Hebrew Bible that this expression appears spoken by God. God repeats what the narrator has told us already in Exod. 2.24-25: God has 'seen' the misery of his people, he has 'heard' their cries and he 'knows' their sufferings (3.7).[6] Now God is going to send Moses to rescue his people. 'To send', שׁלח, is a technical word used for sending a prophet: 'Here am I; send me (שׁלח)' as Isaiah says

---

4. At this point Fretheim (*Exodus*, p. 56) explicitly contradicts Childs who said that Moses' call is 'a radical break with the past' (*Exodus*, p. 73). Fretheim sees more continuity with ch. 2.

5. Cf. R. Rendtorff, 'El als israelitische Gottesbezeichnung. Mit einem Appendix zum Gebrauch von הָאֱלֹהִים', *ZAW* 106 (1994), pp. 4-21, esp. 16-17.

6. This interrelation of Exod. 2.24-25 to 3.7 is another example for the intertextual relations of 'P' and 'non-P' texts. Cf. J.-L. Ska, 'Quelques remarques sur Pg et la dernière rédaction du Pentateuque', in A. de Pury (ed.), *Le Pentateuque en question* (Geneva: Labor et Fides, 1989), pp. 119-20; cf. also Fretheim, *Exodus*, pp. 41, 73.

(Isa. 6.8). Already we have the first elements of the prophetic task of Moses.

There are still more important connections to the patriarchal tradition to be observed. I will mention two of them. When Moses is frightened of the task God is imposing on him, God answers: 'I will be with you' (v. 12). This is exactly what God had said again and again to the patriarchs, in particular to Jacob on his dangerous wanderings, for example, when he fled from Esau (Gen. 28.15), when God told him to return (31.3), and on his way to Egypt (46.4). God will be with Moses as he had been with the fathers. And the word 'I am' אהיה as used in this phrase reappears later in the sentence אהיה אשר אהיה circumscribing the divine name (v. 14). And when Moses says to the Israelites 'אהיה has sent me to you' this element is still included: The one who will be with you has sent me to you. In Hos. 1.9 it sounds like a negative version of this: 'You are not my people and I am not your אהיה'.

The second relationship is perhaps even more important. In Exodus 3 and 4 there is a long, intimate dialogue between God and Moses. Nowhere else in the Hebrew Bible do we find such a direct dialogue between God and a human being, except with Abraham in Genesis 15 and 17. And, particularly, in Genesis 18, looking down on Sodom, God and Abraham talk to each other face to face. No one else had been honoured to speak to God in such a way except these two: Abraham and Moses. This also constitutes the difference between Moses and all the other prophets as is clearly stated in Num. 12.8 and Deut. 34.10. It would go beyond the scope of this paper to scrutinize the relations of the biblical traditions about Moses and the prophets in more detail. My point is to show that already here in the introductory chapters Moses is depicted in a way that shows his relationship to the prophets on the one hand and to the patriarchs on the other hand.

3. I would add one more point. In Exod. 3.12 God gives a sign to Moses saying:

> I will be with you;
> and this shall be the sign for you
> that it is I who sent you:
> when you have brought the people out of Egypt,
> you shall worship God at this mountain.

Most commentators find great difficulty in dealing with this verse. Of course, it points to Sinai. But commentators are rather vague about

the particular relationship this verse has to the later texts speaking of
Sinai. Yet if we are audacious enough just to read the biblical text as
we have it before us, it seems to me to be quite obvious that exactly at
the point where the Israelites arrive at Mount Sinai we find the reference to the words in Exod. 3.12. At the beginning of Exodus 19 it is
reported that the Israelites arrived in the wilderness of Sinai. And
then: 'Israel camped there in front of the Mountain, and Moses went up
to God', ומשה עלה אל־האלהים. How did Moses know what to do? And
how did he know that God was at this mountain? Of course, he knew
the place because he had already been there next to the הר האלהים
(Exod. 3.1), and God had told him when coming out of Egypt they
should worship God at this mountain על ההר הזה. In order to make the
connection clear the narrator uses the term האלהים in both cases: the
sign should be to worship האלהים, and Moses went up אל־האלהים. So
Moses had no problem knowing what to do. God had told him, at least
to begin by climbing up alone.

This is an interesting test of how consistent exegetes are in reading
the text synchronically. Most commentators interpret the text according to the pieces into which they had previously divided it. I have to
confess that even form criticism, the method which I have been trained
in, and which I still believe to be useful, under certain aspects prevents
us from reading the given text continuously. And I would like to
encourage a discussion on the synchronic and diachronic reading of
the text. Of course, I am not so naive as to ignore or be unaware of all
the obvious indications of various diachronic levels within the texts.
But the question is, What happened when the texts came together into
the given context and shape? To what degree were those who brought
the texts together aware of certain elements of continuity? To come
back to my example. Is it scientifically defensible, feasible to read
Exod. 19.2-3 as a continuation of Exod. 3.12? If so, what are the exegetical consequences?[7]

4.   I will close here. I wanted to attempt a holistic reading of the
beginning of the Moses story. My main emphasis was to show the
explicit depiction of Moses as a successor of the patriarchs, in particular of Abraham. This relationship is developed in the narrative texts,

7.   Cf. my contribution to the Festschrift for Klaus Koch: R. Rendtorff, 'Der
Text in seiner Endgestalt. Überlegungen zu Ex 19', in D.R. Daniels *et al.* (eds.),
Ernten, was man sät (FS Klaus Koch; Neukirchen–Vluyn: Neukirchener Verlag,
1991), pp. 459-70.

as well as on the compositional level, in particular with regard to the 'covenant' and 'covenant formula'. God began to be the God of Israel through Abraham, he continued by taking Israel as his people through Moses. But then in the Moses story, certain specific elements of the prophetic image appear which I have not explained in detail in this paper. My main point is that it is not only a Deuteronomic tradition to call Moses a prophet, but that it is an intrinsic element of the Moses tradition from its earliest beginnings. It is the main characteristic of the figure of Moses in the Hebrew Bible to incorporate basic elements of all the main figures of the Israelite traditions. And more than this, for in the field of lawgiving, for example, Moses is not only the paradigm of later institutions, but he represents an authority beyond all institutions that ever existed in Israel. This assertion goes far beyond the scope of this paper.[8] But it seems to me that we should connect these quite different multi-faceted aspects of the figure of Moses. I do not believe that we would succeed in finding out much more about the 'historical Moses', but we should begin to see the different aspects of the biblical, the 'canonical' Moses together, in order to understand his importance and specific relevance for Israel in the time when the canon was taking shape. Understanding the relationship between Moses and Abraham could be one first step.

---

8. See F. Crüsemann, *Die Tora: Theologie und Sozialgeschichte des alttestamentlichen Gesetzes* (Munich: Chr. Kaiser Verlag, 1992), pp. 76-131: 'Mose als Institution?'

BIBLICAL AND EARLY ISLAMIC MOSES

Malcolm Clark

1. Introduction

George Coats in his book *Moses: Heroic Man, Man of God* argued for a tradition rooted in narrative folk storytelling of Moses as Heroic Man.[1] This tradition existed alongside a portrayal which focused on the acts of God and presented Moses, the 'man of God', as basically an instrument of God's acts which brought Israel into being. In this essay, I compare Coats's heroic Moses interpretation to the portrayal of Moses which emerged in early Islamic writings.[2] I will not be examining the development of the Moses traditions in the post-Tanak Jewish material,[3] elements of which were incorporated into the Muslim

---

1. G.W. Coats, *Moses: Heroic Man, Man of God* (JSOTSup, 57; Sheffield: JSOT Press, 1988).

2. I will neither challenge nor affirm Coats's acceptance of the traditional sequence of the Pentateuchal sources (JEDP) nor will I re-evaluate Coats's definition of 'heroic tale'. It is interesting that Van Seters, who views the source sequence as D, JE (exilic), and P (post-exilic), also comments that JE gives a distinctly non-heroic presentation of Moses who is 'totally dependent on the divine word from Yahweh for each action he takes' (summarized in his article on Moses in M. Eliade, [ed.], *The Encyclopedia of Religion* [New York: MacMillan, 1987], X, pp. 115-21). For Coats, it is precisely in the J source that the heroic portrayal of Moses comes through most strongly. I suspect that the difference between Coats and Van Seters rests partly on the particular definition of heroic. It is to be expected that just as mythic forms are substantially affected when incorporated into biblical or Islamic materials, the same would be true of heroic elements. Cf. S.H. Hurreiz, 'Afro-Arab Relations in the Sudanese Folktale', in R.M. Dorson (ed.), *African Folklore* (Garden City, NY: Anchor Books, 1972), pp. 154-63, for comments on what happens to myth in a specific Islamic context. For the modification of myth in the Tanak, cf. B.S. Childs, *Myth and Reality in the Old Testament* (SBT, 27; London: SCM Press, 1960).

3. A useful survey of Moses in the Jewish tradition is found in D.J. Silver,

traditions. The purpose is fourfold: 1) to examine what degree of congruence there is between the image of Moses in the Tanak and in the Muslim sources; 2) to ask if Coats's heroic Moses picture is sustained in the Muslim sources; 3) to see if there is anything in the Muslim tradition corresponding to the dual approach of the Tanak tradition indicated in the subtitle of Coats's book; and 4) to make some observations on the relation of the portrait of Moses in the Qur'an to that found in Ibn Ishaq's *Sirat Rasûl Allâh*.[4]

2. *Islamic Sources*

The two basic sources for the early portrayal of Moses in the Islamic

Images of Moses (New York: Basic Books, 1982). This includes the basic picture in Josephus, Philo and other early (pre-Islamic) sources as well as representative portrayals in mystical and modern Judaism. Josephus tells the Moses story in Book 2, chapter 9 through Book 4, chapter 8 of his *Antiquities of the Jews*. Philo's treatment is found in his *De Vita Mosis*. Easily accessible English translations are found in W. Whiston, *The Works of Josephus* (Peabody, MA: Hendrickson, 1987) and in C.D. Yonge, *The Works of Philo* (Peabody, MA: Hendrickson, 1993). The primary compilation of haggadic treatments of Moses in Jewish tradition is found in L. Ginzberg's *The Legends of the Jews* (7 vols.; trans. H. Szold *et al.*; Philadelphia: Jewish Publication Society, 1942 [1909–1938]), abridged in *The Legends of the Jews* (New York: Simon & Schuster, 1956), pp. 277-506. The representation of Moses in the New Testament is also part of the early Jewish representation and is recently treated by D.C. Allison, Jr, *The New Moses: A Matthean Typology* (Minneapolis: Fortress Press, 1993). Allison also provides the most recent survey of the use of Moses as an interpretive model or prototype for other biblical, intertestamental and early Christian persons: e.g., Joshua, Elijah, Constantine.

4.   For an overview of Moses in Islamic traditions, see B. Heller, 'Mūsā', in C.E. Bosworth, E. Van Denzel, W.P. Heinrichs, and C. Pellat (eds.), *The Encyclopaedia of Islam* (Leiden: Brill, new edn, 1993), VII, pp. 638-40 and the added note by D.B. MacDonald on the title of Moses in the same article. The Heller article is essentially the same found in *The Shorter Encyclopaedia of Islam* (ed. H.A.R. Gibb and J.H. Cramers; Ithaca, NY: Cornell University Press, repr. 1974 [1953], pp. 414-15). To the bibliography listed in this article add Y. Moubarac, 'Moïse dans le Coran', in *Moïse: L'homme de l'alliance* (Paris: Desclée & Cie, 1955), pp. 373-93. The same work contains additional articles on Moses in the Tanak, in Philo, in other Jewish writings, in the New Testament, in post-New Testament Christian writings and other sources, and in Islamic Sufi writings. From a Sufi perspective, Moses is often paired with Aaron, the former representing the exoteric tradition with the emphasis on law (*shariah*) and ritual while Aaron represents the mystical, esoteric tradition expressed in Sufi exegesis.

tradition are the Qur'an and the *Sirat Rasûl Allâh*.[5] The traditional Muslim view, followed by many western (non-Muslim) scholars, regards the Qur'an as having been completed in the first generation after the death of Muhammad (632 CE) and having undergone no significant change since. There is a revisionist approach which allows for a more extended process of compilation and sees the final form of the Qur'an as affected significantly by controversies in the Umayyad and early Abbasid periods. The issue affects the evaluation of the Moses image in that the presentation of Moses (as well as of Muhammad) may reflect early tensions within the Muslim community itself. The other major early source is Ibn Ishaq's biography of Muhammad, the *Sirah*. Ibn Ishaq begins with creation (Adam) and ends with the death of Muhammad. The book was completed before 767 CE, the portion on the life of Muhammad being written first. It was divided into three 'volumes'. The last two volumes concerned the life of Muhammad and its immediate context. The first volume (*Kitâb al-Mubtada'* = 'The Book of Beginnings') covered the earlier period beginning with creation. Thus the *Sirah* is formally similar to the Pentateuch of the Tanak in its focus on the major founding figure of the religion (Moses and Muhammad respectively), placed within a universal context which covers the period from creation to the death of the founder. Just as the basic Pentateuchal narrative in its earlier written form was produced in the time of the Hebrew monarchy and expressed the universalizing claims of the Davidic state, so the *Sirah* was composed in early Abbasid times—the reign of caliph al-Mansur—when Ibn Ishaq was employed by the caliph as tutor to the presumed heir, Prince al-Mahdi. Both 'histories' functioned as legitimation for particular dynastic regimes in a time of controversy but at the same time as a manual for proper rule. Both also served to undergird a universal state which included people of diverse religious, cultural, and ethnic origins.[6] The

5. Hereafter cited as *Sirah*. That portion of the text of the *Sirah* which covers the time before Muhammad is reconstructed by G.D. Newby, *The Making of the Last Prophet: A Reconstruction of the Earliest Biography of Muhammad* (Columbia, SC: University of South Carolina Press, 1989). A series of review essays (by M. Waldman, W. Brinner, R. Firestone, R. Kiener, and S. Wasserstrom, with response by Newby) was published in *Religious Studies Review* 18.3 (1992), pp. 179-89

6. In the case of the Hebrew monarchy this diversity included northern and southern elements, Yahweh and non-Yahweh worshipers, conquered subjects and

parallel appears even closer if we compare the Deuteronomic History which carried the story from the death of Moses to the time of King Josiah (in its earlier form) with the planned (but never written) sequel of Ibn Ishaq which was to cover the history of the caliphs to the time of al-Mansur.[7] From volumes II and III of Ibn Ishaq's *Sirah* derives the standard biography of Muhammad whose basic content and chronology is still accepted in most Muslim and many non-Muslim portrayals of Islamic origins. However, this biography of Muhammad was preserved only in the heavily edited version of Ibn Hisham (dated 834 CE).[8] Ibn Hisham wrote in a time, in contrast to that of Ibn Ishaq, in which the use of non-Muslim sources had become suspect.[9] Thus, he eliminated in his edition most of the pre-Muhammad and non-Muslim materials.[10] However, Ibn Ishaq's full work was extensively quoted in other early Islamic sources. Using these sources—especially the writings of al-Tabari (dated 923 CE)—Gordon Newby has reconstructed

conquering elites, supporters of the house of Saul and of the house of David. In the case of the Abbasid state, it included Muslims (only about 8% of the population), Christians, Jews, and Zoroastrians, Arabs and client (non-Arab) peoples, Umayyad, Abbasid, and Shiite (Ali partisans), groups of divergent views on the qualifications for leadership of and membership in the community. The 8% figure is from R.W. Bulliet, *Conversion to Islam in the Medieval Period* (Cambridge, MA: Harvard University Press, 1979), p. 44.

7. Newby, *Making*, p. 7.

8. The standard English translation of Ibn Hisham is A. Guillaume, *The Life of Muhammad: A Translation of Ibn Ishaq's Sirat Rasul Allah* (Karachi: Oxford University Press, 1955). The most recent Western, scholarly biography of Muhammad, which is more critical in its use of Ibn Ishaq than are many other biographies, is F.E. Peters, *Muhammad and the Origins of Islam* (Albany, NY: State University of New York Press, 1994).

9. Newby, *Making*, pp. 8-9, 11.

10. Ibn Hisham's *Sirah* begins with a genealogy going back to Adam and continues with a genealogy of Ishmael, the ancestor of the Arabs in biblical and Islamic traditions. It then moves to traditions concerning the history of southern Arabia, from which many of the supporters of Muhammad in Medina (the ansar) traced their ancestry. It then recounts traditions directly relevant to Mecca and its sacred precinct and the ancestors of Muhammad in the century or so preceding the birth of Muhammad. The remainder and bulk of Ibn Hisham consists of the story of Muhammad. Thus, in some ways Ibn Hisham's revision of Ibn Ishaq is reminiscent of the treatment of the editor of the biblical book of Chronicles who similarly abridged the earlier history (creation to David) with a genealogy, moving into detailed narrative once he had arrived at his main character (David, rather than Moses).

the 'missing' or 'lost' portions of Ibn Ishaq's *Sirah*. In the case of the Moses material, Newby draws mainly on the Qur'anic commentary (*tafsir*)[11] and the history (*tariqh*)[12] of al-Tabari, with only four references from other sources. Thus depending on one's evaluation of the process of the canonization of the Qur'an, Ibn Ishaq's *Sirah* represents a viewpoint roughly contemporary to approximately 100 years after the compilation of the Qur'an. As reconstructed by Newby, the *Kitâb al-Mubtada'* began with creation, including Adam and Eve, and then moved on to Noah, followed by two non-Tanak prophets,[13] then Abraham and his family, Lot, Job, another non-Tanak prophet,[14] then Joseph, Moses, Ezekiel,[15] Elijah, Elisha, Samuel, David, Solomon, Sheba, Isaiah, al-Khidr,[16] Daniel and associates and Ezra, Alexander the Great,[17] Zechariah and John, Jesus, the companions of the cave,

11. *Jāmi' al-Bayān fī Tafsīral-Qur'ān* ('The Full Exposition of Qur'anic Commentary'). Abridged translation by John Cooper, *The Commentary on the Qur'an*, I (Oxford: Oxford University Press, 1987). Forthcoming volumes are in progress.

12. *Tarikh ar-Rusul wa-l-Muluk* ('History of Prophets and Kings'). In translation, see W. Brinner, *The History of al-Tabari*. II. *Prophets and Patriarchs* (Albany, NY: State University of New York Press, 1987).

13. Hud and Salih.

14. Shu'ayb, who is sometimes (not in the Qur'an) identified with Jethro, the father-in-law of Moses.

15. Cf. Newby, *Making*, p. 145. Perhaps Ezekiel is located at this point in the sequence because the story is given as a gloss to Q 2.243, a text regarded by some Muslim commentators as referring to the Exodus. The brief story in Ibn Ishaq refers to a plague which killed a number of Israelites, leaving their bones uncovered until a later time when Ezekiel called the bones to reassemble and come back to life (cf. Ezek. 37.1-10).

16. Ibn Ishaq identifies al-Khidr with Jeremiah of the Tanak. Al-Khidr ('the green one') is more often identified with the person whom Moses encounters in his search for the union of the two worlds (Q 18.61-82). This story introduces the Moses segment of the *Sirah*. In the Sufi tradition, al-Khidr is identified with esoteric knowledge while Moses can see only the surface reality—a distinction obvious in the story both in the *Sirah* and in the Qur'an.

17. Dhu'l-Qarnaim (Q 18.83-101). According to Newby (*Making*, p. 194), Alexander is included as a role-model of an ideal ruler of an ideal community for the future Abbasid ruler. The identification with Alexander is not unanimously followed in the Muslim tradition but is explicit in Ibn Ishaq. The name ('the two horned') recalls the Vulgate (following Aquila) reading of Moses as 'horned' which was often represented in medieval art. The Hebrew is *qāran*, i.e., the same root as in Q 18.83, 86, 94. The qal form occurs in the Tanak only in Exod. 34.29, 30, 35. The LXX

Jonah, the three messengers, Samson, and (St) George. While most of the figures are from the Tanak, there are some New Testament figures, some non-biblical Arabic prophets, and some post-New Testament figures from the Christian tradition. The sequence follows the biblical chronology (not the sequence of books) with a few exceptions (e.g., Ezekiel, Job, Samson) which have their own explanations.[18] The persons included by Ibn Ishaq are mainly those mentioned in the Qur'an.[19] In writing his *Sirah*, Ibn Ishaq actively sought out Christian and Jewish sources, written and oral. These included the *Isra'iliyat* stories derived from Jewish and Christian sources.[20] There is a dialectic relationship between the biblical, post-biblical (Jewish and Christian), pre-Islamic Arabic, and Qur'anic material in which each informs and sets the context for the others.[21] As already mentioned, this sympathetic use of non-Muslim material as a means to help explicate the Qur'an was no longer acceptable after the time of Ibn Ishaq when Ibn Hisham edited the *Sirah*.

translation agrees with modern renderings ('his face was shining'). Coats (*Moses*, p. 34) suggests the golden calf of Exod. 32 was originally a substitute for Moses, and that bovine symbolism may have been originally a traditional symbol for the leadership of Moses. According to Newby, some Muslim commentators identify Dhu'l-Qarnaim with Alexander on the basis of the representation of Alexander as Jupiter-Ammon on some coins. Whatever the original link here, there seems to be assimilation in the representation of Moses and Alexander (and David) as ideal rulers, predecessors of both Muhammad and the Abbasid caliph (Newby, *Making*, p. 114).

18. The order of characters included and of individual segments for each character is partly hypothetical. Newby (*Making*, p. 16) follows the order of the Qur'an, then that of al-Tabari, and then biblical and historical order, and finally logical order.

19. Exceptions include Samson and George (cf. Newby, *Making*, pp. 229, 231).

20. For a recent discussion of the relationship of biblical material to similar materials in Muslim sources, see Chapters 1 and 2 of R. Firestone, *Journeys in Holy Lands: The Evolution of the Abraham–Ishmael Legends in Islamic Exegesis* (Albany, NY: State University of New York Press, 1990), pp. 3-21. Newby suggests that Ibn Abbas was the main source for the *hadith*s which Ibn Ishaq utilized in incorporating biblical materials into the *Sirah* (Newby, *Making*, p. 10, confirmed by R. Firestone in his review of Newby's book, *Religious Studies Review* 18.3 [1992], p. 182).

21. Newby, *Making*, p. 3. He suggests that Ibn Ishaq had as his primary audience the minority Muslim population, who were thus provided with a Muslim understanding of their biblical sources. Ibn Ishaq also intended his work as an apologetic aimed at the larger Christian and Jewish communities (Newby, *Making*, pp. 22-23).

3. *Moses as Hero*

In his discussion of Moses as hero, Coats argues that the heroic portrayal is original to the narrative exposition of the Moses story,
although a non-heroic reference to Moses in mythopoetic confessional
statements may be older than the narrative heroic presentation.[22] Subsequent development (e.g., the P source in the Pentateuch) tends to
portray Moses in a non-heroic or anti-heroic mode.[23] For an understanding of heroic narrative, Coats first outlines the twenty-two elements isolated by Lord Raglan from eighteen stories (including the
biblical Moses story).[24] Coats favors a more limited list of ten characteristics in a subsequent study by Jan de Vries based on medieval
heroic tales: 1) the hero is begotten; 2) he is born; 3) his youth is threat-
ened; 4) he is brought up; 5) he often acquires invulnerability; 6) he
fights with the dragon or other monsters; 7) he wins a maiden, usually
after overcoming great dangers; 8) he makes an expedition to the
underworld; 9) he returns to the land from which he was once banished
and conquers his enemies; 10) he dies.[25] Heroic is understood as a
literary term which belongs to folklore and the repertoire of the
popular storyteller rather than to the realm of historical fact or authorial intent. Coats retains the use of the term 'saga' for this type of
folkloric narrative, defining it as 'a long prose, usually episodic narration built around a plot or a succession of plots. Its intention is to
capture the audience by the tensions in its story line, thus to entertain
the audience with the skill of its storytelling.'[26] This type of storytelling

22. Coats, *Moses*, p. 168.
23. Coats, *Moses*, p. 79.
24. Coats, *Moses*, pp. 38-39, citing Lord Raglan, 'The Hero of Tradition', in
A. Dundes (ed.), *The Study of Folklore* (Englewood Cliffs, NJ: Prentice-Hall,
1965), pp. 142-57.
25. Coats, *Moses*, p. 39; J. de Vries, *Heroic Song and Heroic Legend* (trans.
B.J. Timmer; New York: Oxford University Press, 1963), pp. 210-26. There are
obviously questions as to how universal all items in this list are. The 'fight with the
dragon' and even the 'wins a maiden' elements seem culturally bound. Without
having done a detailed study, my impression is that not all these features appear, for
example, in West African epic. Cf. D.P. Biebuyck, 'The African Heroic Epic', in
F.J. Oinas (ed.), *Heroic Epic and Saga: An Introduction to the World's Great Folk
Epics* (Bloomington, IN: Indiana University Press, 1979), pp. 336-67. Biebuyck
gives a brief summary of features on pp. 354-55.
26. Coats, *Moses*, p. 42. The genre terminology used in various works

belongs primarily to the oral realm and each telling is a recreation of the story rather than a recitation of a fixed, memorized text.[27] Coats further refines his understanding of heroic saga by asking about the qualifying intention which distinguishes heroic narration from other types of folkloric narration focusing on a central character. Here he draws on Joseph Campbell who emphasizes the element of the fabulous or supernatural, of decisive victory, and of the return of the hero to bestow 'boons' on his community.[28] Coats makes this link between the hero and his community, the intent to benefit the community, decisive for his definition: the 'heroic tradition binds the hero with his people. Either by military might, or by skillful intercession, or by familiarity with surroundings and conditions, he defends and aids his own. He brings "boons" to his people.'[29] Further, Coats notes the tendency of heroic tradition to elevate its hero to god-like status (or to the status of 'perfect man'), something which happens in Philo's life of Moses. The hero is betwixt and between: neither simply ordinary man nor yet a god or demi-god.

4. *Moses in the Qur'an*

There are many references to biblical characters in the Qur'an including Adam and Eve, Satan (Iblis), Cain and Abel, Noah, Abraham, Lot, Isaac, Jacob, Joseph, Elijah, Elisha, Jonah, Saul, David, Solomon, Ezra, Job, Jesus and Mary, Zachariah (New Testament), John the Baptist,

discussing this type of literature varies greatly: epic, legend, saga, tale, etc. Coats distinguishes legend from saga by its focus on a virtue or characteristic of the hero instead of the actions of the hero (Coats, *Moses*, pp. 125-128). R. Dorson, one of America's foremost folklorists, apparently uses legend and saga as synonyms (see R. Dorson, *Folklore: Selected Essays* [Bloomington, IN: Indiana University Press, 1973], p. 159. W. Bascom provides a tripartite division of folk narrative into myths, legends, and folktales ('The Forms of Folklore', in A. Dundes [ed.], *Sacred Narrative: Readings in the Theory of Myth* [Berkeley, CA: University of California Press, 1984], pp. 5-29). Like Dorson, Bascom's 'legend' again includes both legend and saga in Coats's usage.

27. For general discussions of folklore as related to biblical studies, cf. P.G. Kirkpatrick, *The Old Testament and Folklore Study* (Sheffield: JSOT Press, 1988), and S. Niditch, *Folklore and the Hebrew Bible* (Minneapolis: Fortress Press, 1993).

28. Coats, *Moses*, p. 40; J. Campbell, *The Hero with a Thousand Faces* (Princeton, NJ: Princeton University Press, 1949), p. 30.

29. Coats, *Moses*, p. 40.

and Moses. Other characters are mentioned associated with the above, for example, the various characters in the Moses story including Aaron, Miriam, and Joshua.[30] Less certain are possible references to Seth, Enoch (Edris: Q 21.85; 19.56), Jethro (Shuayb: Q 7.83-91), and Ezekiel (dhu-l-kifi: Q 21.85). Many prominent biblical persons are not mentioned in the Qur'an, including the classical prophets (except Jonah and possibly Ezekiel), the judges including Samuel, prominent kings such as Hezekiah and Josiah, Daniel, and many New Testament characters. Nor are there any clear references to characters in the Apocrypha, Pseudepigrapha, or New Testament Apocrypha. Most obviously mentioned in the Qur'an are those persons who are considered prophets and messengers (*nabī* and *rasūl*) in the line beginning with Adam and concluding in Muhammad as the seal of the prophets.

Within this group, the most frequently mentioned are Abraham and Moses. These two figures are presented as the most prominent prototypes and precursors of Muhammad, Muhammad having combined the accomplishments of each.[31] Since the most obvious feature of a prophet in the Qur'an is as a warner sent by God, it is not surprising that Noah is frequently mentioned and Lot to a lesser extent. Abraham is mentioned in about twenty-five surahs and Moses in at least thirty-four, making him the most frequently mentioned biblical figure.[32]

30. Joshua is also mentioned in the *Sirah* as part of the Moses story but not an independent character with his own story.

31. Abraham is a *ḥanīf* (a monotheist from before the time of Muhammad), ancestor of the Arabs, and (re-)establisher of pure religion focused on the rituals surrounding the Kaba in Mecca. Moses is important as the recipient of a major 'book'. Both have functions as warners and both are designated as both *nabī* and *rasūl*. All 'messengers' are also prophets but not all prophets are 'messengers'. A messenger establishes a new religion or stage in the history of salvation by bringing a major new manifestation of the heavenly book. Prophets who are not messengers are mainly warners (*nadhīr*) and bringers of good news (*bashīr*) within the context of an existing revelation. Newby (*Making*, p. 113) notes the following features which emphasize Moses as a predecessor and prototype of Muhammad in the *Sirah*. 1) Both are precious infants. 2) Each has a foster mother. 3) Each protects a believing community. 4) Each has to flee his birth land and makes a *hijrah*. 5) Each receives a revelation. 6) Each sees God. 7) Each observes the proper ritual requirements of a Muslim. 8) Each is a military leader of his people. 9) And as with all prophets, each is rejected when he delivers his warning message.

32. If we include references to Pharaoh as implying Moses, the total number of surahs mentioning Moses is about forty, or more than one third of the 114 surahs of the Qur'an. The texts are: 2.40-102; 3.84; 4.164; 5.12-26; 6.91, 154; 7.103-62;

References to Moses vary from the briefest mention (e.g. scrolls of Moses)[33] to extensive recitation of the story of Moses (e.g., Q 20.9-98). Although some references are extensive, many others are what Wansbrough calls 'referential'. They presuppose that the audience will know the story sufficiently to be able to fill in the details.[34] In terms of the traditional European dating of the surahs, the most extensive references to Moses occur in the middle and late Meccan period, with Q 20.9-98 being the earliest extensive summary of the Moses story.[35]

8.53-54; 10.75-93; 11.17, 96-99, 110; 14.6; 17.2, 101-103; 18.60-82; 19.51-53; 20.9-98; 21.48; 23.45-49; 25.35-36; 26.10-68; 27.7-14; 28.3-50, 76; 29.39-40; 32.23-24; 33.7, 69; 37.114-21; 38.12; 40.23-54; 41.45-46; 42.13; 43.46-56; 44.17-36; 46.12-14, 30; 51.38-40; 63.36; 54.41-43; 61.5-6; 66.11; 73.15-16; 79.15-26; 85.17-20; and 87.19. Both Muslim and European scholarship recognizes that many of the surahs are composite and contain revelations received on different occasions. Some of the surahs which contain different sections referring to Moses represent more than one independent mention of Moses thus slightly increasing the total number of references.

33. Q 53.36.

34. Cf. A. Rippin, 'Literary Analysis of Qur'ān, Tafsīr, and Sīra: The Methodologies of John Wansbrough', in R.C. Martin (ed.), *Approaches to Islam in Religious Studies* (Tucson, AZ: University of Arizona Press, 1985), p. 159.

35. The Muslim tradition already distinguished between surahs revealed in Mecca prior to the *hijrah* and surahs revealed after the *hijrah* to Medina. There is a traditional branch of Muslim Qur'anic scholarship devoted to the 'occasions' of revelation (*asbāb al-nuzūl*) which correlates the occasion of the revelation of individual Qur'anic passages with particular events in the life of Muhammad (according to the traditional *Sirah*). This is reminiscent of the book of Psalms where a number of Psalms are linked to particular occasions in the life of David (e.g., Ps. 18) by superscriptions which are later than the date of composition of the psalm. European scholarship has gone beyond the traditional Muslim dating to distinguish an early, middle, and late Meccan period. Criteria are both stylistic and content based. The most common European dating is that by Nöldeke. Watt presents a survey of the dating question in Chapter 7 of W.M. Watt and R. Bell, *Introduction to the Qur'an* (Edinburgh: Edinburgh University Press, 1970), pp. 108-20. This is an extensive reworking of Bell's earlier book of the same name. Cf. also the table on pp. 205-13 of Watt and Bell which lists the traditional Muslim chronology of the surahs as well as three different European chronologies (Muir, Nöldeke, and Grimme) along with the division for the European chronologies into the three Meccan periods. Bell published an edition of the Qur'an which attempted to rearrange them chronologically, complicated by his recognition that individual surahs contained revelations from different periods (*The Qur'ān, Translated with a Critical Re-arrangement of the Surahs* [2 vols.; Edinburgh: T. & T. Clark, 1937, 1939]).

There are fewer references in both the early Meccan and in the Medinan surahs.[36] On the one hand, one might expect more references from the Medinan period when Muhammad encountered a large and significant Jewish community. On the other hand, to the extent that the use of the Moses tradition is directed at his fellow (non-Jewish) Arabs who were already familiar with the biblical stories but not with the Bible as a written, canonical text, the predominance of use in the Meccan period is not surprising. The intent was to warn his fellow Arabs by citing earlier prophets sent by God to warn humanity and to support the idea of a new revelation which stood in the sequence of earlier revelations sent by God to other peoples. The whole effort to date the surahs (and thus the references to Moses) to specific periods of Muhammad's life is disputed by European scholars such as Wansbrough who reject Muslim views about both the occasions of revelation and the essential completion of the Qur'an shortly after Muhammad's death.[37]

Surahs 7.103-57, 20.9-98, 26.10-68, and 28.3-50 contain long accounts of Moses. They share elements of a common outline which includes the call of Moses from the fire, the two signs of the staff and hand,[38] the confrontation with Pharaoh, reference to the drowning of the Egyptians at the sea, the giving of the book/tablets/covenant,[39] and

36. Surahs referring to Moses traditions: 1) Nöldeke, in sequence. A) Early Meccan (87; 85; 73; 53; 79; 51). B) Middle Meccan (54; 37; 44; 20; 26; 19; 38; 43; 27; 18). C) Late Meccan (32; 41; 11; 14; 40; 28; 29; 42; 10; 7; 46; 6; 13). D) Medinan (2; 8; 3; 61; 4; 33; 22; 66; 5). II) Traditional Muslim attribution, in sequence. A) Meccan (73; 53; 54; 38; 7; 25; 18; 19; 26; 28; 17; 10; 11; 6; 37; 40; 41; 42; 43; 44; 46; 51; 14; 21; 23; 32; 79; 29). B) Medinan (2; 8; 3; 33; 66; 61; 5). Moubarac, 'Moïse', pp. 376-84, has a detailed presentation using Nöldeke's dating.

37. Cf. Rippin, 'Literary Analysis', especially pp. 153, 161. The division of Moses references into Meccan and Medinan surahs would be relevant to the literary and theological evaluation of the Qur'an but would not allow us to draw historical conclusions about when and in what context Muhammad made most use of the Moses tradition.

38. The sign of Moses' hand differs from the Exodus version where he put his hand in his cloak a first time and it was 'leprous, as white as snow' when he removed it, but restored to normal when he put his hand into his cloak a second time (Exod. 4.6-7). In the Qur'an, there is only a single insertion of the hand which is white when removed, this being a sign of moral purity rather than 'leprosy' (Q 20.22; 26.33; 28.32). The white hand is thus one form of the divine light which shines from the prophet and is functionally closer to the shining face of the biblical Moses (Exod. 34.29) than to his leprous hand.

39. Q 26.68 ends with the deliverance at the sea and does not continue the

a reference to Aaron. The following elements occur in one or more but not all four of these Qur'anic accounts: 1) the birth of Moses (20 and 28.7-13): Moses is put in a box in the river; his sister watches; Pharaoh adopts Moses; Moses refuses Egyptian wet nurses; Moses' mother nurses him. 2) The intervention of Moses in the quarrel of the two men and his subsequent flight, having been warned. The killing of the man by Moses is attributed to the influence of Satan (28.15-16). 3) Moses in Midian waters the sheep of two women; Moses serves for eight or ten years and marries one (28.22-28). 4) More details on the call of Moses including: Moses' defect of tongue and the sending of Aaron with Moses (20; 26; 28); and the enlarging of Moses breast.[40] 5) Further details of the encounter with Pharaoh including: a) Moses' rod/snake eating the snakes of the Egyptian magicians (26.45); b) the confession of God by the Egyptian magicians and Pharaoh's threatening their lives (26.46); c) intercession by Moses for Pharaoh and Pharaoh's subsequent denial; d) building of a tower to see God by Haman at command of Pharaoh (28; 40.36-37); e) the killing of the Hebrew sons and the sparing of the Hebrew women (7.127; cf. 2.49; 14.6; 40.25);[41] f) various plagues (7.133); g) the despoiling of the Egyptians; h) the departure by night (20.76; 26.52); and i) the smiting

account on to Sinai. The place of Moses' call is referred to as 'the valley of Tuwa' in 20.12 and 79.15. This could either be a proper noun or an adjectival description. The place to which the people go after the Exodus is referred to (if specified at all) simply as 'the mountain' and so, unlike the biblical account, is not explicitly equated with the location of the call of Moses. The one explicit reference to 'Mt Sinai' is in Q 95.2. I have not used Q 2.48-102 in the primary synthesis because of its different form: a series of 'when' passages addressed to Jewish contemporaries of Muhammad which recall both events from the Moses tradition (not arranged in a single linear sequence) intermixed with references to subsequent and contemporary sins of the Jews. All agree in attributing this surah to the Medinan period and this portion of it seems more concerned with a condemnation of the Jews (in Medina and perhaps understood also the Jews in the time of the early caliphate) than in using the Moses tradition as an example of past prophethood and legitimation of the line of prophets.

40. Q 20.25. Although not identical, this may help draw the parallel to Muhammad for whom the opening of the breast is a significant event in his childhood according to the *Sirah* (Guillaume, *Life of Muhammad*, p. 72). The Qur'anic reference to the opening of Muhammad's breast occurs in Q 94.1 although without specific link to Muhammad's childhood.

41. Unlike the biblical account, the killing of the Hebrew male children is not in the Qur'an placed at the time of the birth of Moses.

of the sea with the rod of Moses (20.76; 26.63). 6) More on Moses
and the people at Sinai: a) his thirty plus ten nights on the mountain
(7.142; cf. 2.51); b) Moses' request to see God; Moses falls unconscious and is revived (7.143); Moses' confession (7.143); Moses is
raised above all men (7.144); c) the making of the calf (7.148-53;
20.85-98; cf. 2.54) in which the major blame is born by Sameri (the
Samaritan) rather than Aaron who does not take more forceful action
to avoid causing a division in the people (20.85; 87, 95-97); d) the
choosing of seventy leaders (7.155; 20); and e) reference to manna
and quail in the wilderness (20.80; cf. 2.57).

Together these four long accounts constitute a fairly complete Moses
story, with elements from the birth, youth, flight to Midian, call,
encounter with Pharaoh, and events on Sinai. Other Qur'anic passages
add the following elements: the Egyptian claim that Moses is a lunatic;[42]
the belief of Pharaoh's wife in God (66.11); some Egyptian youths'
belief in God (10.83); Pharaoh's confessing and submission (i.e.,
becoming a Muslim) and his salvation at the sea (10.90-92); water
from the rock producing twelve springs (2.60); the cloud in the wilderness (2.57); reference to the rebellion of Korah (28.76); the sending
of spies to the land and forty years' wandering (Num. 13–14; Q 5.12-
26); further general references to the rejection of Moses by the Hebrews
and to the book/words etc. given to Moses. The unique encounter of
God and Moses is expressed in 4.164 by a word which provides the
Islamic epithet of Moses—'Confidant of God'.[43] Finally, there is the
unique story in Q 18.60-82 of Moses' search for the meeting place of
the two oceans; the strange companion (identified in the tradition as
al-Khidr); and the three incidents whose true meaning is revealed to
Moses by the companion.

We may also note some items of the biblical account not clearly
alluded to in the Qur'an: the midwives of Exodus 1; the links to the
patriarchal tradition; the revelation of the name of God (Exod. 3.12-
15); the attack on Moses upon his return to Egypt (Exod. 4.24-26); signs
done before the Hebrews; Passover references; the desire of the
people to return to Egypt; the battle with the Amalekites and a number
of other wilderness traditions (conflict with Miriam and Aaron; Moses
as very meek; the bronze snake; the tent, ark and tabernacle); any

---

42. 51.38-40—recalling the similar change against Muhammad.

43. *Kalīm Allāh*—i.e., God spoke to him directly (*taklīman*). See D.B.
Macdonald, in *The Encyclopaedia of Islam* (new edn), p. 638.

reference to or explanation of Moses' failure to enter the promised land; and the succession to Moses.[44]

The implied story in the Qur'an resolves internal tensions and contradictions that exist in the presentation of Moses in the Tanak. Due to this, Moses in the Qur'an seems to fit Coats's definition of a heroic saga more clearly than does the Moses of the Tanak. In neither case is the miraculous conception of the hero portrayed.[45] The birth, threat, and rearing motifs are present in the Qur'anic references. While Moses is not invulnerable (in either Bible or Qur'an), his exceptional status raised above other prophets is emphasized in both. In neither case can we really speak of a 'winning of a maiden' as being a significant element. Coats argued that the relevant traditions in the Pentateuch were really Jethro rather than Zipporah traditions and were non-heroic in their concern.[46] However, in the Qur'an, the focus on Jethro is removed.[47] Neither in the Tanak nor in the Qur'an is there a fight with a dragon or an expedition to the underworld.[48] Both have the return to the land of banishment and the triumph of the hero. The Qur'an does not relate the death of Moses although this is developed in the *Sirah*. Moses does bring boons to his people having triumphed over external forces. Moses' intercessory role on behalf of his people, which Coats sees as part of the heroic Moses portrayal, is emphasized equally in Qur'an and Tanak. But a number of the non-heroic aspects of the biblical Moses traditions are missing in both the Qur'an and the *Sirah*. Coats concludes that the tradition of the Passover as the context for the Exodus is part of the P source's non-heroic portrayal of Moses.[49] Passover links are absent in the Islamic material and only the tradition of a hasty, evening departure is mentioned: part of the original heroic Moses portrayal in Exodus according to Coats. As noted, the

44. Joshua is alluded to but not named in Q 2.246 and 5.23. Moses' servant in (18.60-65) is identified by the subsequent tradition as Joshua.

45. The miraculous conception motif is found in post-biblical Jewish Moses traditions.

46. Coats, *Moses*, pp. 53-55.

47. The father is unnamed. According to traditional interpretation, Shu'ayb of 7.83-91 is Jethro, but is in any case not linked to Moses.

48. The triumph over the sea in some references to the exodus in the Tanak has allusions to the killing of the primordial dragon or sea monster in creation (e.g., Isa. 51.9-10). Such mythological allusions are even less likely to occur in the Qur'an than in the Tanak.

49. Coats, *Moses*, pp. 89-108.

Jethro traditions, also part of the non-heroic portrayal of Moses in the Pentateuch, are attenuated.[50] While there are references to Moses selecting seventy elders and to God appointing leaders after Moses, nothing comparable to the non-heroic Jethro tradition of Exodus 18 occurs. The priestly aspects of Moses in the Pentateuch do not belong to the heroic Moses. Nothing in the Qur'an emphasizes Moses as a priest. The tradition of a sin of Moses at Meribah (Num 20.9-14) is also judged by Coats to be non-heroic. While the production of water from the rock does occur in the Qur'an (7.159-60), there is no hint of a sin or non-heroic action. Rather Moses acts positively in bringing forth a separate spring of water for each of the twelve tribes. Only the tale of Q 18.60-82 presents a distinctly non-heroic Moses.[51] Of course, the Qur'an is even less likely than the Tanak to allow a fully independent role to the 'hero'. Thus, the typical hero tale is modified in both Islam and in Judaism. And in both Qur'an and Tanak there is the dual role of Moses as both active, heroic liberator of his people and as passive recipient of the torah. Overall the portrayal of Moses in the Qur'an by eliminating a number of non-heroic Mosaic traditions presents a more consistent picture of Moses as a hero for his people than does the Tanak.

5. *Moses in the* Sirah

As in the case of the Qur'an, so in the *Sirah* there is more material concerning Moses than any other person before the time of Muhammad, including Abraham. Very little from the Moses references of the Qur'an is omitted in the *Sirah*. This is not surprising as the *Sirah* functions as an explicit narrative complement and commentary to the Qur'an. Examples of minor elements mentioned in the Qur'an but not in the *Sirah* are Haman's being ordered by Pharaoh to build a tower to heaven so that he (Pharaoh) may see the Lord of Moses (Q 28.38; 40.36-37), the reference to the rebellion of Korah (28.76), and the reference to Pharaoh's believing wife (Q 66.11).

The two major expansions in the *Sirah* as compared with the Qur'an concern Moses' vision of God and the death of Moses. There are a

---

50. Coats, *Moses*, p. 149.

51. This passage presented special problems to Muslim commentators. One solution was to suggest that this was a different Moses (Moses the son of Manasseh) than Moses the son of Imran. Cf. Newby, *Making*, pp. 114-15.

number of other elements present in the Bible and in the *Sirah* which are either not present or not explicit in the Qur'an. 1) The genealogy of Moses and the link to the time of Joseph and the patriarchs. 2) The instruction to the midwives (not just two Hebrew midwives as in Exodus) to kill all male Hebrew children. The threat to the male children had been mentioned in the Qur'an but only as a reaction of Pharaoh to the initial confrontation with the grown Moses. This element is further expanded with details of how the newly born were killed and how this happened only in alternate years, thus explaining why there was no threat to Aaron's life. 3) The identification of one of the two Midianite sisters as Zipporah. The other is Leah (or Sharfa).[52] The text is explicitly uncertain as to which of the two sisters Moses married. 4) The link of the white hand of the Qur'anic sign to the (lack) of leprosy.[53] 5) The plagues, simply enumerated in the Qur'an, are amplified.[54] In addition, there is the non-biblical episode of the woman of Pharaoh's family who tries to secure a drink of water directly from the Hebrews, but finds that even when the Hebrew woman spits water into her mouth, it still changes into blood. 6) The finding and taking of Joseph's sarcophagus (and remains) from Egypt to the 'holy land'.[55] 7) The despoiling of the Egyptians is developed with details not in the biblical account. 8) The destruction at the sea is expanded adding to the biblical account a number of details: the 70,000

52. Just as various prominent figures in the Tanak are portrayed with Mosaic features (e.g., Elijah at Horeb; cf. further on other Tanak figures with Mosaic elements, Allison, *New Moses*, pp. 11-95), so in the *Sirah* various 'prophets' are assimilated to each other in certain aspects (without being carbon copies). The intent is to emphasize all the prophets as predecessors and prototypes of Muhammad, the last prophet. The Qur'anic portrayal of Moses' father-in-law as having two daughters (instead of 7 as in Exod. 3) and the mention of Moses' working for his wife for a specific term already emphasized the similarity of Moses to Jacob. Now the naming of one of the daughters as Leah makes this patterning even clearer.

53. Newby, *Making*, p. 126.

54. The plagues are enumerated as flood, locusts, lice, frogs, blood—i.e., five (Q 7.133). Famine is listed but this could be read as either a separate plague or a summary of the effect of the flood. Interestingly, certain aspects of this narrative explication in the *Sirah* of the Qur'anic reference sound almost like Greta Hort's rationalist explanation of the plague sequence in 'The Plagues of Egypt', *ZAW* 69 (1957), pp. 84-102. Q 17.101, 27.12 refers to 'nine (clear) signs' given to Moses. The *Sirah* attributes the number nine to the addition of staff, hand, destruction and sea to the above list of five (not counting famine as a separate plague).

55. Gen. 50.25; Exod. 13.19.

white and 70,000 gray horses which Pharaoh used to pursue Moses; the luring of Pharaoh to pursue the Hebrews into the sea by Gabriel with the rear marked off by Michael so that all the Egyptians would perish in the sea.[56] 9) Moses' vision of God. The Qur'anic tradition had alluded to such a request but had been unclear as to the result. In the *Sirah* this is greatly expanded with an account which is the structural parallel to Muhammad's heavenly journey (*mi'rāj*) to the throne of God.[57] God comes to Moses in seven visions culminating in the crumbling of the mountain (already mentioned in Q 7.143). Moses chooses this vision of God over life itself. 10) The transfiguration of Moses along with the veil seems to be referred to by the 'bright light' that came on the forehead of Moses so that no one could look at him were it not for the screen Moses put near himself. 11) Moses intercedes and (going beyond the biblical text) restores to life the souls of the sinful Hebrews who had been killed as a result of their demand to see God. 12) The names of the spies sent out to scout the land are introduced, including Caleb and Joshua. 13) The Balaam tradition is introduced, along with the role of Phinehas (Num. 22–24; 25).[58] 14) Elements from the biblical Joshua tradition are included (conquest of Jericho, sun standing still). 15) This leads us up to the second major expansion in the *Sirah*, the death of Moses. Here there are echos of various post-biblical Jewish traditions. Moses' death occurs after mention of the conquest of Jericho so that implicitly Moses does not die outside the Promised Land. This removes another non-heroic element from the biblical Moses account. As in Deut. 34.6, the *Sirah* says that no one knows his grave. Then there is a further description of Moses' hesitation in turning over leadership to Joshua and his reluctance to die along with an anecdote of how his death finally occurred when Moses came upon a group of angels digging a splendid grave.

---

56. As in the Qur'an, there seems to be some uncertainty between whether Pharaoh perished in the sea along with the other Egyptians or whether his confession of belief in God converting him to a Muslim sufficed to effect his salvation.

57. Interesting, Moses plays a significant role in the text of Muhammad's heavenly journey in the *Sirah*. It is Moses who encounters Muhammad on Muhammad's descent from the presence of God and tells him to secure from God a lessening of the number of times God had commanded Muslims to pray daily (Guillaume, *Life of Muhammad*, pp. 186-87).

58. This is related to Q 7.175-76 which refers to a prophet who abandoned his commission.

Not in the Bible nor the Qur'an but present in the *Sirah* are the following elements. 1) The prediction by astrologers that a male Hebrew child will overthrow Pharaoh (found in post-biblical Jewish traditions). 2) The explanation that one of Pharaoh's wives was a Hebrew woman and it was this wife who was responsible for retrieving Moses from the river.[59] 3) The addition that the breasts of the Egyptian women who tried to nurse Moses were scorched. 4) The gathering of a group of Hebrews around the young Moses while still in Egypt. 5) The information that Moses fulfilled a term of ten years rather than eight years of service to his father-in-law.[60] 6) The detail that Moses' rod came from the first tree planted on earth (found in the post-biblical Jewish tradition) and the details on the shape of the rod. 7) Some aspects of Moses' appearance: large body, strong, ruddy, with a hooked nose. 8) Moses and Aaron remaining at the door of Pharaoh's palace for two years before coming into the presence of Pharaoh. 9) Pharaoh as a god-claimant, indicated by his attempt to avoid emptying his bowels so that he almost died. 10) A magnification of the contest between Moses and the Egyptian magicians to the point that 15,000 magicians are gathered with the four chief ones being named.[61] 11) Of course the role of as-Sameri in the golden calf incident was already an addition to and an apology for Aaron's role. In the *Sirah*, this Samaritan is specified as 'Moses ben Zafar', thus giving us our third Moses in the *Sirah*.[62]

6. *Conclusion*

Moses in the Qur'an reflects the same tension between Moses the active deliverer of his people and Moses the (passive) recipient of the law that Coats developed in his book. This ambiguity is further attenuated in the *Sirah*. While Moses as the recipient of a 'book' is implied

59. Cf. B. Stowasser, *Women in the Qur'an: Traditions, and Interpretations* (New York: Oxford University Press, 1994), Chapter 5, 'The Women in the Life of the Prophet Moses', pp. 56-61 (also discussing the wife, mother, and sister of Moses).

60. The Qur'an had not said which term he fulfilled.

61. This may be intended to evoke a Mosaic parallel to the contest of Elijah with the prophets of Baal (and Asherah) on Mt Carmel (1 Kgs 18) before King Ahab.

62. Moses ben Imran ('the' biblical Moses); Moses ben Manasseh (the Moses who accompanied al-Khidr (?) Q 18.60-61, whether or not the same as Moses ben Imran), and now Moses ben Zafar, the Sameri of the Q 20.85-7.

by the *Sirah*,[63] this aspect of the Moses tradition recedes before the heroic portrayal of Moses as the confronter of Pharaoh and the leader of his people who delivers them both from the oppressions of Egyptian slavery and from the threats of their annihilation by God due to their own sins. Unlike the picture in Philo, the Moses of the Qur'an and the *Sirah* is not an almost divine man. Further the total portrait is relatively restrained in terms of its divergence from either the biblical or Qur'anic models. Here is a 'hero' appropriate to both the theological constraints of monotheism and the needs of an emerging *umma* (Islamic community). Here is an individual who provides the model for a very human but yet exalted Muhammad.

63. The *Sirah* (Newby, *Making*, pp. 133-34) refers to the promise of a 'covenant', to the 'covenant of God on His tablets' along with a several other references to the 'tablets' and to the 'inscription for Moses in which was an exhortation and elaboration of everything as well as guidance and mercy'. There is also mention of the breaking of the tablets and the retention of only one-seventh of the original (perhaps a reference to the idea that the Jewish scriptures are not a full representation of the heavenly 'mother of the book'). But in this section, the emphasis is not on the reception and content of the book or law but on the vision that Moses has of God. This is in distinct contrast to the Qur'an which especially in the briefer references to Moses associates Moses with the revelation of a book: book (*kitāb*): 2.87; 6.91, 154; 28.43; 46.12; 47.35; 53.36; 87.19; also referred to as a torah (*tawrāt*—3.4; 7.156; 61.7), and (as in the *Sirah*) as 'tablets (7.154). According to Brinner, al-Tabari does not mention the decalogue, but it is referred to in Q 7.143-44. Brinner suggests that Q 17.22-38 (cf. 6.152-54) implies an Islamic 'decalogue' revealed to Muhammad at the time of his heavenly ascension (cf. 17.1 and Brinner in his review of Newby's *Making*, *Religious Studies Review* 18.3 [1992], p. 181). For a fuller discussion of the terminology used to refer to the book of Moses in the Qur'an, cf. Moubarac, 'Moïse', pp. 384-85. Of course, Ibn Ishaq presumes that readers of his *Sirah* would be constantly referring, at least mentally, to the appropriate passages of the Qur'an.

NARRATIVE FORM CRITICISM: DEAD OR ALIVE?

Trent Butler

Narratives in the Old Testament deserve serious attention as examples of ancient literary art. This assertion may appear to be obvious. Yet, its importance as an assumption for form-critical analysis and the difficulties experienced by contemporary cultures in taking it seriously require its consideration at the beginning of this introduction. The difficulties arise from a penchant among members of western audiences, particularly American audiences, for destroying the narrative in an effort to discover the 'real' history experienced by its heroes and hidden behind its forms.[1]

With this introduction to his invaluable FOTL commentary on Genesis, George Coats recited his own scholarly history, a history dominated by a love for Hebrew narrative and the forms, traditions, and history behind those masterful narratives.[2] His personal path crossed my own wanderings through Germany, Switzerland, New York, Kentucky, and Tennessee in good times of scholarly sharing, encouragement, and challenge, and in harder times of illness, heartache, and tears. Each time our paths crossed, George prodded me to new growth and new confidence as a scholar searching down many of the same lines of inquiry. George led me into scholarly lectures, scholarly publishing, and scholarly societies. These finally found fruition in a critical, evangelical commentary,[3] where I plunged into the depths of the form-critical waters. Like George, I found these soothing and healing for a while. As John Muddiman phrases it, form criticism

1. George W. Coats, *Genesis, with an Introduction to Narrative Literature* (FOTL, 1; Grand Rapids: Eerdmans, 1983), p. 3.
2. Beginning with his dissertation, *Rebellion in the Wilderness* (Nashville: Abingdon, 1983), Coats constantly wrestled with the interrelationships of tradition, motif, form, history, and literary word. His scholarly pilgrimage led to ever-deeper appreciation for the literary nature and form of biblical books.
3. *Joshua* (WBC, 7; Waco, TX: Word Books, 1983).

offered a scientific method, which broke through the limitations of
philological and literary study of the texts, to answer current questions
about religious development and about the transmission of historical
memory... It... enabled the literature to be related to society, and the texts
to be related to history, opening a new window on to the lived experience
of those communities... from which and for which the biblical literature
was produced.[4]

Reviewers and friends welcomed my attempt to carry narrative form
criticism deeper into the book of Joshua, but they also showed me the
whirling eddies and steep waterfalls leading to a seeming abyss at the
end of the form-critical road.

The present study examines the whys and wherefores of this abyss.
The abyss seemingly yields only death-defying questions. Does form
criticism necessarily eliminate historical questions from view or, even
by its employment, automatically answer all such questions negatively? Does form criticism presuppose too simplistic a sociological method
and thus claim results at illuminating a social setting for a text (*Sitz im
Leben*) that can never be proven, and if they could, represent a
simplistic history of literature and of society? Does form criticism
enthrone an original form of an oral text and humble all other textual
forms to insignificant servants and descendants of the royal oral form?
Does attention to the canonical form and the literary beauty of the
final text eliminate interest in and need for form-critical inquiries?
Can form criticism be transformed into genre criticism and be applied
to literary texts rather than to oral reconstructions? Succinctly, is form
criticism dead, buried by theological presuppositions, literary methods,
and its own necessarily tentative conclusions? Or, can we breathe new
life into form criticism's forms?

Breathing new life into old forms represents dangerous ground as
our Lord warned the Pharisees.[5] Perhaps a life span of almost a century
suffices. Why not let form criticism die and rest in peace? Because
long attachment breeds desire for further life, but more importantly
because experience shows that we are too often willing to overturn the
old for the new with disastrous results. Let us at least make sure what
we have declared dead before we bury it.

Bo-Krister Ljungberg recently raised a startling question:

---

4.   'Form Criticism', *A Dictionary of Biblical Interpretation* (ed. R.J. Coggins
and J.L. Houlden; Philadelphia: Trinity Press International, 1990), p. 240.
5.   Mt. 9.17.

Has it been once and for all settled what Form Criticism is? Encyclopaedias and introductions give the impression that Form Criticism is firmly established. But current specialized literature does not support this...a leading concern seems to be to establish the limits of Form Criticism. What is *not* Form Criticism?... Has Form criticism aided in interpretation? Knierim is of the opinion that with some modifications, Form Criticism might continue to make a contribution to the exegetical disciplines by being subservient to those factors that dominate texts rather than dominating texts through its own methodological system.[6]

A brief venture through the introductory and historical review books should place us on solid ground to define form criticism, its aims, its accomplishments, its weaknesses, and its right to life.[7] Form criticism rose out of Hermann Gunkel's frustration! He wanted to write a history of Israel's literature, particularly the oldest, secular literature, but ran only into blank walls marked 'Quellenscheidung', and 'religiser Einkleidung', and 'Chronologie der Schriften vieffach unsicher'.[8] Gunkel discovered hope. Only moderns idolized individual poets and writers. Ancient Israel allowed only small roles to individuals. Ancient Israelite writers stood under the intense pressure of the style established by the *Gattung*. Poetry came from *Volk*, not from *Kunst*. Writing a history of Israel's literature became possible again. Only first, produce a history of Israel's *Gattungen*, emphasizing the unique qualities of each. Why bother with such a history of *Gattungen*? Gunkel spelled out his reasoning as he concluded his addendum in 1923: Especially is a history of literature indispensable in the exposition of a text because it is impossible to comprehend the content of a Hebrew text in its fullest meaning when one does not recognize its *Gattung* and form.[9]

Such a history would begin with poetry, since Israel's literature began with popular songs, often accompanied by instruments and dance.

---

6. 'Genre and Form Criticism in Old Testament Exegesis', in R.D. Bergen (ed.), *Biblical and Hebrew Discourse Linguistics* (Winona Lake, IN: Eisenbrauns for the Summer Institute of Linguistics, 1994), pp. 419-20.

7. Following the lead of George Coats and of my personal research interests, I limit examples to 'historical' materials, excluding cultic and prophetic poetry and narrative as well as wisdom.

8. Author's translation of Hermann Gunkel, *Die Israelitische Literatur* (Darmstadt: Wissenschaftliche Buchgesellschaft, 1963), p. 1; reprint from *Kultur der Gegenwart, I, 7: Orientalische Literaturen* (Leipzig: Teubner, 1925; original edition about 1906; see 'Nachtrag zum zweiten Abdruck', p. 53 [105]), p. 1 (53).

9. Gunkel, *Literatur*, p. 60 (112).

Only later did recited poetry arise, then prose. This meant that almost all *Gattungen* existed in oral tradition before being written down.[10] This set up a new task. If literature was not the product of an individual genius but much more of the popular community, then literature had its origin not at the scribal desk but in the life of the community. Where in the community's life did different kinds of literature function? That is, where is the *Sitz im Leben*. What was the extent of such literature? Certainly not large tomes; more probably only a few lines constantly repeated. Writing brought such brief literary units into larger collections. Such collections gain center stage for the history of literature only when independent reworking of the materials has produced something unique and new such as the books of history.

The history of literature focuses on *Gattungen* for one further reason. The oldest *Gattungen* have their own *Sitz im Leben*, focus on a definite audience, and seek to create precise effects on that audience. Such *Gattungen* are almost always totally pure. Writers only complicate and mix such originally pure *Gattungen*.[11] As time passed, older *Gattungen* were bent to fit new situations or revived for new circumstances so that the same narrative material at different times could appear as myths, sagas, fairy tales, legends, short stories, or novels.

In his 1923 addendum, Gunkel defined a *Gattung* more clearly. A *Gattung* is to be presumed when one sees at the same time: (1) a precise store of thoughts and moods (*Gedanken und Stimmungen*), (2) a clear speech form (*Formensprache*) by which the thoughts and moods are expressed, and (3) a *Sitz im Leben* which provides the only way the content and form can be understood.[12]

Gunkel saw two types of historical materials, poetic narrative and

10. Gunkel, *Literatur*, p. 3 (55).
11. Gunkel, *Literatur*, p. 4 (56).
12. Gunkel, *Literatur*, p. 57 (109). Note his warning that only by holding firmly and strictly to these three groups of observations can we avoid failures in the future in fixing (*der Ansetzung*) of *Gattungen* and his reminder that *Gattungen* rise out of oral and not written literature. In 1963, Klaus Koch could still write: 'I found that it was the most venerable father of them all, Hermann Gunkel, who provided me with the most information. All that was produced on this subject during the period of his activity appeared under his auspices alone, and since his death, very little more has appeared in print about the principles of form-critical work.' See K. Koch, *The Growth of the Biblical Tradition: The Form Critical Method* (trans. S.M. Cupitt; London: A. & C. Black, 1969), p. x (= *Was ist Formgeschichte? Neue Wege der Bibelexegese* [Neukirchen–Vluyn: Neukirchener Verlag, 2nd edn, 1967]).

strict history. The poetic was the rule for ancient Israel, strict historical narrative being the exception, because it presupposed a certain
intellectual power of objective observation, limited to educated circles.[13] Poetic narratives, on the other hand, carried the imprint of the
circles that formed, preserved, and transmitted them for centuries.
Such poetic narratives appear in different *Gattungen*: myth, saga, fairy
tale, and fable. Only later do short stories and legends appear. Myths
were narratives in which the active persons were divine. They came
from primeval times and from polytheistic people. Thus true myths
do not appear in the Old Testament even when mythical materials do.
Sagas featured humans in action. Here Israel developed a rich literature with primeval sagas, patriarchal sagas, and historical sagas.
'These sagas belong to the most beautiful, exalted, and charming that
appear anywhere in world literature.'[14] Many sagas represent the
ancient people's attempt to answer basic ethnological, etymological,
geological, and cultic questions of life and so are framed in etiological
forms. The scholar seeks to trace how saga materials came from foreign
sources, settled on certain places, moved from one location to another,
were transported from one person to another, and joined different saga
figures such as Noah, the flood hero, and Noah, the first vineyard keep-
er, together. The historian of literature can see that original sagas were
short and unified, while in later times such short sagas were length-
ened through many means and joined into an artistic unity. Historical
sagas concentrate on public officials and their heroic traits. Only
exceptionally do they depict private people like Ruth or Job.

The wonderful artistic skill of these sagas must be due to a class of
popular narrators. Still, they avoid all outer adornments: poetic expressions, metaphors, images. They have no concern with the hero's inner
life. They maintain the simplicity of the oral tradition from which
they received the materials. Likewise, according to Gunkel, such sagas
must not be confused with modern conceptions of history. 'History
writing is no inborn art of the human spirit, but developed in the course
of human history at a precise point of the development.'[15]

Historical narratives as such deal almost exclusively with political
subjects, particularly wars. The history writer is quite reserved in

13. Gunkel, *Literatur*, p. 16 (68).
14. Gunkel, *Literatur*, p. 19 (71).
15. *Genesis übersetzt und erklärt von Hermann Gunkel* (Gottingen: Vandenhoeck
& Ruprecht, 6th edn, 1964), p. vii.

writing about God and divine things and avoids miracles entirely. Here Israel accomplished something Egypt and Babylon never did.[16] Such history writing had an entirely different *Sitz im Leben* from the sagas. Sagas are oral, while history writing belongs to learned readers who write in book form. Still, many transitional members (*Zwischenglieder*) exist between the two *Gattungen*. Sadly, no pure history book from the older period has been preserved. What we have preserves only pieces from the older history books.[17]

In new hands, form criticism took new directions.[18] Studies of small units of literature dealing with similar content led to conclusions regarding the historical origins of the oral forms behind all the various literary units.[19] Hahn critiqued such work, especially that of von Rad,

16. *Literatur*, p. 24 (76).

17. Literary history and Israelite life experienced transformation, for Gunkel, in the period after 750 BCE. Individualism raised its head along with the world-dominating enemies and national catastrophe. Here prophecy took over center stage.

18. See the survey by H.F. Hahn, *The Old Testament in Modern Research* (expanded by a survey of recent literature by Horace D. Hummel; Philadelphia: Fortress Press, 1966 [1954]), pp. 119-56.

19. Anton Jirku, *Die älteste Geschichte Israels im Rahmen lehrhafter Darstellungen* (Leipzig, 1913) traced the summaries of Israel's early history in Josh. 24, Pss. 78, 105, and Deut. 29, to a literary type much older than the Pentateuch used by priests in their 'sermons'. Martin Noth, *Das System der zwölf Stämme Israels* (Stuttgart, 1930), found the origin of the list of 12 tribes of Israel as preserved in Gen. 49, Num. 1, 26, to belong originally to a list of the members of the earliest Hebrew league in the time of Judges. Kurt Galling concluded that Israel's two election traditions (Abraham and Egypt) had differing origins. Egypt belonged to Israel's earliest living traditions, while Abraham was prefixed to the Exodus narrative by the first literary compiler, the Yahwist. Scandinavian scholars building on the work of Ivan Engnell described traditional sources in the Pentateuch as units of oral tradition crystallized in circles of oral traditionists rather than being literary compositions. Gerhard von Rad, *Das formgeschichtliche Problem des Hexateuchs* (Stuttgart, 1938; ET *The Problem of the Hexateuch and Other Essays* [trans. E.W. Dicken; Edinburgh, 1966]) isolated Exod. 15.4-16; Deut. 26.5b-9; 6.20-24; Josh. 24.2b-13, as representing an early Israelite credo confessing God's work in leading Israel out of Egypt and into Canaan without mention of Sinai or creation. He saw the credo as a central feature of Israel's earliest cultic worship during the Feast of Weeks. Such celebration had its original home in Gilgal. The Sinai materials, on the other hand, developed at Shechem during the ancient feast celebrating and renewing the covenant, a celebration later connected to the Feast of the Booths. To these, according to von Rad, the Yahwist prefixed patriarchal and primeval sagas, encasing all in his own ideological framework. Martin Noth,

as justified isolation of traditions but as being too specific and sure in attaching such traditions to a specific cultic rite instead of to a more general process of repetition from generation to generation as Jirku had done.[20] Such form-critical work on small units laid the groundwork for Eissfeldt[21] and Hempel[22] to carry out more fully Gunkel's dream of a history of Hebrew literature from its oral origins through its massive written collections. Hahn states,

> Hempel's chief accomplishment was that he showed how closely religious interpretation was identified with historical composition in the work of Old Testament writers. This recognition of the religious motivation of Hebrew historiography is the most important development in biblical criticism of the last two decades... Originally, the variety of literary types had led the form critic to treat the units of material as independent entities; now, as Gunkel had first realized with reference to the prophetic literature, an appreciable amount of heterogeneity in literary form was not incompatible with conceptual unity. The latter was more significant than the literary form.[23]

Subsequent work on methodological issues carried form criticism far afield. Klaus Koch made it the overarching category for all exegetical methodology, subsuming literary criticism, redaction criticism, and tradition history all under form criticism.[24] Wolfgang Richter sought to detail an exegetical methodology that would be capable of validation and disproof at each stage. He thus set up a process in which each step must be taken in order. Form criticism became divided into at least two parts: form criticism and *Gattung* criticism, the first of these

---

Überlieferungsgeschichtliche Studien (I, Halle, 1943; II, Stuttgart, 1948) traced the basic elements or themes of the Pentateuch as separate traditions gradually melded into a basic stream (G). He separated Genesis–Numbers from Deuteronomy, Joshua, Judges, Samuel, Kings, the latter comprising a Deuteronomistic history, a literary unity by a Deuteronomic author.

20. *The Old Testament in Modern Research*, p. 144.

21. O. Eissfeldt, *Einleitung in das Alte Testament* (Tubingen, 1934; ET *The Old Testament: An Introduction* [trans. P.R. Ackroyd; New York: Harper & Row, 1965]).

22. J. Hempel, *Die althebräisches Literatur und ihr hellenistisch-jüdisches Nachleben* (Handbuch der Literaturwissenschaft, 21; Wildpark-Potsdam, 1930–34).

23. *The Old Testament in Modern Research*, pp. 153, 155.

24. *The Growth of the Biblical Tradition*, pp. x-xi. Introducing the English edition in 1968 (p. xiii) Koch noted the underlying purpose of his book was 'to try to discover what lies behind the speech of God in the Bible'.

ensuring that the individual Bible text was examined carefully prior to the formation of theories concerning overarching types. In this scheme, form criticism became a study of the individual sentences, sentence series, and paragraphs at the phonemic, morphological, syntactic, and lexemic levels.[25]

Summarizing the state of narrative form criticism in 1983, Coats emphasized the artistic nature of narratives, downplaying their relationship to history. He admitted that the terms used for narrative genres originated outside the field of biblical studies and 'apply, therefore, to the Old Testament literature, only with a limited degree of accuracy'.[26] Coats identified criteria for establishing narrative genre categories as: (1) a distinctive structure, (2) distinctive vocabulary patterns, perhaps appearing as indicators of the structure, (3) a typical setting, and (4) a qualifying function of the literary piece within its setting, thus a distinctive intention.[27] Before beginning his commentary proper, Coats lists the various Old Testament narrative genres: saga, tale, novella, legend, history, report, fable, etiology, and myth.[28]

In practice, Coats follows Koch in subsuming all exegetical methods basically under form criticism. In so doing, he begins to fulfil Gunkel's dream of a history of the literature of Israel from oral *Gattung* through finished literary works. In this spirit Coats looks for form-critical definition not only of oral stories but also of the larger streams of tradition that first united oral narratives into a larger unit and of the postulated written source documents, as well as of the Pentateuch/Hexateuch as a whole. At none of these stages does Coats use a historical category in his form-critical definition.

Form criticism has not been limited to mainstream critical scholars. Conservative scholars have also practised the art to one degree or another as illustrated in the various volumes of the Word Biblical Commentary, a self-proclaimed evangelical series. Still, the more

---

25. W. Richter, *Exegese als Literaturwissenschaft, Entwurf einer alt testamentlichen Literatur Theorie und Methodologie* (Gottingen: Vandenhoeck & Ruprecht, 1971). He argued vehemently against theological and systematic presuppositions that would favor one method or refuse to utilize another method current in general *Literaturwissenschaft*. He also opposed an outdated description of methodology as historical critical studies.

26. *Genesis*, pp. 3-4.

27. Coats, *Genesis*, p. 4.

28. Coats, *Genesis*, pp. 5-10.

conservative evangelical scholars have distanced themselves somewhat from form criticism as a quote from a recent Introduction shows:

> In labelling patriarchal narratives 'sagas' or the narratives of Joshua 'etiologies', form critics exercise great influence on interpretation, for with these identifications comes the implication that these narratives are of less historical value. As with source criticism, the difficulties lie in the speculative nature of the results and the neglect of the final form of the text.[29]

A more recent conservative work, on the other hand, presents a summary of form-critical work on the Old Testament but self-consciously claims to be 'the first book to be devoted specifically to the *literary forms* of the Old Testament' (italics mine).[30] Why? They work with genre analysis, not *Gattung* analysis. Why?

> Genre criticism works with the canonical form of the text and not any form *before* that. Searching for an oral stage for forms and ultimately an original 'setting in life' (German, *Sitz im Leben*) before the written stage is an unnecessary pursuit, in part because the exercise is all too often a biased one. Furthermore, genre may (and often does) change when a piece of communication passes from an oral, isolated stage to that of a written, contextual one.[31]

29. A.E. Hill and J.H. Walton, *A Survey of the Old Testament* (Grand Rapids: Zondervan, 1991), p. 9.

30. D.B. Sandy and R.L. Giese, Jr (eds.), *Cracking Old Testament Codes* (Nashville: Broadman & Holman, 1995), p. 3. Interestingly, the distinction is made between narrative and history, apparently dividing Pentateuch from history books. Narrative is described in purely literary terms of plot, scene, characterization with no reference to form-critical terms, whereas history is described with explicit dependence on the Forms of the Old Testament Literature series with an almost comprehensive list of the sub-genres noted in the volumes on Kings and Chronicles. This process leaves Joshua and Judges basically undiscussed and raises questions about what type of genres or sub-genres appear in 'Narrative'.

31. R.L. Giese, Jr, 'Literary Forms of the Old Testament', in *Cracking Old Testament Codes*, pp. 8-9. Such a turning to literary analysis and literary analysis alone is not a conservative monopoly. Critical scholarship started the process in the 1960s and 1970s as seen in D.A. Robertson, *The Old Testament and the Literary Critic* (Guides to Biblical Scholarship; Philadelphia: Fortress Press, 1977). In some ways, the impetus for such study came from James Muilenburg, 'Form Criticism and Beyond', *JBL* 88 (1969), pp. 1-18. The assessment of this development by Rolf Knierim in 1985 remains true: 'It is evident that the new concentration on the Hebrew Bible as literature has generated an enormous resurgence of literary criticism in our generation. At the same time, the variety and diversity of models indicate that a

The list of works on form criticism and exegetical method can be widely extended.[32] The point, hopefully, has been identified. Form criticism has absorbed so much into itself that it lays itself open to easy criticism. Such criticisms have come forth freely and often from various sources. Following Muilenburg's title, Paul House edited a volume entitled *Beyond Form Criticism: Essays in Old Testament Literary Criticism*.[33] In his introductory essay, House described older methods, particularly form criticism, as having run their course, becoming stale with overuse, and thus producing diminishing returns. House saw literary criticism in all its modern faces as a return to the full biblical text and away from the atomizing, divisive work of form criticism that obscured the unity of and reorganized texts. 'Pre-textual matters subsumed textual issues.'[34]

R.N. Whybray summarized the case against form criticism under five issues.[35]

1. The use of writing. Israel, like others in the ancient Near East, had access to writing at an early date, and oral tradition studies cannot depend on evidence from societies that recited written texts orally. Early Israel cannot be viewed as a

consensus on the description of the literary-critical task is not yet in sight': 'Criticism of Literary Features, Form, Tradition and Redaction', in D.A. Knight and G.M. Tucker (eds.), *The Hebrew Bible and its Modern Interpreters* (SBL Centennial Publications; Philadelphia: Fortress Press, 1985), p. 136.

32. For examples, see G.M. Tucker, *Form Criticism of the Old Testament* (Guides to Biblical Scholarship; Philadelphia: Fortress Press, 1971); J.H. Hayes (ed.), *Old Testament Form Criticism* (San Antonio, TX: Trinity University Press, 1974), where Jay A. Wilcoxen ('Narrative', p. 75) underlined the point of Gunkel and Gressman that history writing in Israel developed from saga, not from historical documents; J.H. Hayes and C.R. Holladay, *Biblical Exegesis: A Beginner's Handbook* (Atlanta: John Knox, 1982); J. Rogerson (ed.), *Beginning Old Testament Study* (London: SPCK, 1983); W.W. Klein, C.L. Blomberg and R.L. Hubbard, Jr (eds.), *Introduction to Biblical Interpretation* (Dallas: Word Books, 1993); D.S. Dockery, K.A. Mathews and R.B. Sloan, *Foundations for Biblical Interpretation* (Nashville: Broadman & Holman, 1994).

33. Sources for Biblical and Theological Study, 2; Winona Lake, IN: Eisenbrauns, 1992.

34. House, 'The Rise and Current Status of Literary Criticism of the Old Testament', in *Beyond Form Criticism*, p. 3.

35. *The Making of the Pentateuch: A Methodological Study* (JSOTSup, 53; Sheffield: JSOT Press, 1987) with conclusions listed on pp. 215-19.

primitive, nomadic people.

2.   Foreign models. Arguments from the study of oral traditions in other cultures lack cogency. Olrik's so-called epic laws could be used by writers as well as oral storytellers. Icelandic family sagas do not have an oral basis, but are purely literary compositions. Also, they represent an entirely different type of family life from that pictured in the patriarchal materials. Modern oral narrative studies, as yet in their infancy, show *Gattung* and *Sitz im Leben* to be flexible, ill-defined, and interchangeable in oral narratives. Modern studies deal with poetry, whereas Israel's materials are prose.

3.   The fluidity of oral tradition. Study of modern oral literature emphasizes the fluidity of the oral texts and the ability of the narrator to change the narrative to fix the context of study. Whybray likewise refuses to accept any argument based on the sacral nature of the materials because the materials cannot be shown to have been preserved in sacral institutions and do not display any intrinsically sacred character.

4.   Storytellers in the Old Testament. The Old Testament yields no evidence of a class of professional storytellers.

5.   Oral and written composition. No techniques are available to differentiate oral bases of written texts. Studies in form criticism and tradition history reach such widely differing results that 'scientific method' is reduced to subjectivity, conjecture, and presuppositions.

Whybray does not deny the probability that the one author he posits for the Pentateuch used oral sources. He simply cannot find any proper methods for isolating and studying those sources.[36] Still, he builds a case for one author of the Pentateuch in the sixth century BCE who retold folktales at his hand, in his own way, and not having a sufficient quantity of such folktales at that late date, he invented some. This means that 'a large proportion of the narratives in the Pentateuch are fiction'.[37]

36.   Whybray, *Pentateuch*, p. 236. He even speaks (p. 238) of a rich vein of folklore and of folklore motifs in Israel of which what has survived is no more than a selection.

37.   Whybray, *Pentateuch*, p. 240. Whybray goes so far at this point as to claim (pp. 241-42) that 'the only tradition which can safely be regarded as ancient is that of the Exodus. Even here it is hardly possible, out of the whole complex of narratives which now enshrine that event in Exod. 1-15, to point to any ancient

Bruce Waltke echoed Whybray's arguments from a conservative standpoint. He notes his theological uneasiness with the fluidity of sacred tradition in the hands of form critics: 'One is still left, however, with the uneasy feeling that the text's original meaning to the people of God has been deliberately obfuscated by the final redactor'.[38] Waltke reviewed briefly the cultures of Ebla, Mesopotamia, the Hittites, Ugarit, Egypt, and Northwest Semitic, as well as Homer and the Classics, the Jews and the Talmud, the Hindus and the Rig-Veda, the Arabs and the Koran, and Old Icelandic and Serbo-Croatian cultures. He concluded: 'We have found no evidence in any Semitic cultures, including Islam, that tradents molded an oral tradition to meet changing situations over the centuries'.[39] Thus for Waltke

> the only reliable information we have about the antediluvian and postdiluvian patriarchs is not from oral tradition but from the written records preserved in the canon. It is gratuitous to assume that the biblical narrators depended on oral tradition. . ... We have no reason to think that it was not revealed to the storyteller himself, who inscripturated it in Holy Writ. The biblical authors are surrogates for God and as such are not dependent on oral tradition.[40]

Nonetheless, for Waltke it is

> difficult to verify or refute the claim that oral tradition lies behind the patriarchal narratives referring to events before the invention of writing. . . the important point is that God's inspired spokesman told the sacred stories in his own way. For this reason, there is no reason to doubt their historicity or to be uncertain about his meaning.[41]

narrative which has been verbally or substantially preserved and incorporated unchanged into the present text.'

38. 'Oral Tradition', in H.M. Conn (ed.), *Inerrancy and Hermeneutic: A Tradition, A Challenge, A Debate* (Grand Rapids: Baker Book House, 1988), p. 119.

39. Waltke, 'Oral Tradition', p. 134.

40. Waltke, 'Oral Tradition', p. 135. Interestingly, Waltke then tries to cover his bases a bit by admitting that successive patriarchs knew the promises of God to their fathers and that the author of Genesis used them. Still, 'it is inapposite, however, to think that he (or any other of the omniscient narrators of the Bible) was dependent on oral tradition.'

41. Waltke, 'Oral Tradition', p. 135. He notes that his objection is not to the indispensable exegetical tool of identifying literary genres and forms but to the subjective practice of tracing the history of tradition.

Most recently, discourse linguistics has entered the fray against form criticism. Ernst Wendland offers a recent example.[42] He sees the form critics as the first to take discourse analysis of the biblical text seriously.

> The problem was that they practised this from a distinctive and often disruptive bias whereby a supposedly original oral context often became the determining factor in deciding textual and interpretative issues... Although stimulating and informative in a general sort of way, most FC analyses need a rather great deal of correction and supplementation. Their overemphasis on the supposed original *Sitz im Leben*, both historical and socio-cultural, often produces very speculative and idiosyncratic reconstructions, with one debatable prop used to support another. Furthermore, there tends to be an unsubstantiated concern with the alleged predominant influence of the communal and/or royal cult upon biblical composition, a hypothesis that is based to a great extent upon pagan, non-Israelite models.[43]

Wendland notes also the dangers of atomism, inflexibility, failure to see possibilities of authorial creativity, and of overgeneralization. Most important for him, apparently, is that 'designations such as "myth", "legend", "fable", and "saga"... convey a notion of fiction-ality and the fantastic that stands in contrast to the strong assumption of historicity and divine action which the Scriptures assert both explic-itly and implicitly'.[44] Thus advising use with caution, Wendland says form-critical information is of an

> extrinsic, organizational, or background nature and hence needs to be followed up by an intensive literary-structural and rhetorical-poetic examination of the textual data... to reveal precisely how (stylistically) and why (functionally) the original author conveyed a definite ethical and theological message with distinct affective force and aesthetic appeal, not only to the intially intended constituency, but also to countless readers and hearers in subsequent ages, right up to the present day.[45]

---

42. 'Genre Criticism and the Psalms', in R.D. Bergen (ed.), *Biblical Hebrew and Discourse Linguistics* (Winona Lake, IN: Eisenbrauns for the Summer Institute of Linguistics, 1994), pp. 374-414.

43. Wendland, 'Genre Criticism', pp. 383-84. See the similar critique by Muddiman, 'Form Criticism', pp. 241-42: 'Underestimation of the role of the authors, abstract idealization and logical circularity, exaggeration of the extent to which communities adapt and even generate tradition to suit their immediate needs, along with discounting of the conservative aspects of oral tradition'.

44. Wendland, 'Genre Criticism', p. 384.

45. Wendland, 'Genre Criticism', p. 385.

Having presented his own discourse-oriented, 'structure-functional' analysis, he has to conclude that this is only a supplement to form-critical methodology and that 'the original form-critical concern for describing indigenous genres (text) in relation to social setting (context) and a given literary tradition, whether oral or written (i.e., the "intertextual context"), must be emulated'.[46]

Ljungberg, wanting to liberate genre, dares question the time-honored form-critical connection of *Gattung* and *Sitz im Leben*: 'The implication, is that a *Gattung* will not predict a *Sitz im Leben* with any accuracy'.[47] He says that 'genre provides the literary context for a given sentence, and thus partly determines what it means. Genre is constitutive of meaning: it conditions reader expectations and thus allows for understanding.'[48] He notes that 'Old Testament Form Critics have often not seen, as others have, that genres are abstractions, and that virtually all human experiences involve a combination of categories applied simultaneously'.[49] But Old Testament genre interpretation is complicated for the Christian reader because the Christian reader reads the Old Testament with a secondary meaning from outside its original context but within the context of the entire Christian canon. Reading within the context of the entire Christian canon means the interpreter cannot de-historicize the Old Testament narrative since the canon consistently presents it as history.

What can we conclude about the health of narrative form criticism? It has seemed to die the death of a thousand definitions and then experience resurrection because no one has found a sufficient replacement. Can we rescue form criticism from this cycle of death and resurrection so often experienced by the gods of Israel's culture? Can we give it life so long as exegetes shall live? Or should we let it rest in peace once and for all? Rescue work can be done only by being quite specific about what form criticism can claim to deliver for the interpreter of narrative and deciding whether the nature of the exegetical task leads us to want what form criticism can deliver. Perhaps the following conclusions drawn from the current status of research and questioning can help clarify the condition of form criticism's health.

    1. With Gunkel against Coats and Koch, we must define form

---

    46. Wendland, 'Genre Criticism', p. 411.

    47. Ljungberg, 'Genre and Form Criticism', p. 420.

    48. Ljungberg, 'Genre and Form Criticism', p. 421.

    49. Ljungberg, 'Genre and Form Criticism', p. 429.

criticism as an attempt to identify one stage in the history of a definite text, and, indeed, the original, oral stage of the history of the text. This is done to maintain the clear distinction between methodological steps. One would hope that scholarship would take more seriously Richter's lead in seeking to find methodological steps whose results can be verified and whose work takes seriously the literary text before jumping too quickly to theoretical stages and generalizing theories. Isolating form criticism from tradition history allows the Bible student to ask proper questions in discovering biblical *Gattungen* and their functions in Israel's life before too quickly making judgments based on the life and literature of Israel's neighbors. It should lead to literary decisions that do not automatically create historical decisions, thus meeting some of the criticism of people like House, Hill and Walton, and Wendland.

2. This means form criticism is applicable only to those texts that in some fashion have an oral basis. Such texts can be divided into at least two categories: texts that themselves originated and were preserved in oral form before achieving the written form we now work with, and texts that reflect the language and customs of 'oral life' in an everyday culture even though the present text never had an oral form. Texts as simple as greeting formulas, written eulogies, and literary laments belong to the second category. Full understanding of such elements includes to some extent an understanding of a real life *Sitz im Leben* as well as a literary *Sitz im Leben*.

3. Some narrative texts in the Hebrew Bible do reflect an oral stage of composition and transmission.[50] Against Whybray and Waltke, we must contend that arguing that writing was known at a particular stage in a people's history and was used by surrounding cultures to preserve parallel types of literature does not eliminate oral literature from Israel's culture. One must not only show that Israel had the capability to write literature, but that it had the sociological, institutional means to create a class of people who had time and resources to create,

---

50. Certainly much of the prophetic, psalmic, and wisdom literature also has oral origins. One must apply the same theological processes and draw the same theological implications in regard to the passage of narrative literature from oral to written form as is done for the other types of literature which are not so explicitly historical. After all his critique, Muddiman ('Form Criticism', p. 242) concludes: 'Despite these reservations, form criticism is an indispensable tool of biblical interpretation'.

preserve, and store a written literature. The patriarchal society on the fringes of Canaanite city states, the slave society in Egypt, the wandering society of the wilderness period, the warring society of Joshua's day, and the unsettled, leaderless, squabbling society of the judges do not reflect any type of institution that would support a class of people engaged in writing literature for the entire nation. Prior to the united monarchy, the sociological situation of Israel may well have produced isolated instances of writing, especially sacred literature, and its preservation at a worship site such as Gilgal, Shiloh, or Shechem. Yet it remains quite doubtful that any of these worship places had sufficient staff or storage resources to accommodate any large amount of literature. [51]

4. The existence of oral literature raises methodological issues. a) How can one recognize oral literature within the present written text? Whybray correctly argues that no sure answers are available at this point. Still, Whybray must admit that oral materials lie at the basis of much of Israel's texts. This admission requires that we find the most likely means of isolating oral materials behind the present written literature. To say that a written author could be creative enough to use different styles and different literary forms is to generalize too far in the opposite direction from those who would follow Gunkel in attributing almost everything to an oral stage. The best prospects appear to remain with the following procedure: (i) determine major stylistic features of the framework of a biblical book or related group of books: Pentateuch, Deuteronomy, Chronicles; (ii) isolate brief portions with clear poetic structure or narrative structure that do not reflect the style and vocabulary of the controlling framework.[52] Still, we can probably never be sure that we have absolutely separated originally oral literature and written literature imitating oral formulations.

---

51. For those who would postulate a suddenly creative exilic community producing all of Israel's historical literature for the first time, one must raise the similar sociological issue: Did exilic, post-exilic, or Judean Israel of the sixth and fifth centuries have a social class and institution with the resources to create, preserve, and store such literary works? Does not such literary activity presuppose some kind of established governmental institution such as the city states of second and third millennium Syria or Mesopotamia or of the late post-exilic Judean society dominated by a priesthood with religious and political powers?

52. See my brief discussion based on Westermann and Dommershausen in *Joshua*, p. 29.

b) Oral literature, or writing that imitates oral literature, may employ conventional forms and content that appear to point to the sociological setting where either the form, the content, or both, originated. Distinction must be made at this point between reality of sociological history and a reality of relevance to the author of the biblical text. To isolate a narrative form used in a biblical text and to compare it with and include it in a category with other biblical and extra-biblical texts to form a *Gattung* does not mean that the writer of the biblical text was aware of that *Gattung* nor that the original readers or listeners to the written text were supposed to recognize and identify with that *Gattung* any more easily than do modern readers.

c) Oral literature may continue to have a life of its own, separate from and parallel to written literature. This may present for the writer's audience a point of contact to recognize and understand oral forms and their functions. If this is the case, understanding of the oral *Gattung* and *Sitz im Leben* paints an emotional tone and living identity with the written situation for the reader. Use of such recognized *Gattungen* is part of the literary artistry of the biblical writer. This provides the modern exegete the task of recreating the emotional tones and living identity as much as possible for the modern reader.

d) The content of written literature may reside originally in an oral *Gattung* and point the reader more easily than form to a place, a worship setting, a political or family institution. Through such content the author may seek to lead the reader to personal recollections of participation in similar settings or to remember other narratives and other history connected to such settings. Such connections may be part of a writer's artistry in helping the reader to anticipate the course of the larger literary work.

e) Oral literature for Israel may well be distinctive from the traditional descriptions of oral literature in its central sociological settings. I agree with Whybray that Israel's oral literature did not find its chief settings in institutions or personalities dedicated to entertainment.[53] Israel's oral literature, on its own witness, was placed in the hands of the worship leaders[54] and in the hands of educators, especially

53. This is not to say that some biblical literature did not find use in entertaining situations such as the victorious return from battle pictured as settings for the early poems of Miriam (Exod. 15.18) and Deborah (Judg. 5).

54. The tie between Exodus and Passover in Exod. 12, for example. Whybray is certainly overstating the case when he claims that Israel's materials do not have

parents.[55] One must expect that for Israel, wherever narrative material originated, it lived because worship leaders and family[56] preserved it.

f) Oral literature at home in worship and family education expects a different fate than literature at home in community entertainment. Worship and family settings seek to pass on materials as they have been handed down, not change materials to suit a new audience or demonstrate the ability of the storyteller. Worship and family preserve the old rather than inventing the new.

g) Oral literature existing in Israel appears to promise continued life to form criticism. Such life is not life in absolute freedom. It is life within clear limits. Form criticism of Israelite narrative literature can hope only to indicate that certain narratives apparently originated in oral forms. Form-critical methodology may well determine that a narrative is structured according to a pre-given form, a *Gattung*, and connect the narratives to what seem to be obvious sociological, institutional settings in early Israel. Insofar as this is done successfully, form criticism is commissioned to give names to such newly discovered *Gattungen*. These names, however, need to be Israelite names, reflecting the sociological reality of Israel.[57] Working successfully, form criticism may shed new light on the sociological life of ancient Israel and how oral literature functioned for Israel. The task then becomes to demonstrate how this information from sociological history

intrinsically sacred character. Materials such as are found in patriarchal stories tied to Bethel and Shechem, and exodus narratives such as Josh. 24 have not only sacred content, but show that they quickly acquired a sacred role in Israel's worship. The alternative to this is to follow Whybray and others in claiming that all Israelite historical narrative is late, based on few surviving sources, and basically fictional. This goes against all of Israel's own claims for its religion and gives credit to a stage of Israel's political and sociological history for creating and preserving mass amounts of literature when no Israelite institutions existed to serve as the initiator and/or preserver of such literature.

55. The catechetical demands in Josh. 4.6-7, 21-23, for example.

56. Such is to be expected in the patriarchal materials so centered upon family history.

57. If one readily admits that Israel did not use myths, why use the term myth in relationship to Israelite literature? If Israel told materials as family history or as promise narratives, why load ambiguous titles such as saga or legend to such materials? Form criticism must not try to establish universal *Gattungen* with as few categories as possible, with all categories applicable to all cultures. Form criticism must be careful to establish categories that are descriptive of the sociological reality within the culture that used the categories.

sheds light on the written text. Methodologically, this becomes the territory of redaction criticism, literary criticism, or discourse analysis. The task of the form critic stops at the boundary of written literature. Here a new methodology takes over. Writing, too, has component units with particular form, content, mood, and structure. Writing, however, is a different stage in the history of literature and presupposes different issues and sociological realities than does the oral stage. Methodological clarity demands that form-critical work differentiate levels of activity between analysis of oral and written literature.[58]

5. The existence of oral literature also raises historical issues. Too readily, form criticism either hailed the discovery of the earliest form of a pure *Gattung* and made historical claims or has melted too quickly into tradition history, tracing materials and motifs into pre-Israelite stages, giving *Gattungen* pre-Israelite names, and making historical judgments based on non-Israelite information and institutions. If the judgment above is correct—that Israel's oral literature found two and most likely only two basic homes, worship place and family—then Israel's oral literature needs to be evaluated in terms of the functionality of Israelite cult and Israelite clan educational practices. Form criticism isolates a narrative and determines its *Gattung* and the sociological function of that *Gattung* in Israel. Form criticism, as such, does not place a historical judgment upon the contents of the materials used within the *Gattung*.[59] The name form criticism gives to the *Gattung* should not make such historical judgments. Form criticism may determine if the particular *Gattung* was originally used to transmit historical information, to impart moral instruction, to give content to liturgy, to entertain, to polemicize against enemies, etc. The function of an original *Gattung* does not often label the contents of that *Gattung* as necessarily unhistorical. History writing is not a form-critical category. It is a category of written literature that utilizes materials gained from many different sources, including oral sources.

58. This is the point where George Coats's beloved FOTL project needs to be much clearer in its methodological definitions and operations. Blessing may cover an oral *Gattung* and a structure in a written text, but blessing is a different entity in each situation and must be given clearly different definitions.

59. An exception would be a clearly metaphorical, parabolic, or fabular narrative such as appears in Judg. 9. At this point, form criticism can make a judgment that this is not told as a historical event but cannot make the historical judgment that the material was only secondarily placed in the mouth of Jotham.

Oral sources used in the conservative institutions of family and cult for the conservative purposes of education and celebration may well be expected to preserve historical memory with a strong degree of accuracy. Historians supported by Israelite political and religious institutions would be expected to look to such sources to find contents for their written history writing.

6.   The existence of oral literature in Israel also raises theological issues. These are far spread. In the forum of contemporary church and academy, the most pressing is in the area of the nature of Scripture itself. Must word of God be written word? In the area of prophecy and liturgy, the quick and obvious answer is, No. At least in the area of the universe's and Israel's beginnings, the same answer applies. The answer becomes crucial at this point because of the nature of the religion of Israel. No matter how many other cultures shared a belief in a deity having control of and directing a nation's or a universe's history, no nation produced a religion and a religious literature centred totally around the relationship between a God, a people and the people's history. For Israelite history, not fertility nor ecstasy, is the beginning point of apologetics. The historical verity, if not verfiability, is the kernel to its religious reality. To deny Israel its historical claims for its God is to deny the central characteristic of its God, his unabashed, undeterrable covenant love that creates and preserves a historical people throughout all history's changes. If oral tradition means tradition laden with the myths of neighbors, the amusements of storytellers, and the inventions of centuries-later writers, then Israel's basic liturgy loses all content. Thus, the theological issue of oral tradition is central for the nature of Israel's and Christianity's religion. Can oral tradition preserve reliable information? Study of oral tradition in contexts outside Israel always seems to emphasize the negative side of the answer. Form criticism that locates the basic *Sitz im Leben* for Israel's oral literature in the conservative environments of cultic reenactment and the family education may point in a different direction. It still does not point in a direction that ensures total historical accuracy. No human direction can do that. Whatever mode of composition one speaks of in relationship to biblical materials, the accuracy of its materials is not ensured by the mode of composition: oral, one creative author, *Volkliteratur*, editors, compilers, redactors. The accuracy of the historical narrative is a matter of theological dogma and faith confession. It is entirely dependent on the working of

the author of history. Perhaps, form criticism is one way the author has given us to see a little bit of his working procedures to create the Bible. If so, long live form criticism.

BEYOND REALITY: POETIC DISCOURSE AND PSALM 107

John W. Roffey

1. Introduction

Form criticism looks in two directions: seeking reference in the genre and world of the text, and searching for the text's life in the world of reality. However, form-critical work on the Psalms, as expressed in most commentaries on the Psalms, has failed to maintain that true Janus-like perspective. It has primarily focused on the world of reality for its reference. It is impossible for one who had the privilege of studying under George Coats to be content with such a betrayal of literary reference. It is a further privilege to contribute this essay in his honour and in appreciation of his ability to inspire students and to open for them the world of the Old Testament literature.

Two examples will clarify the above claim that form criticism has betrayed poetic discourse in its search for cultic origins, betraying literary for historical reference.

Concerning Psalm 8, Hans-Joachim Kraus claims that it is

> obvious that we assume a cultic *Sitz im Leben*. We might think of a festival at night, in the course of which the song of praise was intoned antiphonally.[1]

In asserting that the cultic setting for such a hymn is an outdoor, night liturgy, that this is the location of its experience, Kraus makes no allowance for its poetic reference to an experience that is both universal and personal: the archetypal memory of standing under the stars. This existential sense of wonder and awe, both archetypal and individual, does not at all obviously find its meaning in cultic intonations.

In reference to Psalm 90, Kraus places the psalm in a time of historical affliction, when the nation is under threat and life is

1. H.-J. Kraus, *Psalms*, I (Minneapolis: Augsburg, 1988), p. 179.

endangered.[2] It could well be that the contrary applies. Existentialist philosophers and social psychologists alike have recognized that personal or communal *Angst* is greatest when the external threat is least.[3] Psalm 90 speaks of what the existentialists call a universal sense of *Angst*, the crisis that comes to us as we experience our mortality, our finitude and our search for meaning.

While I am critical of Kraus's tendency to read cultic or historical referents into poetic discourse, I believe that he is not atypical of psalm criticism in the last century. Indeed, my decision to engage in a dialectic with Kraus on this issue is related to my conviction that his is the best available commentary of this genre on the Psalms.[4] While more recent years have seen a growing focus on the psalms as poetry,[5] contemporary insights from the hermeneutics of poetic discourse have not yet been adequately applied in commentaries on the Psalms.

In this paper, I undertake a reductive hermeneutic of psalm criticism, utilizing Paul Ricoeur's hermeneutics of reference and engaging Psalm 107 in order to demonstrate the failure to take seriously the poetic language of the psalms. Paradoxically, the reductive critique of the form-critical bias in commentaries then leads to some hypotheses about the *Sitz im Leben* of Psalm 107. This paper therefore also offers a recollective hermeneutic of Psalm 107, arising out of its second-order referential reading. The recollective hermeneutic also serves to demonstrate that reading the psalms as poetic discourse does not leave us with timeless, ahistorical abstractions.

Finally, full engagement with the poetics of Psalm 107 helps

2. 'The people obviously suffer from an affliction of long duration.' H.-J. Kraus, *Psalms*, II (Minneapolis: Augsburg, 1989), p. 217. Although, in fairness to Kraus, it must be noted that he recognized, with von Rad, that the final form of the psalm was more reflective as in the wisdom tradition.

3. E. Becker, *The Denial of Death* (London: Collier Macmillan, 1973), ch. 1.

4. On the claim that such form-critical, literalist readings of the psalms are dominant, cf. A.R. Johnson, 'The Psalms', in H.H. Rowley (ed.), *The Old Testament and Modern Study* (Oxford: Clarendon Press, 1951), pp. 162-209, and J.H. Eaton, 'The Psalms and Israel's Worship', in G.W. Anderson (ed.), *Tradition and Interpretation: Essays by Members of the Society for Old Testament Studies* (Oxford: Clarendon Press, 1979), pp. 238-73.

5. Compare the summary articles in the previous footnote with E.S. Gerstenberger, 'The Lyrical Literature', in D.A. Knight and G.M. Tucker (eds.), *The Hebrew Bible and its Modern Interpreters* (Philadelphia: Fortress Press, 1985), pp. 409-44.

identify it as a poem of instruction based on thanksgiving. It comes from the historical world of the sages who shaped the Psalter in post-exilic Israel.

2. *Reading the Psalms as Poetic Discourse and the Question of Reference*

Crucial interest in Psalm 107 has been concerned with three areas:

1. the cultic setting of the psalm, particularly the liturgical reference to Thanksgiving sacrifices (זבחי תודה) in v. 22;
2. the dating of the psalm, particularly the introduction, with its reference to the redeemed of the Lord (גאולי יהוה) and to the sea or the south (ים); and the dating of the concluding poem; and
3. the unity of the psalm, particularly the four groupings in the body of the psalm, the introduction and the concluding poem.

An important characteristic in discussions on these three areas has been the tendency to read the psalm not as poetic discourse but as language of signification. If we are to break with this, we need to have a hermeneutic theory that addresses the question of reference in poetic discourse.

In discussing what he means by a language of signification, Ricoeur refers to Aristotle's concern with the defining role of language; language that is formulated in such a way as to contain the locus of the true and the false.[6] This recourse to a direct reference for language was used to refute the sophistical arguments: 'Not to have one meaning is to have no meaning'.[7] Such signifying purpose for language highlights its function in a direct one-to-one reference between word and reality.[8] Nevertheless, Aristotle's claim was that the language of signification contains the definitions: that in its reference to reality we find the locus of truth.

6. K. Hart, 'Ricoeur's Distinctions', in P. Craven and M. Heyward (eds.), *Scripsi* (Melbourne: Penguin Books, 1989), p. 111.

7. Aristotle, 'Metaphysics', in *The Works of Aristotle*, VIII (trans. J.A. Smith and W.D. Ross; Oxford: Clarendon Press, 1908), ch. IV, 1006b, 8.

8. Aristotle, of course, recognized in his 'Metaphysics', 1006b, 19, that words could carry ambiguity. He also acknowledged that metaphor operates as another level of reference, cf. his 'Poetics', in *The Works of Aristotle*, XI (trans. J.A. Smith and W.D. Ross; Oxford: Clarendon Press, 1924), 1457b, 7.

It is this agreement type notion of truth which Martin Heidegger rejected. Heidegger pointed out that the semantic root of truth (*alētheia*) is properly understood as not hidden.[9] Thus the word, or discourse (*logos*), is the act of uncovering, of not hiding, the phenomena rather than of defining them. Truth, and meaning, need not be grounded in univocal language which has only one referent. Meaning and truth are also to be found in symbolic language that is equivocal.

Following Heidegger, Ricoeur distinguishes between signification and symbol:

> The notion of signification requires univocity of meaning: the definition of the principle of identity, in its logical and ontological sense, demands it. Univocity of meaning is ultimately grounded in essence, one and self identical.[10]

However, hermeneutics, in its concern with symbols and the meaning of being, rejects this univocal definition of language for all discourse. Ricoeur argues that literary works, legal texts, symbolic language, even ordinary language, all involve equivocal language.

> Being is said in several ways: being means substance, quality, time, place, and so on. The famous distinction of the many meanings of being are the categories, or figures, of predication; hence, this multiplicity cuts across the whole of discourse.[11]

Psalm commentators generally make reference to the symbolic language of the psalms, yet the import of this has not been incorporated into much of psalm criticism. It is not enough simply to assert that psalms are poetry. We need a theoretical basis from which to argue that the language of the psalms is more properly read as equivocal language, as *poiēsis*, that does not have direct, ostensive reference to reality. We can do this in three steps.

Firstly, the psalms are composed in ordinary language. Not even the theological claim for scripture as revelation or truth is inconsistent with this fact. Hymnic discourse, the language of humans addressed to God, is one of the five forms of revelatory discourse outlined by

9. M. Heidegger, *Being and Time* (trans. J. Macquarrie and E. Robinson; London: SCM Press, 1962), p. 56.

10. P. Ricoeur, *Freud and Philosophy* (New Haven: Yale University Press, 1970), p. 22.

11. Ricoeur, *Freud*, p. 23.

Ricoeur.[12] Its power to reveal lies in its very nature as ordinary language. Ordinary language is poetic discourse, that is, equivocal, symbolic.[13] The contextual nature of ordinary language, the language of speech and of discourse, gives the language a variety of meanings; it becomes equivocal rather than univocal signification. James Beshai expresses it:

> Once speech or discourse is set as the objective of the study of language, the entire course of investigation becomes altogether different from the 'language of bees', the 'language of computers', 'verbal responses', or 'verbal mediation'.[14]

Secondly, the psalms are poetic. If even ordinary language is to be understood as *poiēsis*, as symbolic or equivocal, then how much more must this apply to psalm language that is self-consciously poetic. In discussing the self-consciously poetic form of the psalms, Robert Alter speaks of them as,

> an act of singing or chanting, a way of using language... rhythmically and regularly, to implore, to admonish, to reflect—and above all, to celebrate... Many of the psalms devote special attention to the activity of song or utterance enacted in then, making it their virtual subject, 'foregrounding' the act of speech.[15]

Finally, there is a question of reference: the connection between poetic language and the world of reality. If language is to have meaning, then it must have reference. To argue that poetic language is not a univocal language of signification containing the locus of the true and the false does not mean that poetic language is without reference or truth value. Some structuralist and formalist schools in contemporary literary criticism would deny this, seeking the 'destruction of reference'.[16] We need to be wary of this, for, 'Without reference, there can

---

12. P. Ricoeur, 'Toward a Hermeneutic of the Idea of Revelation', in *Essays on Biblical Interpretation* (Philadelphia: Fortress Press, 1980), pp. 73-118.

13. P. Ricoeur, 'From Existentialism to the Philosophy of Language', in C.E. Reagan and D. Stewart (eds.), *The Philosophy of Paul Ricoeur* (Boston: Beacon Press, 1978), pp. 86-93 (92).

14. J.A. Beshai, 'Is Psychology a Hermeneutic Science?', *Journal of Phenomenological Psychology* 5.2 (1975), pp. 425-40 (426).

15. R. Alter, *The Art of Biblical Poetry* (New York: Basic Books, 1985), p. 133.

16. P. Ricoeur, *The Rule of Metaphor* (Toronto: University of Toronto Press, 1977), p. 224.

be no truth; and without truth, we are left open to the abuse of power'.[17]

In his search for the meaning of reference in poetic language, Ricoeur acknowledges that:

> In written language, the reference is no longer ostensive; poems, essays, works of fiction speak of things, events, states of affairs and characters are evoked but which are not there. And yet literary texts are about something. About what?[18]

Poetry further complicates the problem of reference in referring to itself and to other literary texts, removing it even more from the world about us.[19] This is the problem of reference.

One possible solution to the problem of reference is that even where poetry does not show the thing it talks about, it can situate it in 'a unique spatial temporal network' to which the writer and reader belong. We move from the ostensive world of reality to the phenomenological world of the text. The natural world still exists, but it is no longer the *ground* of our experience.[20]

In this phenomenological life-world (Husserl's *Lebenswelt*), we are no longer concerned with first-order reference between language, reality and truth (nor do we deny its truth claims). Rather, we attend again to Heidegger's truth as manifestation: we are confronted with our being within the world of the text (Heidegger's being-there, *Dasein*). This radical question of being is the hermeneutic of *Dasein*, rather than the more rational hermeneutic of the *cogito*.[21] Poetic discourse invites us into this second-order reference, into the truth of the possible worlds in which we may live.

In claiming even a second-order reference between poetry and reality, Ricoeur stands in the tradition of Plato's belief that the poetic

---

17. Hart, 'Ricoeur's Distinctions', p. 114. Hart details Frege's point that sentences without reference are open to political, demagogic abuse. This is an important reminder in biblical studies, given the dangers of abuse made possible through ahistorical, pietistic misappropriation of the text.

18. P. Ricoeur, *Hermeneutics and the Social Sciences* (Cambridge: Cambridge University Press, 1981), p. 177.

19. P. Ricoeur, 'Philosophical and Theological Hermeneutics', cited in Hart, 'Ricoeur's Distinctions', p. 115.

20. Hart, 'Ricoeur's Distinctions', p. 116.

21. P. Ricoeur, 'Heidegger and the Question of the Subject', in D. Ihde (ed.), *The Conflict of Interpretations* (Evanston, IL: Northwestern University Press, 1974), pp. 223-35 (230).

does represent in some way the forms of reality: that *poiēsis* is *mimēsis*.[22] However, following Aristotle and against Plato, Ricoeur argues that *poiēsis* reflects reality not by imitating it through idealism, but through re-creating its phenomenal reality by means of *muthos*, literature. Here Ricoeur follows similarly, with Auerbach, whose *Mimēsis* is subtitled, 'The representation of reality in western literature'. Thus, Ricoeur in *Time and Narrative* argues that in reading, the world of the text and the world of the reader intersect.[23] The reader appropriates the projection of the world contained within the text.

The argument that the psalms are to be read as equivocal language has therefore been established on the grounds of their being both ordinary language and self-consciously poetic. Furthermore, they are to be read symbolically, with only a second-order reference to reality. We can now proceed to a reading of Psalm 107 as poetic discourse.

3. *Psalm 107 as Poetic Discourse*

Many of the references in Psalm 107 have traditionally been read as univocal language of signification, particularly its image of the redeemed and its cultic references. This is largely because of attempts to resolve the critical concerns outlined earlier: that is, the search for possible cultic settings, the dating and the unity of the psalm.

The following structural analysis helps establish the fallacies in such a univocal hermeneutic. This structure identifies four units of the psalm: Invitation, Memory, Response and Instruction.

Invitation		*Verses*		
Invitation	1-3			
Memory (in four parts)				
Distress	4-5	10-12	17-18	23-27
Prayer	6	13	19	28
Deliverance	7	14	20	29-30
Response				
Thanksgiving	8	15	21-22	31-32
Motivation	9	16		

22. Hart, 'Ricoeur's Distinctions', p. 118.

23. P. Ricoeur, 'Mimēsis, Reference and Refiguration in *Time and Narrative*', in Craven and Heyward (eds.), *Scripsi* , pp. 99-100.

Instruction (in two parts)		
Curse	33-34	39-40
Blessing	35-38	41
Reflection	42-43	

We will return later to the Invitation, and start with the images contained in the Memory.

a. *Memory—Distress, Prayer and Deliverance*

In the body of the psalm (vv. 4-32), under the headings of Memory and Response, is a four-part embellishment of the redeemed who have been gathered in from trouble (vv. 1-3). While most would agree with this overall structure, attention has been focused on the possible historical origins of the individual parts, denying their unity of structure.

The pattern within each grouping is consistent. Despite this, much has been made of the diversity in length across groupings: both the development of the sea segment in vv. 23-27 and, to a lesser extent, the additional reflection within vv. 10-12 concerning the prisoners in v. 11. However, Johannes de Moor has demonstrated that it is

> one of the leading principles of versification in the West Semitic world that especially on the level of the smaller structural units... the singers were allowed a certain freedom to expand or to contract their text.[24]

In Psalm 107, de Moor argues that each of the four canticles has to be divided into three strophes (using my headings of Memory and Response)

(Memory)					
Strophe I:	Distress	4-5	10-12	17-18	23-27
Strophe II:	Prayer & Deliverance	6-7	13-14	19-20	28-30
(Response)					
Strophe III:	Thanksgiving & Motivation	8-9	15-16	21-22	31-32

De Moor concludes that even though the length of each strophe varies considerably, it is not necessary to explain this by assuming a number of glosses. The psalm conforms to his principle of expansion within Semitic poetry.

I would also argue that the unity of the psalm is reflected in the four archetypal images within the Memory. The traditional reading of the four groups has sought to separate them by reading them as univocal

---

24. J.C. de Moor, 'The Art of Versification in Ugarit and Israel III: Further Illustrations of the Principle of Expansion', *UF* 12 (1980), pp. 311-15.

language of signification with first-order reference to the world of reality. So Kraus, quoting Gunkel, argued that,

> in the festival days, perhaps at the time of the great autumnal festival, it was impossible to make arrangements for the individual offerings of the large number of those giving thanks; time and space would not have sufficed. 'Therefore the priests arranged a common festival of thanksgiving offerings for all of these people, something that might be compared with the mass baptisms or mass marriages seen in our large cities.'[25]

A second-order poetic reading of the memories would suggest that we are not being invited into four groups of separate experiences. We are being invited into 'a unique spatial-temporal network', into the phenomenal world of the text. This phenomenal world becomes the ground of our experience as we encounter what it means to be 'redeemed from trouble' (v. 2).

The poet has drawn on four images of distress that we can all understand even if never having experienced them in reality. It is in this sense that they are archetypal and hence, in Jungian typography, collective or universal.[26] Thus, for example, it is misleading to suggest that the psalm is written for travelers,[27] or to enter into discussions about whether or not or when the Hebrew people were sea-going and hence able to identify with vv. 23-37.[28]

It is particularly interesting that Oswald Loretz accepts that vv. 4-22 cover the whole spectrum of human need, while claiming that vv. 23-27 cover only seafarers. Yet biblical poetry, especially in the post-exilic period, is replete with references to God and the sea, to God's ordering the chaos of the deep and to the taming of Leviathan.[29]

The world of the text, to which Psalm 107 makes second-order

---

25. Kraus, *Psalms*, II, p. 326. Also, S. Mowinckel, *The Psalms in Israel's Worship*, II (Nashville: Abingdon, 1962), p. 42. Against this, J.H. Eaton, *Psalms* (London: SCM Press, 1967), p. 256.

26. C.G. Jung, 'The Archetypes and the Collective Unconscious', in *C.G. Jung, The Collected Works*, IX.1 (London: Routledge & Kegan Paul, 1968), p. 3.

27. Cf. M. Dahood, *Psalms*, III (New York: Doubleday, 1970), p. 80.

28. See O. Loretz, 'Baal-Jahwe als Beschützer der Kaufleute in Ps. 107', *UF* 12 (1980), pp. 417-19, both for a summary of views on this pericope and for his own conclusion that this pericope evidences a close connection between Ps. 107 and Canaanite literature concerning merchants on both sea and land.

29. Gen. 1; Job 38, 41; Pss. 18, 33, 74, 89, 114, 148; Jonah; and (especially relevant to this study) Isa. 42.10, 50.2, 51.10, 15.

reference, is our experience of distress from which we are redeemed. All four images combine to express the whole spectrum of human needs through the archetypal language of desert and watery chaos, of imprisonment and illness. The reader, then and now, can enter into such experiences of distress and redemption whether or not all its details have been experienced in reality.

b. *Response—Thanksgiving and Motivation*

Just as the structure I have proposed for Psalm 107 highlights the parallelism of the four archetypal images in the Memory, it also points to a poetic parallelism within the Response.

Psalm 107 is generally classified as a psalm of thanksgiving. Kraus (following Crüsemann) suggests that, rather than a thanksgiving psalm, it is a summons to give thanks, 'a cultic introduction to the innumerable individual thanksgiving'.[30] Those called to give thanks are to bring forward the priestly thanksgiving offering, the תודה of v. 22. Largely as a result of this one cultic reference, Kraus suggests that the psalm's origin is very old, located in the pre-exilic cult.

Kraus's analysis is another example of a univocal reading of signification with a first-order reference to a historical event, in this case the pre-exilic sacrificial cult.[31] Yet the parallelism of the four archetypal images introduced in the Memory is maintained within the Response.

We are asked to thank God in vv. 8, 15, 21, 31 in response to God's answer to our prayer for deliverance. Verses 22 and 32 expand on the nature of the thanksgiving response. In thanks for God's steadfast love, we are invited to offer thanksgiving sacrifices, to tell of God's deeds, to extol God in the congregation and to praise God in the assembly of the elders. The offering of sacrifices of thanksgiving should not be read as one literal expression over against the other suggested ways of expressing thanks.

Alter claimed that the psalms devote special attention to the act of speech. In his analysis of Psalm 30, he demonstrates how the bias is tilted along the poet's medium, language.[32] I would claim that this bias to language is also true in Psalm 107. In its structure it invites us to *remember* our memories of deliverance from distress, to *recall* our

---

30. Kraus, *Psalms*, II, p. 327.

31. Kraus, *Psalms*, II, p. 327. Also Mowinckel, *Psalms*, II, p. 17.

32. Alter, *Biblical Poetry*, p. 135.

thanks for that deliverance and to *reflect* on the nature of God's stead-fast love. These are all language activities and they draw us into the language medium of the psalm. Should not the offering of sacrifices of thanksgiving also be read as a language activity rather than as the one isolated 'act-reference'?

If we place the weight of meaning of the psalm on one isolated 'act-reference' (the cultic זבחי תודה), then we misinterpret the language medium of the psalm. In v. 22, sacrifices of thanksgiving are to be read symbolically as 'language-reference' along with the other language acts of thanksgiving in vv. 8, 15, 21-22 and 31-32. The claim for a poetic reading of תודה is not entirely new. For example, Walter Beyerlin claims a double *Sitz im Leben* for the זבחי תודה of v. 22 and for the 'travelers' within the psalm.[33] He recognizes the post-exilic wisdom shape of the psalm, but sees other origins in the individual sacrificial cult and travelers' thanksgiving songs. However, there is no need to conclude that v. 22 has to be from an earlier cultic setting.

The parallelisms in vv. 22 and 32, together with the language medium bias of the psalm as a whole and the linguistic ties to הדו in v.1 and יודו in vv. 8, 15, 21 and 31, all point to a second-order reference reading of תודה as language-event. Given the long and continuing association between sacrificial offerings and healing, it is not surprising that the poetic image of thanksgiving sacrifice is used in this healing context as another language image to complement speaking, extolling and praising.

A language-reference reading of תודה is also consistent with Harvey Guthrie's recognition that the function of von Rad's *credo* in the Hexateuch has parallels with the function of תודה in the Psalter.[34] Both ground the people's sense of identity in a ritualized memory of their experience of God. Whatever its origins in the cult, the תודה has become a language-event, articulating the people's memories of distress, deliverance and response.

c. *Instruction—Curse, Blessing and Reflection*
The final part of the psalm, the Instruction, invites reflection on the nature of God's steadfast love. Its language reflects the wisdom

33. W. Beyerlin, *Werden und Wesen des 107 Psalms* (Berlin: de Gruyter, 1979), p. 97.

34. H. Guthrie, Jr, *Theology as Thanksgiving* (New York: Seabury, 1981), pp. 43-59.

tradition. Each of the two parts (vv. 33-38 and its parallel in vv. 39-41) follows the traditional two ways theme of wisdom instruction (*torah*) (as in Psalm 2). Each contains a curse (the wicked impoverished and the mighty brought low) and a blessing (the hungry nourished and the needy enriched). Each follows the wisdom literature style of reversal of fortunes.[35]

However, this wisdom style of reversal of fortunes is not limited to the final section of the psalms. It is present in, and consistent with, the psalm as a whole. Within each of the four parts of the Memory there is reversal: distress followed by deliverance. Also present across the psalm's sections are other reversals. There is the way of an inhabited city (דרך עיר מושב [Zion?], v. 4) with the chaos of no way (תהו לא־דרך, v. 40). There are those who are wise (מי־חכם, v. 43) with those in the storm, when 'all their wisdom was gone' (כל־חכמתם, v. 27).[36]

The final part of the Instruction is reflection on the steadfast love (חסד) of the Lord. The psalm has moved from the initial invitation to give thanks for the Lord's steadfast love, an invitation repeated throughout, through to reflection (בין) on that steadfast love.

While many have accepted that the psalm received its final shape in the post-exilic wisdom tradition, recognizing in this period the language and style of vv. 1-3 and 33-43,[37] the same wisdom reversal style, imagery and language of vv. 33-41 are found throughout the psalm (the desert, the way, the inhabited town, hunger and thirst). The Introduction and the Instruction on God's steadfast love are not simply later developments that have enabled the psalm, 'freed from its cultic past',[38] to be shaped into a sage's reflection.

Kraus, after Duhm, suggests that it is not surprising that a 'supple-

35. Dahood, *Psalms*, III, p. 80.

36. Kraus's translation of v. 27b. Yet he does not draw the association with v. 43. Given the carefulness in language and the structure of the psalm, it is even harder to credit Gunkel's comment that vv. 25-27 are 'conspicuous because their frivolous manner departs from the seriousness of the rest' (Kraus, *Psalms*, II, p. 326).

37. See Beyerlin, *Werden und Wesen*, pp. 107-108, for both a summary of hypotheses concerning the mixed origins of the psalm and for the argument that while it does come from mixed origins, it is nevertheless a poem rather than a mere compilation of parts. Beyerlin refers to the creative activity of an editor poet who was both a speaker of wisdom sayings and a biblical scholar.

38. Contra Kraus and Beyerlin. As argued, the reference in v. 22 does not in itself necessitate a cultic heritage and is better read as a language-act.

mental poem' would reflect the language of what has gone before.[39] I would argue, on the grounds of consistency of language, themes and structure, that the entire psalm is composed as a unity.[40] It is also possible to identify the literary world to which this composition belongs.

4. *A Recollective Hermeneutic of Psalm 107*

I have argued for a reading of the psalm as poetic discourse, with its own language world and with only a second-order reference to reality. The following recollective hermeneutic demonstrates that even with such a second-order rather than ostensive reference to reality we are not left with a timeless, ahistorical abstraction. It is possible to place the psalm in a historical setting and in relation to its role in the shaping of the Psalter.

I have already noted the characteristic of poetry to make reference to itself and other literary texts. Using this phenomenon, the literary world of the whole of Psalm 107 can be seen to be the post-exilic world of Israel that was defined in the language and images of Deutero-Isaiah.

Common Imagery and Language	Psalm 107	Isaiah
The desert turning fertile	35-36	41.17-18; 43.19-21; 44.3
The drying up of the fertile	33-34	44.27; 50.2
The way through the desert	4-7, 40	40.3-4; 43.19-21 *et al.*
Affliction, offering and healing	17-20	51.21; 53.10-12; 54.10
Imprisonment and deliverance (note direct parallel)	10-14 16	42.7, 22; 45.2b; 49.9-12 (45.2b)
The control of the sea, of chaos (תהו)	23-30 40	43.16; 50.2, 51.10, 15; 54.11 (45.18)
YHWH as redeemer (גאולי יהוה)	2, 3 2	43.1 *et al.* (62.12)
Redemption and sea	2-3, 23-30	51.10, 11, 15
From the north and from the sea מצפון ומים	3	49.12

We need to be cautious about claiming a common literary world on the basis of word associations alone. However, in addition to the sheer

---

39. Kraus, *Psalms*, II, p. 325.
40. See also Dahood, *Psalms*, III, p. 89.

dominance of desert/water/way/prisoners language and imagery, there are a number of strong indicators of a common literary milieu.

The title 'redeemed of the Lord' is only attested in Ps. 107.2 and Isa. 62.12. However, its origin as a reference to the post-exilic community is readily traced to the dominant use in Deutero-Isaiah of גאל in reference to YHWH both in its verbal form and as a title.[41]

The imagery and language of the sea has long been an issue in the study of this psalm, with focus on the degree to which Israel was a sea-going nation. I have already argued that the archetypal image of the sea has meaning even for those who have never traveled it. There is evidence for this also in the literary world of Deutero-Isaiah, where there are two categories of references to the sea.

The first category is the mix of sea, chaos and the creative power of God. The God who has power to raise up and control the sea is able to act to redeem Israel. The second category associates the memory of God's action in history (the exodus from Egypt) with the crossing of the sea. This association of sea and exodus is particularly relevant to another important literary tie between Psalm 107 and Deutero-Isaiah: the use of מצפון ומים normally translated 'from the north and the south'. The Deutero-Isaiah references to the crossing of the sea and the southern exodus make it unnecessary to emend ים in 107.3.[42] John Jarick has also recently argued for retaining the reading as 'sea', noting that the four directions in v. 3 then parallel the four stanzas in our Memory section of the psalm.[43]

We can therefore conclude that Psalm 107 is a product of the post-exilic literary world that was shaped by the prophecies of Deutero-Isaiah. We have seen that not only the Invitation and Instruction, but also the Memory and Response with their images of desert, imprisonment, illness and sea, all belong in this literary world. It is neither a summons to thanksgiving or a thanksgiving psalm located within the pre-exilic cult with its sacrificial offerings. It is a psalm of instruction

41. 'The redeemed' as a title is also used in Isa. 35.9, 51.10, 63.4. Note the 51.10d, 11a chiasm, the redeemed to pass over, and the ransomed of the Lord shall return (ופדויי יהוה ישובון and גאולים לצבד), and its similarity to the other two instances of the 'redeemed of the Lord' as a title.

42. Here I have sympathy with Dahood and his translation, 'southern-sea', *Psalms*, III, p. 81.

43. 'The Four Corners of Psalm 107', paper presented to IOSOT Fifteenth Congress, Cambridge, 1995; forthcoming in *Catholic Biblical Quarterly*.

based on thanksgiving: beginning with our memories of redemption, inviting a response of thanksgiving and finally moving towards reflection on the nature of God's steadfast love.

As a psalm of instruction, we can more clearly see the role of Psalm 107 within the Psalter as a whole. J. Clinton McCann has argued that the Psalter, through editorial activity, was 'appropriated, preserved and transmitted as instruction to the faithful'.[44] McCann draws heavily on Gerald Wilson's work on the editing of the five-book structure of the Hebrew Psalter.[45]

Wilson refers to the roles of Psalms 106 and 107, with their invitations to give thanks, in relation to the fourth and the fifth books of the Psalter. Whereas in 106, the people are looking forward to being gathered from among the nations, for 107 this event is in the past. It is the answer to the plea for redemption, introducing the fifth book with its 'attitude of dependence and trust in YHWH alone'.[46] Likewise, Psalm 118 with its invitation to give thanks, introduces the reflection of Psalm 119 on *torah*. Wilson concludes that the Psalter 'assumed final form at a time when the sages had the upper hand in restructuring the community's perception of these cultic traditions'.[47]

Psalm 107 can be seen to serve this function within the Psalter. However, I am suggesting not only that it serves a function in the sage's editing of the Psalter, but that the psalm itself is a wisdom composition. Wilson and Mays have detailed the role of other wisdom psalms (1, 18, 19, 90, 106, 119, 145) in marking the beginning and endings of books and groupings within the Psalter.[48] My contention that 107 is a wisdom psalm supports Mays's, Wilson's, and McCann's work on the Psalter. Likewise, their work on the creative activity of the sages in the development of the Psalter provides a valid context for the wisdom composition of Psalm 107.

44. J.C. McCann, Jr, 'The Psalms as Instruction', *Int* 46.2 (1992), pp. 117-28 (118). See also G.H. Wilson, 'The Shape of the Book of Psalms', *Int* 46.2 (1992), pp. 129-42.

45. G.H. Wilson, *The Editing of the Hebrew Psalter* (SBLDS; Chico, CA: Scholars Press, 1985). See also B.S. Childs, *Introduction to the Old Testament as Scripture* (Philadelphia: Fortress Press, 1976), ch. 33.

46. Wilson, *Editing*, p. 227. See also J.L. Mays, 'The Place of the Torah Psalms in the Psalter', *JBL* 106.1 (1987), pp. 3-12.

47. Wilson, 'Shape', p. 138.

48. Wilson, 'Shape', p. 134; Mays, 'Place', p. 8.

My reading of Psalm 107 incorporates what many form-critical scholars refer to as 'mixed genres'.[49] It is a psalm of instruction that begins with a call to thanksgiving, invites memories of suffering and redemption along with responses of thanksgiving, and then moves towards reflection on the nature of God's steadfast love. Mays has suggested that many 'mixed genre' psalms 'are a type of literature whose generic characteristic is the gathering and combination of styles and materials into a new kind of unit'.[50]

To claim that this is a thanksgiving psalm only is to overlook its role in instruction. Even the 'definitive hymn',[51]

O give thanks to the Lord for he is good;
for his steadfast love endures forever!

that introduces the psalm is more than an expression of praise.[52] The reference to חסד calls to mind God's covenantal faithfulness which grounds the experience of redemption. It provides the rationale for reflection which the upright see and the wise heed.

McCann has argued that within the psalms of praise there is a movement from hymns of praise to teachings on how to live.[53] Likewise, Psalm 90 moves from lament to wisdom (cf. Ps. 90.12).[54] In a similar manner, Psalm 107 teaches that an attitude of thanksgiving leads to a greater wisdom about the nature of God. The grounds for our thanksgiving are not just the historical redemption from exile (vv. 2, 3), but also the archetypal memories of distress and deliverance, expressed poetically in vv. 4-32. In giving thanks, something of God's nature as the one who raises up and brings down is revealed to us.

49. Mays, 'Place', p. 5.

50. Mays, 'Place', p. 5.

51. P.D. Miller, Jr, 'Enthroned on the Praises of Israel', *Int* 39.1 (1985), pp. 5-19 (10). Miller refers to this as the Old Testament paradigm of the song of praise, cf. 2 Chron. 5.13; 7.3, 6; 20.21; Ezra 3.10-11; Jer. 33.10-11; Pss. 106.1; 118.1, 29; 136.1ff.

52. Note Westermann's distinction between declarative praise (Gunkel's song of thanksgiving, תודה) and descriptive praise (Gunkel's hymn, תהללה), *Praise and Lament in the Psalms* (Atlanta: John Knox, 1981). While Westermann's distinction is not generally agreed to, there is a valid distinction between primal, immediate forms of prayer and more reflective praise or lament.

53. McCann, 'Psalms as Instruction', pp. 123ff.

54. W. Brueggemann, *The Message of the Psalms* (Minneapolis: Augsburg, 1984), p. 110.

Psalm 107 comes to us as a poem of instruction based on thanksgiving. It comes from the historical world of the sages who shaped the Psalter, but it is not tied to that world. The power of this psalm lies in the way in which its archetypal symbols of distress and deliverance are able to be recognized and known across the centuries. In recognizing the second-order reference reality of the psalms as poetry, we are freed from the danger of limiting the psalms to a moment in history. As Ricoeur argues, poetic discourse does not speak to us of the world around us, only of possible worlds in which we may live.[55]

55. Hart, 'Ricoeur's Distinctions', pp. 116-17.

REDACTION CRITICISM: WHENCE, WHITHER, AND WHY? OR, GOING BEYOND SOURCE AND FORM CRITICISM WITHOUT LEAVING THEM BEHIND

Lawson G. Stone

I begin with a word of appreciation for the personal enrichment afforded by the scholarly labors and personal contribution of the man whom we honor in this volume, George W. Coats. For me, he has been a vital link to the great figures of Old Testament interpretation such as Gerhard von Rad and Walter Zimmerli, not just because he knew and worked with them, but also because of the quality and spirit of his own interpretation. When I first came to the Lexington area five years ago, I found in George a ready wit, a provocative conversation partner, a valuable mentor, and a loyal friend. My scholarly pursuits have been fuelled by Professor Coats, especially in his role as one of the leading practitioners and theoreticians of the traditio-historical approach to biblical interpretation.

1. *The Problem with Redaction Criticism*

I have long been concerned that the discipline of redaction criticism has never attained in Old Testament studies the kind of methodological clarity and fruitfulness that one finds in New Testament studies, especially in the period just after the Second World War, when New Testament redaction criticism enabled us to rediscover the evangelists, seeing each of the four Gospels as a distinct literary entity worthy of independent study, thus opening the way to defining the precise and unique contribution made by each to the theological vision of the New Testament. Unfortunately, Old Testament redaction criticism has always looked much as New Testament redaction criticism looks today: over-refined, over-preoccupied with hypothetical historical reconstructions of 'communities' behind the redactors, and completely preoccupied with intermediate levels of redaction prior to the final form of the text, leaving the received text largely unexplored as an editorial creation with its own distinctive contours and emphases. In New Testament studies this constitutes a degeneration, a kind of fall from grace. In Old Testament studies, it is reflective of a failure of the method to find its proper location in the context of the other historical-critical disciplines. Old Testament redaction criticism essentially went from childhood to senility in one generation! In 1969 James Muilenberg called Old Testament scholars to go 'beyond' form criticism to the study of the distinctive literary features of the present text, a discipline he christened 'rhetorical criticism', thus launching in Old Testament studies a powerful movement emphasizing the literary analysis of the text.[1] Unfortunately, although Muilenberg saw this literary emphasis as derived from and related to form criticism, his subsequent interpreters quickly abandoned that connection. They moved 'beyond form criticism', leaving it behind in the process. Thus we find in Old Testament studies a great dichotomy between source, form, and redaction criticism on the one hand and studies of the literary structure, themes, and even theological emphases of the finished Old Testament books on the other. Old Testament studies is trapped between diachronic and synchronic modes of interpretation, between analysis and synthesis. One often hears calls to move 'beyond' traditio-historical study, with the strong implication that such study is not simply transcended, but abandoned as well, and that with some relief.

But must this be? From the outset I must say I am not yet ready to join the post-modern, anti-enlightenment chorus in its chant that historical criticism is dead or, worse, should never have lived. I suspect we will find that historical criticism is like an intellectual Elvis—its supposed death will always remain problematic and debatable, and it will ultimately become even more influential (and profitable!) 'dead' than it would be if it continued living as a puffy, wheezing, overweight and overdressed performer. My own efforts recently have focused on a reconsideration of the role of redaction criticism in order to see if its basic principles may be formulated so as to serve as a point in interpretation where the insights of the diachronic, historical, analytical disciplines, most notably source criticism and form criticism, are brought into conversation with the insights of synchronic literary criticism.

1.	J. Muilenberg, 'Form Criticism and Beyond', *JBL* 88 (1969), pp. 1-18.

2. *Whence?*

The problem in describing the method of redaction criticism in Old Testament studies derives partly from the fact that the term 'redaction' was used in very different ways by the two most important methods of Old Testament exegesis: source criticism and form criticism.

'Redaction' in Source Criticism

The term 'redaction' was first used to explain how the Pentateuch could be composed from four distinct literary source documents, and yet still possess an overarching unity of plot and theme.[2] Right from the start, source criticism understood redaction to be the process by which separate documents were successively combined to produce the present text of the Pentateuch as well as other books, most notably Joshua–Kings. Hypotheses about redaction were thus the means by which scholars sought to account for the *ultimate conceptual unity* of documents such as the Pentateuch which, to all appearances, had *emerged from diverse origins*.

Despite the possibility that the redactors might be seen as creative writers weaving a unified theological narrative out of their sources, the tendency of source criticism was to view the redactors negatively. The profound recontextualizing of the material in the sources resulting from the redactor's combing of the documents was felt only as a historical annoyance. The possible interpretative significance was missed entirely. Most interpreters hoped to penetrate behind the redactor's work to the pre-existent sources, which, they thought, were both historically and religiously more pristine. This preoccupation with historical originality and purity thus caused the early source critics to view the work of the redactors as a species of textual corruption. There was simply no chance that anyone would find here a profound theological dynamic.

'Redaction' in Form Criticism

With form criticism, a whole new vision of the Old Testament

2.   An initiation into source criticism appears in N. Habel, *Literary Criticism of the Old Testament* (Guides to Biblical Scholarship: Philadelphia: Fortress Press, 1971). Note the continuation of the term 'literary' criticism in reference to what I am calling 'source' criticism.

literature came into play that focused on the dynamics of oral composition, performance, and transmission. Here the emphasis shifted to the communal context of the tradition and its performative function in ancient society. As units of tradition served new functions, their forms developed and changed. Thus the tracing of the alteration of the form of stories, hymns, prayers, laws, or even motifs and themes revealed profound dynamics of communal interpretation and reinterpretation. Form criticism generally took a dim view of the stage when the oral traditions were written down, a point which they designated by the word 'redaction'. According to the early form critics, the transformation of the material into written texts was in no way creative, but merely preservative. The move to writing was seen by early form critics as something approaching a tragedy. Either the tradition had died in the popular consciousness, or, overburdened with accretions and additions, it required writing simply to survive. Upon its being written, Hebrew tradition became the private bailiwick of scribes and scholars. This transformation from oral traditions to written texts was called *redaction* by form critics, and though in theory the whole process from oral composition through intermediate stages of literary development to the final written form belonged to the history of the transmission of tradition (*Überlieferungsgeschichte*), the final stage in which the tradition was written down was rarely taken seriously. Orality ruled the day.

It is difficult to overstate the disparaging of writing expressed by the early form critics. For Gunkel, the great tradition of Hebrew literature was the move to writing. A text is simply the coffin in which a dead tradition was entombed, or the prison in which ancient academic scribes incarcerated it. Worse still for Gunkel was canonization, which he considered the greatest tragedy of all. Material once alive in the oral tradition of the people, which once served a vital, concrete function, had now become the copy-book of religious clerics who dissected it in order to moralize upon it. Not even the arrangement of the material was regarded as providing an opportunity for creative imagination. The redactors, according to the early form critics, were driven solely by the mechanics of preservation and textual transmission.

Rehabilitating the Redactor: A Pioneer and Five Critical Insights
But were the early form critics correct in their devaluation of writing? Before long there were signs pointing to a reassessment. This

trend was most apparent in Gerhard von Rad's ground-breaking study of the J document (the Yahwist).[3] Von Rad first used form criticism to reconstruct the oral source material lying behind the J document. He propounded his famous thesis that, prior to the composition of the J document, the basic narrative of salvation which forms the structure of the J narrative, the Sinai material, and the primeval history were fully separate, self-contained traditions used at different places in Israel where they served distinct functions. Von Rad then analyzed the implications of this thesis for understanding the integration of these separate oral traditions and their transformation into writing, a transformation von Rad argued was not only a literary achievement, but a triumph of political and theological formulation as well. For von Rad, such a writer could be no 'mere redactor', but must be seen as a creative theological writer of the first magnitude, and, one is tempted to suggest, a theologian with Lutheran sympathies! Although von Rad rejected the term 'redactor' for his Yahwist, it is incontrovertible that von Rad's Yahwist fulfilled all the functions form critics had assigned to the role of redactor. What had to change was not the term, but the negative evaluation. Clearly if von Rad were even partly right, the redactors needed to be seen much more positively.

Over time, interpreters came to realize that von Rad was right about the transformation of these traditions from oral form to written form—redaction. We have also realized that the combination of written documents involved much more than mere 'scissors and paste' work, but flowed out of a profound interpretative mindset.[4] The development of the Old Testament traditions involved both the transformation of the medium of the material from oral tradition to written literature, and the related impact of the successive reordering undergone by the tradition as the literary documents were compiled and edited.[5] Five insights into this phenomenon triggered a rehabilitation

3.   G. von Rad, 'The Form-Critical Problem of the Hexateuch', in *The Problem of the Hexateuch and Other Essays* (Edinburgh: Oliver & Boyd, 1966), pp. 1-78.

4.   Cf. M. Fishbane, *Biblical Interpretation in Ancient Israel* (Oxford: Clarendon Press, 1985); B.S. Childs, 'The Exegetical Significance of Canon for the Study of the Old Testament', in *Congress Volume: Göttingen 1977* (VTSup; Leiden: Brill, 1978), pp. 66-80; *idem*, 'The Canonical Shape of the Prophetic Literature', *Int* 32 (1978), pp. 46-55.

5.   For a terse summation of these ideas, cf. von Rad, 'Form-Critical Problem', pp. 48-50.

of the redactor and gave birth to redaction criticism. These insights were shared, in varying degrees of clarity and explicitness, by von Rad and his colleagues and crucial New Testament scholars such as Wrede, Schmidt, Bultmann, and especially Marxsen, Bornkamm, and Conzelmann.

1. First, these interpreters recognized the *pervasiveness* of redactional activity. If the standard critical theories of their day were even partly true, then virtually the entire Old Testament and the four Gospels have come to us wholly through the work of one or more redactors. The Pentateuch appeared to have passed through three or four stages of editorial composition, the Former Prophets (Joshua, Judges, Samuel, Kings) through at least one comprehensive editorial compilation followed by one or more revisions. Clearly when most of the Bible in its present form is the result of redaction, this phenomenon is worthy of more focused study.

2. Second, interpreters realized that the process of redaction had transformed the *setting* of the material. Form criticism had previously emphasized the heuristic potential of exploring the life context of an individual unit of the biblical tradition in its oral state. The context within which the text had its meaning was the life, worship, and institutions of ancient Israel, and the meaning of the text derived from oral presentation of the text. For the Old Testament traditions, these settings were almost always *sacral*, that is, situations in which Israel came before Yahweh in collective liturgical acts. This communal and sacral context that had served as an echo-chamber for the traditions now fell away and was replaced by a *literary* context. As a result, the traditions were, in von Rad's terms, *desacralized*. Their setting was no longer necessarily Israel's sacred, communal encounters with Yahweh. No longer did the realities of communal life and worship—debate at the city gate, preparation for battle, collective confession, singing— provide the referent for the tradition. The material had been loosened, even detached from these moorings. This loss of context required that the reader now find a new framework of association and reference to understand the texts. Here the redactor's role as anthologist came into play. The sacral life context was replaced by a literary context. Stories, songs, sayings, and laws, which had previously never been heard together, suddenly stood side by side, interacting with each other, mutually conditioning each other's meaning, and creating a new network of literary association from which new meanings and applications

arose. This process continued and deepened as the documentary sources were combined into larger accounts.

3.   Third, interpreters recognized that the move to written texts also transformed the potential *audience* of the tradition. As long as the stories of the promises to the ancestors were part of Israel's oral traditions, as long as the story of salvation was bound to the liturgy of Israel, no one could appropriate Israel's revelation without participating directly in the life, culture, and worship of Israel. The audience for the oral tradition was thus limited to the territory, culture, and practice of the nation. Once the material became a literary text, its potential audience was greatly expanded both geographically and ethnically. First, the literate Israelite could reflect in depth on the whole array of Hebrew religious tradition *without actually participating directly in any of its religious institutions*. Living in the land of Israel was no longer a prerequisite for appropriating the tradition. A very profound reversal had occurred: originally, Israel's life in the promised land had been the home for the text; now the text could become the home for the exiled Israelite.[6] But the expansion of the potential audience of the tradition went further, not merely in theory, but in reality. The written text made it possible for *anyone* to draw on Israel's record of Yahweh's dealings without ever placing oneself in the Israelite community. Thus the shift of medium made it possible for Israel's religious traditions to transcend their ethnic cultural origins and become accessible to any audience regardless of its social and ethnic location. Whether one was an Israelite stripped of the temple worship by the Babylonian exile, or a Jew living in the dispersion, or a Gentile seeking to know Israel's God, it was no longer necessary to participate liturgically and socially in Israel's life. One could now read it in a book. Again, this profoundly reversed the previous order. Before, the Israelite community had defined the tradition; now it became possible for the text to define the community.

4.   Fourth, the shift from an oral to a written medium for Israel's traditions not only changed the potential audience for the material, it also drastically altered the *function* of the traditions, that is, what they actually did for those who used them. The previous form of the material involved a *performative* function in which the words *did* something, such as renew the covenant; the written form of the materials

6.   For a provocative exposition of the notion of a text as homeland, cf. G. Steiner, 'Our Homeland, the Text', *Selmagundi* 66 (1985), pp. 4-25.

quite naturally shifted the emphasis to their *communicative* function, to the events and ideas spoken of in the texts. Von Rad referred to this shift as *spiritualization*. Consequently, one responded to the tradition in a new way. In the sphere of public worship, Israel had experienced the text as the actualization of God's past acts for the present as the liturgy dramatically portrayed the continuing power of the mighty acts of God narrated in the tradition. Readers, of course, can 're-experience' the exodus, but the mode of experience is mainly interior and imaginative.[7] As texts, the traditions now invite us to read them and reflect on the events and ideas presented.[8] Put schematically, the manner by which the tradition is interpreted shifted from the liturgical actualization to the theological exposition.[9] The written traditions thus opened up the possibility for the material to function devotionally and theologically for the individual reader. Consequently, the character of the religious life changed as well. The study of the texts, meditation on them, and conforming one's life to their teaching became essential to piety.

5.   Fifth, Old Testament interpreters recognized the *seriousness and sophistication* of the literary activity comprehended under the term 'redaction'. The manner in which the materials were arranged, the ways in which they appeared to have been altered to fit their new context, their obvious pertinence to the needs of various stages of Israel's history, all pointed to *serious theological intention* on the part of the compilers and editors. Alongside von Rad's interpretation of the Yahwist, other works, such as Noth's stimulating work on Joshua–Kings[10] and emerging studies showing that the prophetic traditions had been organized literally under the pressure of theological concerns

7.   J. Groves offers an analysis of von Rad's use of the concept of actualization in *Actualization and Interpretation in the Old Testament* (SBLDS, 86; Atlanta: Scholars Press, 1987). See my review of Groves in *Asbury Theological Journal* 44 (1989), pp. 91-93.

8.   That von Rad saw spiritualization in theological terms is suggested by his linkage of 'rationalization' (*Rationalizierung*) to 'spiritualization' (*Spiritualizierung*).

9.   We should note here, however, that the power of the Old Testament traditions to actualize the past action of God for the present *via* liturgical use has not been lost, as the liturgical use of scripture in Christian and Jewish worship clearly shows. Even here, however, Christian use is possible only because the textualization of the tradition has permitted its audience to be redefined so as to include non-Jews.

10.   M. Noth, *The Deuteronomistic History* (JSOTSup, 15; Sheffield: JSOT Press, 1981 [1943]).

fuelled the rehabilitation of the redactor in the minds of biblical critics. These insights were summed up cleverly by Franz Rosenzwieg, who suggested that the siglum 'R', far from signifying 'Redactor', should be taken to signify *rebbenu*, 'our teacher'![11]

3. *What and Whither?*

It will be helpful to present a summary definition of redaction criticism both as a description of present practice and as a proposal for future development. Redaction criticism is the exegetical method that assesses *conceptual unity* in texts thought to possess *original diversity*.

Recognition of Compositional Diversity

First, redaction criticism works with texts thought to possess *diversity in origin*. Redaction criticism comes into play whenever the interpreter detects those phenomena of style, structure, perspective, diction, and detail that point to the individual components of the text having separate origins. Whether the component materials from which the text was compiled be oral traditions or written source documents is not as important as the simple recognition that, in its origin, the text is not 'of a piece', but is composite. A corollary of this recognition is that redaction criticism maintains a direct and positive relationship with both source criticism and form criticism, analytic disciplines which search behind the present text for the materials from which it was created.[12]

The dependence of redaction criticism upon source and form criticism distinguishes it from modern literary methods which not only posit the unity of the text as an assumption, but often fail to assess the varying degrees and kinds of unity possible in texts. Redaction criticism is not simply a literary study of the final form of the text, with a few nods toward Wellhausen and Gunkel. It would also resist an approach that, while conceding the text has an involved compositional history, nevertheless asserts this to be irrelevant to interpretation

---

11. Alluded to in M. Buber, *The Kingship of God* (London: George Allen & Unwin, 3rd edn, 1967), p. 167 n. 10.

12. Often the case is more complex. A text might have been compiled from both oral and written materials, or from written materials whose oral prehistory is still discernible.

since 'the final form of the text' is our primary focus. Such limitation of exegetical perspective may be defensible, but not in an interpretative approach aspiring to be holistic and comprehensive. Redaction criticism undertakes a systematic assessment of what the compositional process actually achieved. It focuses on the *processes*, oral and written sources and the manner of their combination, with a view to understanding the *product*, the final text in all its density and multifaceted unity. Both are understood in a mutually illuminating relationship.

Conceptual Unity

Starting with analytical insight into the *diversity* of a text's *origins*, redaction criticism turns to discern synthetically *unity of conception*. This quest for the text's unifying principles requires that the interpreter assess precisely those dynamics noted above whose recognition gave birth to redaction criticism. Such study is, by nature, synthetic, discerning 'the special new shape of the tradition as it leaves the redactor's hand—the inner character of the new constellation of tradition achieved by the redactor'. This requires discerning 'the way in which the received traditions modify and condition each other when perceived in the intended unity'.[13] Necessarily, this approach will pay special attention to the final form taken by the tradition. In fact, some interpreters have argued that the particular concern of redaction criticism must be 'the final written form or composition of a passage, the final stage of the tradition that has become crystallized in written form'.[14]

As a synthetic discipline that discerns unity, redaction criticism stands in a positive relationship with those methods of interpretation that assume the text's unity from the outset, such as rhetorical criticism and recent forms of literary criticism. Indeed, it functions as a bridge by which one may move from a *diachronic* analysis of the text's formation to a synchronic analysis of its present composition. Redaction criticism differs from purely synchronic methods, however, by its recognition that unity in a text that has been composed from previously

13. J.A. Wharton, 'Redaction Criticism, OT' (IDBSup; Nashville: Abingdon, 1976), p. 730.

14. John H. Hayes and Carl R. Holladay, in *Biblical Exegesis* (Atlanta: John Knox Press, 1982), p. 94. Cf. also the discussion in J. Barton, *Reading the Old Testament: Method in Biblical Study* (Philadelphia: Westminster, 1984), pp. 45-47.

EXODUS 18: ITS STRUCTURE, STYLE, MOTIFS AND FUNCTION IN THE BOOK OF EXODUS

Eugene Carpenter

1. *Introduction, Thesis and Methodology*

Exodus 18, its form, content and function, has been a center of attention for various reasons.[1] Brevard Childs calls it a conclusion to the Midianite foci, the first focus being chs. 2–4 and the second focus being ch. 18 itself.[2] The Jewish commentator Cassuto says, 'With fine artistic understanding, the Torah prefaces the account of the central theme of this part of the book of Exodus [chs. 18–24] with a prologue, the purpose of which is to prepare the reader's mind for the narrative that follows'.[3] Such differing positions by competent scholars must have a reasonable basis for their existence. It seems that both claims are partially correct. In fact, it seems to me that Exodus 18 is perhaps the major transitional chapter in the book of Exodus, summarizing the past events (Exod. 1–17) and preparing for the coming revelations at Sinai (Exod. 19–40). To be sure, there are other transitional passages (e.g. 1.1-7; 15.22-24) that are vital to the structure of the book. But ch. 18 seems to be the major hinge in the structure of the total

---

1. B.S. Childs, *The Book of Exodus* (OTL; Philadelphia: Westminster , 1974), pp. 321-22, 326-27, 332-34: U. Cassuto, *A Commentary on the Book of Exodus* (Jerusalem: Magnes Press, 1951), pp. 211-12. See Knierim's comments on Exod. 1–18 in his SBL seminar paper: R.P. Knierim, 'The Composition of the Pentateuch', in K.H. Richards (ed.), *SBL Seminar Papers* (Atlanta: Scholars Press, 1985), p. 396 and *passim*. Rashi's comments are always interesting, if not convincing: M. Rosenbaum and A.M. Silbermaner, 'Exodus', in *Pentateuch with Targum Onqelos, Haphtaroth and Rashi's Commentary* (New York: Hebrew Publishing Co., n.d.), pp. 91-96; R.P. Knierim, 'Exodus 18 und die Neuordung der mosäischen Gerichtsbarkeit', *ZAW* 73 (1961), pp. 146-71.

2. Childs, *Exodus*, p. 327.

3. Cassuto, *Commentary on Exodus*, p. 211.

composition, serving both as a prologue *and* an epilogue. This paper will examine this possibility.

It is a skillfully constructed, unified chapter that both unites and divides Exodus. As Durham notes, it is a chapter with a unity lacking in most other narrative portions of Exodus.[4] The various sources per JE(D?)P (if there were such) and sources from other oral and written materials are united here to conclude and to begin, to emphasize and to get under way some major new themes in Exodus. Documentarians normally assign the chapter to one source (usually E) to account for the extraordinary unity.[5] The chapter serves artistically as both an epilogue to the preceding materials of Exodus and as a prologue to the remaining sections of the book. Its positioning helps the reader grasp the overall content and meaning of the book. It helps to emphasize and make clear two ways of knowing Yahweh, that are, indeed, complementary: (1) the knowledge of Yahweh available in and through the event of the exodus itself and its recitation (18.7-8); and (2) the knowledge of Yahweh found in the way (דרך) of Yahweh—his Torah. The author accomplishes this task by forming and carefully controlling the structure, style, and motifs of the chapter.[6] Even though ch. 18 separates Exodus into two discernible parts, at the same time it unifies and connects these sections and continues the action of the book. Viewing the book as a whole, the chapter provides a respite

4. J.I. Durham, *Exodus*, III (WBC; Waco, TX: Word Books, 1987), p. 238.

5. For a summary of how it is usually assigned, see Durham, *Exodus*, p. 240-41. Durham prefers to stress the chapter's unity.

6. Several current books and articles have helped to partially form and inform my approach and understanding of Exod. 18 in a general way. Only a few are listed here: R. Alter, *The Art of Biblical Narrative* (New York: Basic Books, 1981), pp. 3-22, 178-89; R. Scholes and R. Kellogg, *The Nature of Narrative* (New York: Oxford University Press, 1966); D.W. Baker, 'Diversity and Unity in the Literary Structure of Genesis', in A.R. Millard and D.J. Wiseman (eds.), *Essays on the Patriarchal Narratives* (Winona Lake, IN; Eisenbrauns, 1980), pp. 197-215; S. Tengström, *Die Hexateucherzählung: Eine literatur geschichtliche Studie* (ConBOT, 7; trans. H. Zeiter; Uppsala: Almqvist & Wiksell, 1976), pp. 1-24. In general, see the bibliographical listings in R. Cully, 'Exploring New Direction', in D.A. Knight and G.M. Tucker (eds.), *The Hebrew Bible and its Modern Interpreters* (Chico, CA; Scholars Press, 1985), pp. 167-89; see also pp. 458-63; R. Weiman, *Structure and Society in Literary History* (Baltimore, MD: Johns Hopkins University Press, 1984). The entire book is a needed corrective to some radical positions taken in the New Criticism school. R.W.L. Moberly, *At the Mountain of God: Story and Theology in Exodus 32–34* (JSOTSup, 22; Sheffield: JSOT Press, 1984), pp. 15-38.

(שׁלם is used twice) between two storms, the storm at the Red Sea (chs. 14, 15) and the storm at Sinai (ch. 19). The chapter moves all of the actors and action into 'the vicinity of Sinai, the Mountain of God' (18.5) where the sacred traditions of the acts of Yahweh can be recounted in sacred space (18.5, 7-8)[7] and where provision for the dissemination of the sacred *tôrôt* (תורות), instructions of Yahweh, can be made.

The first half of the chapter (vv. 1-12) brings the exodus deliverance motif of the preceding chapters to a meaningful conclusion (τελός), but also addresses the issues raised by the Midianite traditions, both essential and incidental, found in chs. 2–4. The second half of the chapter (vv. 13-27) points forward to the dissemination of *mišpaṭ* (משׁפס) and therefore, to Sinai. The second half creates a totally new ambience appropriate to the ongoing activities of Sinai. By moving the action of the chapter into the 'vicinity of the Mountain of God' (Exod. 18.5 אל־המדבר אשׁר־הוא חנהשׁם הר האלהים) the author has provided for both the cosmic and the historical significance of everything that occurs in Exodus from this point on.[8] More specifically, everything will be tied to Yahweh who reveals himself as Israel's unique God.

In this study I will discuss the basis for these observations and similar ones. The literary structure and style of the chapter will be noted, as well as its leitmotifs. Then the functional relationships sustained by this structure, style, and leitmotifs to the larger structure of Exodus will be briefly observed.

The approach taken here is first of all literary and proceeds upon the assumption that the book of Exodus is a literary unity until proven

---

7.   M. Eliade, *The Sacred and the Profane* (New York: Harcourt Brace, 1959), pp. 8-113. Two other helpful books are J.W. Rogerson, *Anthropology and the Old Testament* (Sheffield: JSOT Press, 1984), and B. Land (ed.), *Anthropological Approaches to the Old Testament* (Philadelphia: Fortress Press, 1985): chapters 6, 7, 9, 10 are especially relevant. And of course, R. Otto, *The Idea of the Holy* (London, rev. edn, 1929), *passim*.

8.   J.D. Levenson, *Sinai and Zion: An Entry into the Jewish Bible* (Minneapolis: Seabury, Winston Press, 1985). This book is an interesting work that presents a new reading of the Hebrew Bible from a Jewish perspective, emphasizing the nature of the Old Testament as partaking of both the genre of imaginative literature and historicity: see e.g. p. 8. The cosmic and historical interplay of Sinai/Zion is developed. See pp. 142-43 for material relevant to note 5 above. Israel remains in this sacred area for nearly a year. Its departure begins in Num. 10.11-13.

otherwise.[9] The methodology is similar to the New Criticism and narrative criticism and techniques and concerns; but, even though it is not
fully developed here, it gives due concern to the socio-historical
phenomenon of the text—or one might say due concern not only for
the structure, but for the relationship of structure to its historical
social setting.

The procedure used has been to work from the issues raised in
ch. 18 by such features as leitmotifs, stylistics and poetics in general,
to these issues as they are found in chs. 1–17 and 19–40 of Exodus,
tacitly assuming the literary unity of the book. Reciprocal themes are
traced back to ch. 18 to discern any conscious literary/content relationships. A tradition-oriented and form-critical study would, indeed,
inform this study in various important ways, but has not been
attempted.

2. *The Structure, Style, Motifs of the Chapter*

a. *Features of the Whole Chapter as a Unit*

The chapter as a whole can cogently be considered a literary unit, as a
brief overview will show. The symmetry and balance of the chapter is
displayed in its arrangement, an arrangement that reflects parallelism
and expansion often found in lines of Hebrew poetry. It divides
chronologically into two parts (vv. 1-12; 13-27) separated by the
chronological divider 'on the next day' (מחרת). Each of these parts
contains an introduction (v. 1 serves as a 'flashback' for the reader
and as a general introduction and transition piece to the chapter) that
paints the scenario (vv. 1-7; [1] 13-16), a central portion given to a
report (vv. 8; 17-23), and a concluding section to the central report
(vv. 9-12; 24-27). In addition, each part contains its share of the
inclusio to the chapter: 'After Moses had sent away...[Jethro] came to
him in the desert' (vv. 2; 5) and 'Moses sent his...away...he returned
to his own country' (v. 27). The parenthetical comment (which is
important to the total structure and intent of the chapter) about Moses'

---

9.   Cf. Weiman, *Structure and Society*, pp. 18-56. Cf. also S. Bar Efrat, 'Some
Observations on the Analysis of Structure in Biblical Narrative', *VT* 30.2 (1980),
pp. 154-73. The methodological comments in Moberly, *Mountain of God*, pp. 15-
38, are also relevant. Finally, see also Tengström's methodological comments,
Hexateucherzählung, pp. 1-24, esp. 7-18. See relevant materials mentioned above in
note 4.

two sons (vv. 3-4) is sandwiched between the two statements that make up the first part of the inclusio contained in vv. 1-12. This portion is balanced in the conclusion to the second half of the chapter by the repetition of the essentials of Jethro's direct speech, first given in vv. 12-23 (vv. 24-27). The small middle section of vv. 1-12 is balanced by a ballast expansion in the second half of the chapter (vv. 17-23). Or, conversely, the larger introduction (vv. 1-7) and the conclusion (vv. 9-12) of the first part of the chapter are balanced by the larger middle section of the second half. Also, it is evident that each major section begins with a parallel phrase. In v. 1, 'Jethro heard...', while in v. 14, 'Jethro saw...', and the story develops from there.

The use of direct speech in the chapter is also formally and substantively important.[10] It indicates that the direct speech of vv. 10-11 of the first part forms the conclusion to the first section, both formally (or externally) and according to content. The direct speech of vv. 17-23 of the second part presents the leitmotif formally (or externally) and according to content. The amount of space devoted to Jethro's advice in vv. 17-23 also indicates this same point.

An essential dialogical encounter takes place in each of the major parts of the chapter. In the first half, Moses recounts the exodus story (v. 8) for the first time as Jethro listens and then responds favorably. In the second half of the chapter (vv. 17-23) this sequence is reversed. Moses and Jethro each respond favorably in attitude and action toward each other.

Several other stylistic devices tie the chapter together. In every subdivision of these two parts, there is direct speech, or unreported dialogue is in process. The presence of so much direct personal communication enables the chapter to bear the heavy action and content that it does. This also helps focus on two things at least. First of all, as noted, it indicates the importance of those things reported in direct speech, and secondly, it creates throughout the chapter an ambience of filial interpersonal relationship between Moses and his father-in-law. The author's skill is evident as he forms his story.

Finally, the inclusio of vv. 2, 5 and 27 brackets the action of the chapter in the vicinity of the Mountain of God, the place of holy space and holy time (worship and instruction), thus giving the chapter a unity of location. The inclusio does not include the material in vv. 1

10. Alter, *Biblical Narrative*, pp. 182-83; Efrat, 'Structure in the Biblical Narrative', p. 170.

and 4 because that material does not reflect events that took place in the holy space of the vicinity of the Mountain of Yahweh, nor during the two days of holy time there. Some of this is set forth in the following outline:

Symmetrical Outline of Exodus 18

Flashback (v. 1)

On the next day (v. 12)

First Section (vv. 1-12)	Second Section (13-27)
Scenario (2-7)	Scenario (13-16)
First half of inclusio (2/5)*	
(Parenthetical report/repetition, 3-4)	
Moses relates the story (8)	Jethro relates his advice (17-23)
	(large d.s. balances Introduction/
	conclusion to 1-12; d.s. indicates
	importance of material)
Jethro responds (9-12)	Moses responds (24-27) (report/
	repetition)
—in attitude(9)	—in　　attitude
	(24)
—in word (10-11)	—in　　word
	(25)
—in action (12)	—in　　action
	(26)
—(d.s. indicates importance of material)	Second half of inclusio (27)*

*Everything between the inclusio takes place in the holy space and time, at the Mountain of God.

Significant words are used throughout the chapter to tie it together.[11]

---

11. The word counts are based on the concordance by Abraham Even-Shoshan: A. Even-Shoshan, *A New Concordance of the Bible* (3 vols.; Jerusalem: Kiryat Sepher, 1977–80). The Baker Book House edition was used for this paper. The Baker edition is entitled, *A New Concordance of the Old Testament* in one volume (1984). The importance of exploring semantic and lexical issues is an important study and is developed well in the following works: J.F.A. Sawyer, *Semantics in Biblical Research: New Methods of Defining Hebrew Words for Salvation* (Naperville, IL; Allenson, 1972); M. Silva, *Biblical Words and their Meaning: An Introduction to Lexical Semantics* (Grand Rapids; Zondervan, 1983); J. Barr, *The Semantics of Biblical Language* (London: Oxford University Press, 1961); B. Kedar, *Biblische Semantik, eine Einfuhrung* (Stuttgart: Kohlhammer, 1981).

Cassuto notes only a small number of these.[12] Leading the list is the use of Moses' name twenty times (2 × 10). Yahweh and Elohim are used a total of twenty times (El in 18.4). Elohim is used fourteen times, seven times in each section to tie the chapter together. The name Jethro is used seven times in vv. 1-12 and the appellative 'Moses' father-in-law' is used thirteen times throughout the chapter, making the mention of Jethro plus Moses' father-in law equal to twenty times (2 × 10). עשׂה is used ten times throughout the chapter, as is בוא. The word שׁלום is used twice, once in each half, and contributes to the personal and relational dimension of the chapter, especially high-lighting the שׁלום that exists between Moses and his father-in-law. The use of שׁלום also increases the intimacy of the direct speech.

The separation in time of the two major events in the chapter by only one day actually unites the chapter and indicates unified holy time at the holy place. A unity of awareness and response is evident in the use of שׁמע (vv. 1, 19, 24) and ראה (v. 14). ידע is found once in each half (vv. 11, 20), each time referring to the knowledge of Yahweh or making him known to others. דבר in the singular is used ten times in this chapter. It is used once in the concluding verse of the first part (v. 11) and helps to relate the two major sections to one another. From this survey, it is clear that there is enough conscious external stylistic art alone in this chapter to demonstrate that the author has formed intentional unity with specific purposes in mind.

The two leading characters, Moses and Jethro (his father-in-law), dominate the chapter. Their continuous peaceful interaction leads to a literary unity and the 'presence' of an ambience of intimacy through-out the chapter. The clear identity of Jethro as Moses' father-in-law leaves no doubt or ambiguity about the intimate relationship between them,[13] and ties the first part of the chapter to the earlier mention of Jethro in Exodus 3; 4.18. The religious and theological significance of this close interaction and relationship is important. It legitimizes the action that takes place. The basic action in the second half of the chapter, when Moses' father-in-law provides a structure for the dissemination of משׁפט and the knowledge of Yahweh in Israel, is possible because of the result of the action in the first half. After Jethro has gone through a basic religious change from hearing the sacred deliverance story

---

12. Cassuto, *Commentary on Exodus*, pp. 211-22.
13. Efrat, 'Structure in Biblical Narrative', pp. 161-63; Alter, *Biblical Narrative*, pp. 182-83.

(vv. 7-8), responded favorably, confessed Yahweh above all gods, presented sacrifice and praise to him and worshiped him with a representative group of Israel in the vicinity of the Mountain of God, then he, as the father-in-law of Moses, has a privileged place in Israel's history.[14] He is now capable and qualified to offer the advice that he does in the second part.

b. *Features of Each Major Section of the Chapter*
1.*Verses 1-12*. Each of the two major parts of the chapter has, however, its own key concerns. The first part gives a climactic picture of several major events. First, the leitmotif word נצל, 'to deliver', is featured. It is used five times in four verses (18.4, 8, 9, 10 × 2). The word is used thirteen times in Exodus. It is scattered seven times before ch. 18, in chs. 2–17 (the use of the word in 8.22; 33.6 reflects irony by the writer).

The verb יצא is found in v. 1 (and once in v. 7), then followed by נצל five times as the deliverance of Yahweh is recounted. The word נצל (18.11) provides the consummate seventh step in Jethro's character change. יצא and נצל both contain the sibilant צ and the equation of 'going out' (יצא) = 'deliverance' נצל is evident. Hence, the exodus is referred to seven times. Jethro says in response to the story, כי־גדול יהוה מכל־האלהים עתה ידעתי. The fact and the purpose of the deliverance of Yahweh finds expression in microcosm in Jethro, a pagan priest of Midian, who is also Moses' father-in-law. The same thing in macrocosm occurs in Exodus 5–17 among Israel and the Egyptians. Jethro's response to Moses' telling (ספר) of the exodus story is one of faith. This 'seven-step' leitmotif employed by the author shows that the true knowledge of Yahweh through the exodus event results in the worship of Yahweh, 'in the presence of God', in sacred time. This is clearly the purpose for which Yahweh called out his people and exercised judgment upon the Egyptians. Even Jethro worships Yahweh at the Mountain of God (cf. Exod. 3.12).

The name Yahweh is used five times in three verses (8 × 2, 9, 10, 11) to stress his identity as the God who delivered Israel. Yahweh 'brings out' Israel (18.1) and this portrays him in his act of deliverance, his mighty acts of משפט concerning (כדבר) the Egyptians. And it is this name, Yahweh, that was revealed to Moses at this mountain

14. For a further discussion with bibliography, see Childs, *Exodus*, pp. 321-32, *passim*.

when God called Moses to deliver his people (Exod. 3.12-16). In vv. 1-12, Israel moves into the sacred space, 'the vicinity of the Mountain of God', then the sacred story is told, not merely in the sacred space of the Mountain of God, but even in the Tent (האהלה), a concentrated 'holy space'[15] that points forward to the tabernacle (Exod. 25.8) and the portable personal tent of Moses (Exod. 33.1-7).

2. *Verses 13-27*. The leitmotifs of the second half of the chapter cluster around משפט and related issues. The root שפט is employed six times (18.13, 16, 22 × 2, 26 × 2) by the writer, but is clearly implied a seventh time (18.14, sitting [יושב; to judge]) in this section. There appears to be good reason for the writer's leaving it out in 18.14, while also strongly implying it. The word דבר is used in the singular nine times (14, 16, 17, 18, 22 × 2, 23, 26 × 2) in this section and once in the plural (18.19 דברים), giving a total of ten usages (note the single usage in 18.11 listed above) that foreshadow the ten words. The 'ten words' are soon to be Israel's new and best way of knowing Yahweh (20.1; 1-17; cf. Deut. 5.5-21).

Other key words in these verses cluster around implications of משפט and righteousness: זהר, יעץ, דרך תורה צוה, חק. The motif of this section is clearly concern about the establishment of an administrative structure by which משפט in Israel can become a functional reality and the דרך Yahweh can become a lived reality.

The name Jethro is not used to designate Moses' father-in-law in this section so that the inherent right of Jethro by virtue of being Moses' close relative by marriage can be stressed. For Moses is God's approved and appointed lawgiver and dispenser of justice. After Jethro's qualifications have been recounted in vv. 1-12, the writer stresses only the relationship of Jethro to the great 'lawgiver of Israel' in this second part. Note that it is administrative wisdom, not content, however, that the father-in-law of Moses shares. Yahweh is not used in vv. 13-27, but Elohim is employed seven times, probably because Moses' father-in-law is dominant and because the writer is talking about a vehicle for the dissemination of Elohim's teaching, not the specific content of Israel's covenant Torah.

These observations show that there is a structural, stylistic unity and a unity of motif running through ch. 18 as a whole, but also that

15. This idea is developed to some extent in the works mentioned in notes 7 and 8 above.

specific leitmotifs are found in each part. The relationship of this chapter to the rest of Exodus will now be examined.

3. *Relationship of the Chapter to the Larger Structure of Exodus*

Some repetition of some points noted above will be evident and necessary, but here they are recounted for the purpose of showing the relationship of the chapter to the larger structure of Exodus. The chapter is closely related to the Midianite materials in chs. 2–4 of Exodus. This will be treated first. Then the relationship with the rest of Exodus will be covered more briefly. The two major divisions of the chapter will be dealt with first; then, the chapter as a whole will be treated.

a. *Relationship of the Two Sections to the Rest of Exodus*
1. *To the Midianite section in chapters 2–4.* Verses 1-12 contain many allusions and references to major motifs found in Exodus 2–4. The major motif of vv. 1-12, deliverance, is found in 2.19 and 3.8. נצל as noted above is used five times in 18.1-12. It is found twice in the Midianite materials of chs. 2–4. This seems to be a conscious tie-in by developing seven usages of נצל, five in 18.1-12 and two in the preceding materials in chs. 2–4. The fact that the writer recounts to us how Moses rescued (נצל) the daughters of Jethro demonstrates an interesting parallel motif, as well as a conscious parallel word usage.

The sons of Moses are mentioned in 18.2-4 to resolve an issue present in chs. 2–4. Their names serve to emphasize the deliverance theme, but also seem to consciously tie together Israel's stay in Egypt and Moses' stay in Midian as a synonymous motif of 'a stranger in an alien land' (2.22; 18.2-4). The 'bringing out' (יצא) motif is found in 18.1 and in 3.10, 11, 12. The purpose for the deliverance in chs. 2–4 is the worship of Yahweh (3.12; 4.23) and is paralleled in 18.11, 12, where Jethro, Moses, Aaron and the elders of Israel worship Yahweh in the vicinity of Sinai. The place of revelation and worship is noted as the Mountain of God in chs. 2–4 and in ch. 18. The שלום that was spoken to Moses by Jethro is mentioned again (4.18; 18.7) and the hospitality of Jethro in chs. 2–4 is returned by Moses in 18.6-7. An evident purpose for relating ch. 18 to chs. 2–4 is to demonstrate the fufillment of issues first raised there.

The second half of ch. 18 goes beyond the specific issues raised in chs. 2–4 of Exodus. However, the reference to Moses as a judge

(שׁופט) is especially noticeable in Exod. 2.14. Moses' right to act as a judge of cases among Israelites is challenged by the Israelites. In 18.13, Moses indeed does sit and judge as a prince! Yahweh has made him a judge over all Israel. The verb שׁפט, it will be recalled, is used six times explicitly in vv. 13-27 and strongly implied a seventh time. The single usage in the Midianite materials gives seven explicit usages of שׁפט in chs. 2–4, 18, as is the similar case with נצל in 2.19; 3.8; 18.1-12. Even though the reference in ch. 2 is not in the materials dealing with events *in the land* of Midian, it is closely connected to the Midianite complex and was probably always a part of those traditions. And it ties those materials to Egypt and God's purposes there as well. It relates why Moses fled to Midian. So the use of שׁפט and נצל serves to tie together the halves and likewise the whole chapter to Exodus 2–4. The use of שׁלום in this section is found in 18.23 also.

The word דבר, as noted above, appears ten times in 18.13-27, nine times in the singular and once in the plural. The plural usage is found four times in the Midianite materials in a usage comparable to its use in 18.19. Moses uses it three times and Aaron once. In ch. 18, Moses is to take the דברים before Yahweh. (The plural occurs only once in a general way in the Egyptian traditional materials [5.9] throughout chs. 5–17.) The inclusio in 18.27 brings the Midianite complex to a close by relating the separation of Jethro from Moses.

2. *To the non-Midianite sections of Exodus.* Key motifs tied to specific words appear in vv. 1-12 and are directly related to these same motifs in chs. 5–17 of Exodus. Three key words are נצל, and ידע נצל is found in four places before Exodus 18 (5.23; 6.6; 12.27; 12.36). The word is used six times before ch. 18 as it is used here. It is not so used after ch. 18. יצא is used twenty-nine times to refer to Israel's deliverance from Egypt in chs. 5–17 and once in ch. 18. It is used four times after ch. 18 in retroactive references to the exodus event. The use of יצא shows a similar distribution. It is used fifteen times before ch. 18 to refer to knowing Yahweh by the acts of God in the exodus or by accompanying phenomena. It is so used once in 18.1. It is not used this way after ch. 18. This survey of motifs by specific word usage clearly demonstrates that 18.1-12 is used to celebrate and conclude these issues in the non-Midianite sections, as well as in the Midianite sections, as shown above.

The goal of Israel's journey into the desert in chs. 5–17 was to

worship Yahweh.[16] Exod. 5.1-2 is a programmatic piece that illustrates
the concerns to be dealt with throughout chs. 5–17. In fact, 5.1-2 can
easily be arranged to show the issues raised and dealt with in the following materials.[17] Moses' direct speech to Pharaoh conveys the following motifs (5.1):

> –Israel is to be 'let go'
> –in order to worship me
> –in the desert

Pharaoh's response is also programmatic, for the following chapters
will respond to issues raised in his response. He says (5.2):

> –Who is Yahweh (מִי יְהוָה)
> –that I should obey him?
> –I do not know Yahweh!
> –I will not let Israel go.

16. This is clear from the usage of the words עבד and זבח in chs. 5–17. עבד is
found 13 times before ch. 18 (as well as in 3.12, 4.23 noted above in the text).
Jethro's worship fulfils this motif in a preliminary, but essential way, in 18.12,
although the word is not used in ch. 18. It is used only one more time, in 23.25 to
refer to the worship of Yahweh, Israel's God. It is used six times before ch. 18 and
seven times after ch. 18 in a different sense. The numerous usages in chs. 5–17
(plus two in chs. 2–4) all point to the future. When Israel arrives, they do worship.
עבד is used 13 times before ch. 18, once in 18.12 and 12 times afterwards. It is, of
course, evident that the use of this word would necessarily continue throughout the
remaining chapters of Exodus, but that a fulfillment of Israel's purpose in coming to
the vicinity of Sinai is claimed in 18.12 is certain. The process of worship includes
the giving of sacrifices continually. Even Israel, Moses (assumed) and Aaron take
part in the offering and sacrifices in 18.12. The purpose of Israel, to worship
Yahweh, will necessarily continue. Jethro offers up a burnt offering (עלה) which
also has been mentioned in chs. 5–17 as an explicit goal of Israel when they arrive in
the vicinity of Sinai. עלה is found before ch. 18 in only 10.25 where the presenting
of burnt offerings is a future goal of Israel. It is found in 18.12 and 15 times after
ch. 18, since, as with sacrifices, the worship of Israel continues. Sacrifices and
burnt offering are presented to Yahweh in 24.5 when the covenant is sealed.
17. The 'dramatic' dimension, as well as the skillful literary development of the
material within the block of materials now given to the exodus (chs. 1–14[15])
tradition has not been developed fully by commentators. For a helpful discussion of
Exod. 1–15, see D. Robertson, *The Old Testament and the Literary Critic*
(Philadelphia: Fortress Press, 1977), pp. 16-32, although the comparison with the
Bacchae is not sufficiently aware of contrasts (differences) between the nature of the
genre of the materials compared.

Moses' response is programmatic:

> –Let us go... into the desert
> –to sacrifice to Yahweh.

The above motifs are picked up and resolved numerous times throughout chs. 5–17. Yahweh's redemptive purposes are defined even more specifically to include the Egyptians and even the whole earth. 9.13-19 declares the goal of Yahweh's plagues to be the knowledge of Yahweh in all the earth (9.14) and the proclamation of Yahweh's name in all the earth (9.16), a powerful use of what Zimmerli has called 'the recognition formula'. In 14.4, 18, the purpose of the plagues is to cause the Egyptians to know Yahweh. The concern for the worship of Yahweh is mentioned again in 10.8 and in 10.17. Pharaoh asks for prayer to Yahweh for himself. In 12.12, the purpose of the plagues is judgment upon all the gods of Egypt. This sentence concludes with אני יהוה, 'I am Yahweh'—a clear answer to Pharaoh as to who he is and not unrelated to the meaning of Exod. 3.13-16.[18] In 12.31-32, Pharaoh recognizes Yahweh and asks to be blessed by him and sends out Israel. Exod. 14.31 declares the religious result of the exodus event to be trust and worship among the Israelites themselves when they *saw* what Yahweh had done for them. Compare this to 4.31 which is placed in Egypt. 15.11 sings a song about the uniqueness of Yahweh among the gods.

The scheme of going out–deliverance–confession–worship is present in microcosm in vv. 8-12 of our chapter as noted above. Jethro, the non-Israelite, not only confesses and praises Yahweh above all gods and worships him, but he does so in the desert, in the vicinity of Sinai along with Moses and a representative group of Hebrews. All of the motifs found in chs. 5–17 are included at least in germ in this incident and now, not only Pharaoh, but a Midianite priest has proclaimed Yahweh's name in all the earth, and Jethro's, 'Now I know' (18.11) contrasts beautifully with Pharaoh's, 'I do not know' and his reluctant 'admittance' of the power of Yahweh (10.17). Sacrifice and a burnt offering conclude Jethro's worship experience with Israel and Moses in the presence of Yahweh near Mount Sinai. The contrast between Pharaoh's tragic end and Jethro's comic rebirth is based upon their individual response to 'Who is Yahweh?' Verses 1-12 clearly serve as

---

18. J.G. Janzen, 'What's in a Name? "Yahweh" in Exodus 3 and the Wider Biblical Context', *Int* 33 (1979), pp. 227-28.

an epilogue (conclusion) to the major motifs in chs. 5–17 of Exodus and demonstrate that whoever blesses Israel will be blessed and whoever curses Israel will be cursed (Gen. 12.1-3).

The second half of ch. 18, vv. 13-27, relates even more basically, as to content and ambience, to what follows and forms a fitting prologue to the second half of the book. The motif words are words dealing with cultic and judicial issues. The words as noted above are listed here with their distribution in Exodus:

Exodus		1–17		18.13-27		19–40
שׁפט	-	6	-	6	-	9
תורה	-	4	-	2	+	1
חוק	-	2	-	1	-	2
זהר	-	0	-	1	-	0
דרך	-	0	-	1	-	2^{19}
צוה	-	13	-	1	-	41
יעץ	-	0	-	1	-	0
ידע	-	0	-	1	-	3^{20}
דבר	-s	26	-	11	-	24
דברים	pl.	4(5)	-	1	-	16

This word list shows that basically vv. 13-27 of this chapter have motifs that are *carried forward beyond* ch. 18. The section has a much tighter relationship with what follows than with what precedes, although understandably the motif words also pick up the incipient beginning of Israel's concern for *mishpaṭ* in some places in preceding chapters. There the words tend to adumbrate what is to follow. The key words are דרך, צוה, ידע, שׁפט, and דבר (דברים). These words demonstrate a much more organic relationship with what is in chs. 19–40 than to preceding chapters. For instance, צוה is found thirteen times before ch. 18, but forty-one times after it. דברים is found four (five) times before ch. 18, once in 18.19 and sixteen times after it, and of course, is used to indicate the ten 'words' (Exod. 20.1). Every usage, except perhaps 23.8, is akin to its usage in 18.19.

דרך is used in 18.20 in a theological sense (moral/religious) and again in Exodus in 32.8; 33.13, all after ch. 18. זהר occurs only in 18.12, and ידע in the sense of knowing Yahweh through his Torah is

---

19. Used in a moral/religious sense, indicating 'the way of Yahweh'.

20. *yd'* is used in these cases in a way which indicates knowledge of Yahweh through instruction (*tôrâ*). See above for use of *yd'* in chapters preceding ch. 18.

found in 18.20 and then in 29.31, 33, thereafter. The council (יָעַץ) of Moses' father-in-law is designed to provide a reasonable method of dissemination for the instructions to come to Israel, although it does resolve a past problem as well. The author has judiciously placed it here, probably to keep it from breaking up the materials in chs. 19–40, where it would have been clumsy to insert it, as well as anachronistic.

Placed here, this section helps to emphasize the break between chs. 1–17 and 19–40 by gathering up some themes and incidentals of chs. 1–17 and pointing forward in an essential way to chs. 19–40. The tent of meeting is, as already noted, mentioned in 18.7 and the Mountain of God in 18.5; this indicates the appropriate location for these vital judicial/cultural issues to be raised. The Tent of Meeting is developed fully in Exodus 25–31. The administrative structure necessary to execute the total judicial/cultic/jurisprudence program of Israel needed to be presented before the content of that program. The structure itself needed to come into existence in the sacred space, the vicinity of the Mountain of God. And, to keep from breaking the tightly knit narrative that follows in chs. 19–40, the writer has placed it here. According to theological logic, practical logic, and narrative logic it belonged here. Chronologically, it may belong later,[21] although this has been vigorously debated.[22]

b. *Relationship of Chapter 18 as a Whole to the Rest of Exodus*
1. *To the Midianite section in chapters 2–4.* As is now clear, ch. 18 is especially closely related to the Midianite material in chs. 2–4. The heading of the chapter in v. 1 serves beautifully to reintroduce us to Jethro, the priest of Midian and father-in-law of Moses, thus repeating all of the important information about him found in Exodus 2-4, the major block of Midianite traditions. This extended heading introduces the chapter as a whole. Zipporah and Moses' sons are reintroduced (vv. 2–6). The chapter answers the question of the religious relationship of Jethro to Moses and to Israel and satisfies the reader's questions that have arisen about Zipporah and Moses' sons (cf. 2.22 and 4.20).

Even more pertinent are the theological motifs that are mentioned

21. This is, of course, a major concern of the New Literary Criticism. See Cassuto's commentary on Exodus and the literature mentioned in note 6 above.

22. See W.C. Kaiser, Jr, 'Exodus', in *The Expositor's Bible Commentary* (Grand Rapids: Zondervan, 1990), p. 411.

in chs. 2–4 and that are picked up here in ch. 18. These were considered above in the context of the two major sections of the chapter.
The whole chapter clarifies Jethro's past influence on and relationship
to Moses and his people and the groundwork is laid for dealing with
the relationship of Israel and Jethro's descendants.[23] Israel's administrative judicial system originates with Jethro. So his continued
contribution and influence in Israel is evident. This contribution to
Moses and Israel is worthy of a covenant blessing (cf. Gen. 12.1-3;
Exod. 1.1-7).

The physical movement of Moses and Jethro in chs. 2–4 and 18 is
interesting. In Exodus 2–4, Moses flees to the wilderness where he is
welcomed and received hospitably by Jethro. Here Jethro is received
likewise in the wilderness by Moses. In Exod. 4.18, Jethro sends off
Moses in שלום. שלום is used three times in Exodus: 4.18; 18.7, 23. All
usages are in the Midianite materials and involve Jethro and Moses.
Here Moses receives Jethro in שלום and sends him off. The final usage
in 18.23 includes Israel and God. The reception and blessing received
by Moses, God's representative of his people, results in Moses, Israel,
and their God blessing Jethro in return, a clear demonstration of
covenant hospitality.

2. *To the non-Midianite sections of Exodus.* Chapter 18 also picks up
the major motifs found in Exodus 5–17, and it points forward to
major issues in chs. 19–40. Specifically, the motifs of deliverance,
coming out of Egypt, knowledge of Yahweh and worship of Yahweh
are key motifs picked up in Exodus 18 and found throughout chs. 5–
17. The commands (מצוות), decrees (חקים), judgments (משפטים), and
instructions (תורות), given in chapters preceding ch. 18 (5, 6, 7, 12, 13,
15, 16) are also of some concern to the author of ch. 18. The reader
is aware that these decisions, laws and issues must be administered
among Israel.

The location of the chapter between two literal storms, the storm at
the ים סוף and the storm at the Mountain of God is strategic, for it provides a respite of shalom for Israel and the reader, and the tension of
the exodus deliverance has been lifted. As has been noted above,
ch. 18 moves Israel into the vicinity of Sinai and marks a new

---

23. Cassuto, *Commentary on Exodus*, pp. 212, 217-21. This is rejected as an
answer in Childs, *Exodus*, p. 322. Cf. F.C. Fensham, 'Did a Treaty Between the
Israelites and the Kenites Exist?', *BASOR* 175 (1964), pp. 51-54.

position for Israel in the narrative, for now Israel is in holy space. The term 'the Mountain of God' (הר האלהים) and its synonyms are used forty times in chs. 18–40, a clear theological usage of the name. The sacred location, the sacred time, and the administrative needs for the Sinai events are present.

The location of the chapter right after the section on the Amalakites (Exod. 17.8-16) is strategic. They serve as Israel's archetypal enemy, displaying only violence (חמס) toward them. *Shalom* is the attitude of Moses, Israel and their God toward Jethro and his descendants, but war (מלחמה) is the eternal declaration of Yahweh against the warlike Amalakites (Exod. 17.16). The juxtaposition of these two sections emphasizes and illustrates the blessing of Yahweh upon those who are kindly disposed to Israel, and the curse of Yahweh upon those who are hostile toward God's covenant people. The relationship of Israel to the descendants of Jethro is developed in other Old Testament books. By placing the chapter between the Amalakite story and the Sinai event, the point is even more clearly emphasized. Those who would harm Israel have no part in his Torah. Those who bless them can have a share in that torah.

4. *Conclusion*

The above discussion seems to warrant the following conclusions on ch. 18 itself and its relationship to the broader structure of Exodus as a whole.

1. Chapter 18 is a consciously constructed composition that exhibits overall unity and features two skillfully structured parts that interlock formally and according to content. In its broader context, it shows how the writer has organized his material theologically rather than chronologically.

2. It is a major transitional chapter that serves both as an epilogue (vv. 1-12) to the first half of Exodus (chs. 2–17) and as a prologue (vv. 13-27) to the second half of Exodus (chs. 19–40). It takes up and resolves, gathers and adumbrates major issues on earlier/later chapters.

3. It brings the Midianite foci to a satisfactory conclusion, but signals the continuing contribution to Israel by one of the ancestors of the Midianites, thus opening up room for continued peaceful relationships between the two peoples.

4.	It integrates the motifs raised in the land of Midian, but also the motifs of the Egyptian sojourn, exodus, wilderness wanderings, and the Sinai experience, the latter in a preparatory way, into a meaningful whole.

5.	It creates an *Anknüpfungspunkt* between knowing Yahweh through the exodus and knowing him through the Torah, the דרך Yahweh, the way of Yahweh.

6.	As a whole, it moves the reader from the exodus to the verge of Sinai. It moves us from profane space (the wandering in the desert, Egypt and the ים סוף) to sacred space, the Mountain of God and the Tent. It moves us from profane time (listless wandering and murmuring in the desert) to sacred time when stability, praise, worship and divinely approved administrative acts occur. It presents the incipient worship of Yahweh by Israel at the Mountain of God.

7.	It bridges the gap between two storms, at the ים סוף and at the Mountain of God, where Yahweh causes history and cosmic significance to coalesce in him and his purposes for his people. It is artfully, psychologically and theologically pleasing in its present position.

8.	It separates Exodus into two parts, but at the same time unites the two parts in such a way that the significance of the events in chs. 1–17 is caught up in a new way and carried on into chs. 19–40. The religious destiny and significance of Israel continues to be developed after a pause for שלום. The *theme* of Exodus continues through the interweaving of numerous *motifs*: that theme is the continuing creation of a people of God and their development under the Lordship of Yahweh,[24] as he seeks to dwell among them.

---

24. The theme is programmatic in Exod. 6.7, 8; 19.5-6. The rest of the Torah sees these programmatic plans worked out in detail. See also 29.45-46; 33.15-17; 40.34-38.

STRUCTURE AND MEANING IN THE SINAI–HOREB NARRATIVE
(EXODUS 19–34)

Joseph Blenkinsopp

Introduction

One of the most anomalous features of the Pentateuch is its narrative tempo. The Israelite stopover in the wilderness of Sinai on their way to Canaan occupies considerably more than a fifth of the total length of the Pentateuch (Exod. 19.1–Num. 10.28) yet lasts only about one year out of the 2,706 from creation to the death of Moses. To the historical-literary exegete this extraordinary feature suggests the possibility of an intrusion, especially since the account of Moses' meeting with his father-in-law the Midianite priest at 'the mountain of God' immediately preceding the Sinai pericope is taken up and completed immediately following it (Exod. 18.1-27; Num. 10.29-34). It might seem, then, that the entire narrative of what transpired at Sinai–Horeb has been inserted into an earlier and in some respects parallel account of what happened at another special mountain in the wilderness. At this point we link up with the discussion of the Kadesh traditions initiated by Julius Wellhausen and Eduard Meyer about a century ago and taken up sporadically since then.[1] This is not the place for a thorough review of the hypothesis, but certain parallels between Kadesh and Sinai may be recalled: legal enactments and judicial activity take place at both locations (Exod. 18.13-27; Num. 11.10-17, 24-30; Deut. 33.8-11, etc.), both feature a sacrificial ritual and meal in which Moses, Aaron and elders share (Exod. 18.12; cf. 24.1-2, 9-11), both

---

1. The Kadesh hypothesis in its older form (Wellhausen, Meyer, *et al.*) is discussed by E.W. Nicholson, *Exodus and Sinai in History and Tradition* (Atlanta: John Knox, 1973), pp. 4-6; G. Widengren, 'What Do We Know about Moses?', in J.I. Durham and J.R. Porter (eds.), *Proclamation and Presence* (Macon, GA: Mercer University Press, 2nd edn, 1983), pp. 21-47.

take place on or near a mountain (Exod. 18.5), and the question of guidance through the wilderness is raised in both (Num. 10.31; cf. Exod. 23.20).

It has also been noted that the hypothesis is consistent with those narrative traditions dealing with the wilderness journey from which the Sinaitic covenant and law are conspicuously absent. In the itinerary of Numbers 33, generally assigned to P but incorporating older traditions, the wilderness of Sinai occurs as the fifteenth of the forty or forty-two stages (mas'îm) but nothing is recorded as having happened there (Num. 33.15-16). The omission could, of course, be deliberate, but we would then have to explain why the Priestly editor, who mentions the death of Aaron at the thirty-seventh station (33.38-39), had nothing to say at this point. In the course of negotiations, Jephthah gives the Ammonite king an account of the Israelite journey from Egypt to Kadesh. He not only does not mention Sinai, but gives the clear impression that Kadesh was the goal of the journey from the start (Judg. 11.14-18). We note, finally, that in the (generally agreed on) pre-exilic occurrences of Sinai (i.e. Deut. 33.2; Judg. 5.5; Ps. 68.9, 18), the name is never connected with Moses and the giving of the law.[2]

The hypothesis of a massive insertion, described by Wellhausen as 'a most melancholy, most incomprehensible revision',[3] would not of course lead to the conclusion that the narrative in Exodus 19–Numbers 10 had no connection with anything else in the Pentateuch. Much of the same sequence of events is reproduced, for example, in Deuteronomy 4–5. Nor would it necessarily support von Rad's thesis of a distinct law tradition rooted in the Shechem covenant festival, though it might motivate us to dust it off and have another look at it.[4] What the insertion hypothesis suggests is that, in the period of reconstruction after the disasters of the early sixth century BCE, it was felt necessary to create a more complete, coherent and paradigmatic foundational narrative which would serve to place the emergent commonwealth on a firm basis of law. If in the process of elaborating

2.   Add that no prophetic text prior to Jer. 15.1, with the possible but unlikely exception of Mic. 6.14, mentions Moses at all.

3.   *Prolegomena to the History of Israel* (New York: Meridian Books, 1957), p. 342.

4.   G. von Rad, *The Problem of the Hexateuch and Other Essays* (Edinburgh: Oliver & Boyd, 1966), pp. 1-78.

this narrative existing traditions about origins were pushed into the background, this must have seemed a small price to pay.

The paradigmatic nature of the Sinai–Horeb narrative can be detected in the surface structure which manifests the sequence: the making, breaking, and remaking of the covenant between Israel and their God. This sequence corresponds to the religious history of Israel interpreted by the Deuteronomists as a history ending in spiritual and political collapse and indicating the need for a new and better basis for the future. The same pattern is detectable in the early history of humanity in Genesis 1–11—old creation, destruction, new beginning— which also anticipates the pattern according to which the history of the nation unfolds.

Before looking into the theological implications of this pattern and of subsidiary structures in the Sinai–Horeb pericope (restricted for practical purposes to Exodus 19–34) I may be permitted to state in summary fashion what I take to be a probable account of the composition of this most complex section of the Pentateuch.[5] First, I take Exodus 19–34 to be a relatively coherent and thematically unified narrative rather than a work of bricolage assembled by random accumulation or even by a combination of distinct accounts of the covenant made (19–24) and the covenant broken and remade (32–34). This result has been achieved by inserting a basic Deuteronomic account (D) into the Priestly history (P), the latter beginning with creation and ending with the setting up of the wilderness sanctuary in the Promised Land (Josh. 18–19). I find the clue to the relation between these two narrative corpora in the economical and elegant way in which Deuteronomy has been incorporated into the P schematic narrative by the simple expedient of adding a date of the P type at the beginning (Deut. 1.3) and a revised version of the commissioning of

---

5.   A fuller account is given in my *The Pentateuch: An Introduction to the First Five Books of the Bible* (New York: Doubleday, 1992), pp. 33-37, 134-38, 183-97. Other recent contributions include B. Renaud, *La Théophanie du Sinaï (Ex 19–24). Exegèse et Théologie* (Paris, 1991); T.B. Dozeman, *God on the Mountain: A Study of Redaction, Theology and Canon in Exodus 19–24* (Atlanta: Scholars Press, 1989); H. Cazelles, 'Le Théophanie au Désert: Montagne de Dieu, Sinai, Horeb', in *Tradicio i Traduccio de la Paraula: Miscellania Guiu Camps* (Montserrat, 1993), pp. 19-32, the most recent of Père Cazelles's many contributions to the subject; R.W.L. Moberly, *At the Mountain of God: Story and Theology in Exodus 32–34* (JSOTSup, 22; Sheffield: JSOT Press, 1983).

Joshua, followed by the death of Moses, towards the end of the book (32.48-52 + 34.1, 7-9; cf. Num. 27.12-23, both of Priestly origin). The implication is that the inclusion of Deuteronomy necessitated postponing the death of Moses, originally recorded after Num 27.23.[6] I do not doubt that the D Horeb account has incorporated elements of old narrative tradition, perhaps associated with Shechem and even Kadesh, and that narrative material continued to be added after the pericope was essentially complete.[7]

1. It is relatively easy to disengage the main line of the P version of what happened at Sinai. Israel arrived in the Sinai wilderness on the first day of the third month dating from the exodus (Exod. 19.1-2a) and departed processionally on the twentieth day of the second month in the following year (Num. 10.11), the latter date chosen to accommodate those who had incurred ritual uncleanness and who therefore had to celebrate the delayed Passover as prescribed in Num. 9.1-14. We may note, in passing, that for P the celebration of Passover marks the foundation of the commonwealth of Israel (*^{a}dat yiśrā'ēl*) in the wilderness ('this month shall be the first month of the year for you', Exod. 12.1). Immediately on arriving in the Sinai wilderness,[8] Moses went up the mountain and was granted a vision (24.15b-18a) in which he received detailed specifications for the construction of a mobile sanctuary with its appointments, the cult to be carried out in it, and the cultic personnel who were to officiate (Exod. 25.1–31.17). Like Gudea of Lagash, he was also given a model or blueprint (*tabnît*) of the sanctuary to be built (25.9, 40; cf. the *toknît* of Ezekiel's temple, Ezek. 43.10). The construction was to conclude with the celebration of sabbath, at this point officially instituted (31.12-17; 35.1-3) though

---

6. See my *Prophecy and Canon* (Notre Dame, IN: University of Notre Dame Press, 1977), pp. 83-85.

7. The short passages describing the passing of the divine effulgence (*kābôd*) before Moses (Exod. 33.17-23) and the latter's facial transfiguration (34.29-35) share features with midrash and may be late additions.

8. Several narrative fragments between the arrival and the vision are occasionally assigned to P, namely, the much-discussed 'a kingdom of priests and a holy nation' (19.6) and the ritual preparation for the theophany (some or all of 19.11-13, 15-16, 21-25); but not all allusions to priests or ritual matters need derive from one and the same source. Whatever the origin of the tradition in 24.1-2, 9-11 about a vision and a meal involving Moses, Aaron, his sons and seventy elders, also occasionally assigned to P, it is distinct from the account of the vision granted to Moses alone in the same chapter (24.15b-18a).

anticipated earlier in the trek through the wilderness (Exod. 16.4-30). The detailed account of the implementation of the visionary instructions (chs. 35–40) was probably the work of a clerical editor anxious to make the point that the instructions retained their validity in spite of the fact that Aaron had compromised himself in the Golden Calf incident.

All of the cultic and ritual enactments in Leviticus and the first part of Numbers (to Num. 10.28) are recorded as issued or implemented at Sinai. For our present purpose these do not call for comment, but some of the internal correspondences and lines of force within the P version should be noted. According to my reading, the nodal points of the P narrative as a whole are the creation of the world as a precondition for worship (Gen. 1.1–2.4a), the erection and dedication of the wilderness sanctuary (Exod. 40.1-33), and the setting up of the same sanctuary at Shiloh, an action which put the seal on the occupation of and settlement in the land (Josh. 18–19).[9] This meaning-conferring structure is reinforced almost redundantly: the vision on the mountain takes place on the seventh day (24.16), the creation of the sanctuary is followed by the solemn day of rest (31.12-17; 35.1-3), and worship can finally be initiated after the seven-day sacerdotal ordination ceremony (Lev. 8.33; 9.1). The wilderness sanctuary is erected on the first day of the first month, that is, New Year's Day (40.1, 17), corresponding to the first New Year's Day of creation and the date at which the purified earth emerged from the water of the deluge (Gen. 8.13).

The most notable feature of P's Sinai narrative is not, however, what it says but what it omits: it has nothing to say about the *making of a covenant*. The standard explanation of this remarkable omission is that P never existed as an independent narrative but was intended to be read as an expansion of a narrative already in place dealing with the making, breaking and remaking of a covenant.[10] But even if this were so, we would still have to explain why at all important junctures of the story except this one P either has an independent account of its own (e.g., the Abrahamic covenant, the call of Moses) or a significant contribution to a conflated version (e.g., the deluge, the plagues).

9. See my 'The Structure of P', *CBQ* 38 (1976), pp. 275-92.

10. The case for P as tradent rather than as originally independent work is argued by F.M. Cross, *Canaanite Myth and Hebrew Epic* (Cambridge, MA: Harvard University Press, 1973), pp. 293-325.

Moreover, the highly distinctive structural features of the P narrative referred to a moment ago strongly support an originally independent narrative. The narrative logic of P will emerge more clearly if we identify the turning point, the *peripateia*, of this section with the revelation of the divine name in Egypt, at which point the groaning of his oppressed people cause God to remember the covenant with the ancestors (Exod. 6.2-13). The subsequent course of events, culminating in the inauguration of worship in the wilderness of Sinai, flows from that moment of reactivation and retrieval.

I therefore conclude that the absence of any distinct or conflated P version of covenant-making at Sinai signals a distinctive feature of Priestly theology. According to P the first covenant was with humanity in the restored but damaged world after the deluge (Gen. 9.8-17) and the first and only covenant with Israel was made with the ancestors (Gen. 17.1-21). Both are described as perpetual (*bᵉrît 'ôlām*), meaning a type of covenant which did not require periodic renewal and revalidation as was the case with contractual arrangements in the political sphere. In the P Sinaitic narrative sabbath is referred to as *bᵉrît 'ôlām* (Exod. 31.16), but the scope of the term as used here is quite restricted. Sabbath is certainly of obligation, but it also serves as a sign (*'ôt*, 31.17) analogous to the rainbow and the circumcised foreskin (Gen. 9.12-17; 17.11). The context is that of the restored post-exilic commonwealth when sabbath assumed confessional importance and could stand metonymously for the God–Israel relationship in general (cf. Ezek. 20.10-24; Isa. 56.1-8).

It seems, then, that P has substituted for a serial or sequential covenant-making process a once-for-all double dispensation with the damaged postdiluvian world and with Israel at the beginnings of its history. Continuity, linkage between these past moments and the changing present, is maintained by God *remembering* his covenants especially at times of world crisis or when his people have been carried into exile (Exod. 2.24; 6.5; Lev. 26.42, 45). The P covenant is also distinctive in that adhesion to certain commitments on the part of God *qua* originator of the covenant is not contingent on the observance of stipulations imposed on and accepted by the human partner. It is therefore unilateral not bilateral. In P we have moved away from the idea of contractual arrangements and in the direction of an antecedent divine disposition or dispensation.[11] At a later point we will consider some implications of this shift in emphasis.

2. Leaving P aside, there never has been a consensus on source division in the Sinai pericope. The initial address of YHWH to Moses, in which the description of Israel as 'a priestly kingdom, a holy nation' occurs, has, for example, been assigned at different times and by different scholars to E, D and P. The situation is even worse in the sealing of the covenant in Exodus 24 in which, as Lothar Perlitt put it, sources might as well be assigned 'durch Losorakel'.[12] Some progress may, however, be made if we begin with the corresponding narrative section in Deuteronomy presented as reminiscence of Moses on the day of his death. The sequence is as follows: YHWH promulgated the decalogue to the people gathered about the mountain after which 'he added no more' (Deut. 4.10-13; 5.22); he then wrote it on two stone tablets and confided detailed stipulations to Moses alone with a view to later promulgation (4.13-14; 5.22, 31-33); Moses went up the mountain to receive the tablets (9.9-11); the people led by Aaron took advantage of his absence to engage in illegitimate cult acts (9.12-14); on coming down from the mountain and discovering what had happened Moses smashed the tablets, fasted, interceded for Aaron and the people, and was told by God to make new tablets and a box (*ᵃrôn*) in which to put them (9.15–10.5).

When taken together with the many indications of Deuteronomic language and themes in Exodus 19–34,[13] the close correspondence of the latter with the version in Deuteronomy suggests the conclusion that our pericope is basically a Deuteronomic composition, though one which has incorporated older traditions probably associated, as suggested earlier, with Shechem and Kadesh. At a later stage this D composition was positioned within the P narrative complex, and later still other additions could have been made in the manner of midrash, for example, the passage about Moses' shining face (Exod. 34.29-35). This is at least a position which may serve as a working hypothesis for diachronic access to the text at different points of its history. It results

---

11. In linguistic terms the shift is from covenant to testament, hence *diathēkē* rather than *sunthēkē* in LXX.

12. L. Perlitt, *Bundestheologie im Alten Testament* (Neukirchen–Vluyn: Neukirchener Verlag, 1969), p. 181.

13. Exod. 19.3-9a; 20.21-22; 23.20-33; 24.3-8; 32.11-14, 30-35; 33.1-3; 34.1-16, 27-28.

that, in reading through the text, we come upon different, even irreconcilably different, perspectives on such central religious categories as
covenant and cult.

In order to explain this apparent lack of cohesion we would need to
know much more than we do about the circumstances under which the
final redaction of the Pentateuch took place and the identity and point
of view of the redactors. On the assumption that the Pentateuch is a
production of the intellectual and religious elite in Judah under Persian
rule, we might note that Achemenid imperial policy mandated the
drafting of law codes in the provinces as an instrument of the *pax
Persica*, and that these codes had to reflect a compromise between
different interest groups at the local level.[14] If this applied to the
province of Judah, it would help to explain the presence of different
legal compilations and, on the further assumption that the practice of
presenting laws in a narrative context was already established, the juxtaposition of different narrative strands each with its own distinctive
approach.

According to the D narrative line, then, the covenant-making at
Horeb begins with an address of YHWH/God to Moses on the mountain:

> Thus you shall say to the house of Jacob and proclaim to the Israelites:
> 'You have observed what I did to the Egyptians, and how I bore you up
> on eagles' wings and brought you to myself. And now, if you will indeed
> obey my voice and observe my covenant, you shall be my own special
> possession from among all the peoples, for all the earth is mine. You shall
> be for me a priestly kingdom and a holy nation.' These are the words you
> shall say to the Israelites (Exod. 19.3-6).

The appeal to experience with special reference to exodus and wilderness as motivation for fidelity ('you have observed...'), the divine
promises as contingent on Israel's obedience, Israel as a special
possession (*s^egull^a*, cf. Deut. 7.6; 14.2; 26.18)—these traits among
others are unmistakably Deuteronom(ist)ic. Following on this address
Moses proclaims the 'words', the people give their assent, and Moses
reports back to YHWH on the mountain (19.7-9). The context makes it
clear that the 'words' (*d^ebārîm*) now refer to laws, as at Exod. 24.3

14. The principal source is the Demotic Chronicle = papyrus 215 Bibliothèque
Nationale, Paris. On the situation in Judah under Persian rule see my 'Temple and
Society in Achemenid Judah', in P.R. Davies (ed.), *Second Temple Studies. 1.
Persian Period* (JSOTSup, 117; Sheffield: JSOT Press, 1991), pp. 22-53; E. Blum,
Studien zur Komposition des Pentateuch (Berlin: de Gruyter, 1990), pp. 336-60.

where the same formula of assent occurs, which would seem to imply that the laws have already been promulgated and may be presumed to be known. This chronological displacement has puzzled exegetes from ancient times. The simplest solution would be to read the entire passage (19.3-9) as a summary of the Horeb event placed at the beginning to alert the reader to the way in which it is to be understood.

We saw that according to the D version only the decalogue was given at Horeb, while 'statutes and ordinances', that is, detailed stipulations of law spelling out the implications of the decalogue norms, were communicated privately to Moses with a view to later promulgation (cf. Deut. 5.2-33). The postponement is explained by the fear of prolonged exposure to the divine presence, but its real function was, first, to legitimate the office of Moses as prophetic intermediary, and, second, to allow for a later covenant on the eve of entering the land. The insertion of the compilation of laws known as the Covenant Code (20.22–23.19) has occasioned some confusion since the narrative line has had to be adjusted to accommodate it, especially at the ceremonial conclusion of the covenant when Moses promulgates the laws and the people assent to them twice (24.3-8; it is not clear that 'words of YHWH and ordinances' in v. 3 refers to the same text as 'the book of the covenant' in v. 7). Bracketing the Covenant Code for the moment, we see that after the promulgation of the decalogue Moses is told to go up the mountain to take delivery of the stone tablets inscribed by God himself. He does so, leaving Aaron and Hur in charge at the base of the mountain, and in the course of a forty-day retreat receives the tablets (24.12-15a + 18b + 31.18). This narrative tradition introduces the Golden Calf episode, the smashing of the tablets, the making of new ones on which God (or Moses) writes the decalogue (or a different set of laws) (chs. 32–34).

The point at which the proceedings are brought to a conclusion is one of particular exegetical density. Exod. 24.1-18 has preserved four versions of the concluding ceremony each with its own cast of characters, location (on or below the mountain), and account of what happened. Only the briefest summary of these interwoven traditions can be given.[15] The first (1-2, 9-11) features Moses, Aaron, his two sons and seventy elders and consists in a vision and a meal on the mountain. It has no account of covenant-making. The lapis pavement seen in the

---

15. Blenkinsopp, *The Pentateuch*, pp. 189-92.

vision recalls Ezekiel's mobile throne vision (Ezek. 1.26; 10.1), but
the closest parallel is with the meal 'before God' shared by Moses,
Aaron and elders and located at another 'mountain of God' at or near
Kadesh (Exod. 18.12). Into this brief notice about a vision and meal
an editor has spliced an account of a covenant-sealing ceremony at the
foot of the mountain (24.3-8). Moses reads the laws to the people who
accept them, they are written down, an altar with twelve steles
(*maṣṣēbôt*) is set up, sacrifices are carried out by 'young men'
(*ne'ārîm*),[16] and a blood ritual uniting the altar (i.e., the deity) and the
people is carried out. The features which this account has in common
with the Shechem covenant-making tradition (Deut. 27.1-8; Josh.
8.30-35) are easily detected; they include the public reading and
writing of the laws, twelve commemorative stones, and an altar and
sacrifices. Its insertion by a D editor into the brief vision-meal
account, following a well-attested bracketing technique, was intended
to give explicit expression to the covenant character of the Sinai–
Horeb event, connecting it with the promulgation and solemn acceptance of laws as basic for the life of the community.

A similar editorial technique accounts for the arrangement of the
second half of the chapter in which the P version of the vision in
which Moses receives the specifications for setting up the cult (24.15b-
18a) breaks into the continuation of the mainline D narrative (24.12-
15a + 18b + 31.18). The latter leads directly into the Golden Calf
episode and its sequel. As noted earlier, this sequence of events is confirmed by the version of Moses' retrospective survey of what happened as related in Deuteronomy.

3. The 'message' inscribed in this D version of the Sinai–Horeb
event is that Israel's relationship with God rests on a contractual basis
the terms of which are available in writing. Hence only in this
version, and in related D texts elsewhere, do we hear of stone tablets
(*lûḥôt hā'eben*) on which the stipulations of the agreement are
engraved, and which are therefore referred to as 'covenant tablets',
with either *be rît* (Deut. 9.9, 11, 15) or *'ēdût* (Exod. 31.18; 32.15;
34.29), the latter, therefore, not an exclusively P term. The fundamental moral obligation into which Israel has contracted by accepting
the terms of the agreement ('all that YHWH has spoken we will do',

---

16. As resident cult official of the wilderness tent Joshua is called *me šārēt* and
na'ar (Exod. 33.7-11), as is Samuel at Shiloh (1 Sam. 2.18; cf. 1 Sam. 1.24 and
2 Kgs 9.4, the latter referring to Gehazi, prophetic acolyte of Elisha).

Exod. 19.8; 24.3, 7) is encapsulated in the decalogue inscribed on the tablets (Exod. 34.28; Deut. 4.13; 5.22; 10.4). The ultimacy of its authority is expressed through the *topos* that YHWH is both author and engraver of the decalogue (Exod. 31.18; 32.16; 34.1; Deut. 4.13; 9.10). The choice of writing surface, in contrast to the *sēper* (book, scroll) in which the stipulations were written, presumably on papyrus (Exod. 24.7), likewise indicates permanence and permanent relevance. The 'ten utterances' are, literally, written on stone.

It seems that the Deuteronomic school assigned great importance to the distinction between the decalogue, containing the basic moral norms defining the kind of community Israel is meant to be, and the individual stipulations of law which spelled out the decalogic requirements in detail and applied them to specific situations. At the linguistic level the distinction is between $d^e b \bar{a} r \hat{i} m$ (words, utterances) and *ḥuqqîm ûmišpāṭîm* (statutes and ordinances). The former remain forever the same while the latter may be updated, expanded or even abrogated in keeping with contemporary needs. Both the distinction and the connection will explain why the decalogue is repeated in juxtaposition with the laws in Exodus 20–23 and Deuteronomy 12–26. The decalogue tablets are also preserved with much greater care than the 'books' containing the legal compilations. The tablets are placed in an ark or chest (*^{a}rôn*) specially made for them (Deut. 10.5; 1 Kgs 8.9) located in the inner sanctum of the sanctuary, while the book of the (Deuteronomic) law is deposited at the side of the chest (Deut. 31.26). The different perspective of the P source is apparent in the description of the contents of the ark as, simply, 'the testimony' (*hā'ēdût*, Exod. 25.16, 21; 40.20, etc.). No explicit connection is made with covenant, and the nature of the *'ēdût* is not further specified. The focus of the divine presence is above the ark cover (*kapporet*) between the two cherubim, and it is from that point that divine communications were thought to proceed (Exod. 25.22; Num. 7.89).

The frequent mention of stone tablets thoughout the entire D version (Exod. 24.12; 31.18; 32.15-16, 19; 34.1, 4, 28-29) is one of several indications of continuity, coherence, and a basic unity of composition. The narrative structure turns on the hinge of the breaking of the tablets subsequent to the Golden Calf episode, which in its turn opens up the paradigmatic character of the narrative. The connection between the cult offered to the calf (Exod. 32) and the cult establishment of Jeroboam in Bethel and Dan (1 Kgs 12) is well known: the same icon is greeted with the same acclamation, an altar is set up, and an unauthorized feast proclaimed. The vengeance taken by the sons of Levi against the apostates aided and abetted by Aaron (Exod. 32.25-29) recalls the exclusion of Levitical priests from Jeroboam's cult establishment (1 Kgs 12.31), and may even offer a clue to the origins of the Aaronite priesthood. Moreover, the near-identity of the names of Jeroboam's sons (Nadab, Abijah) with those of Aaron's sons (Nadab, Abihu) is curious, to say the least. The Golden Calf incident, therefore, encodes a theological evaluation of the Northern Kingdom in its religious-cultic aspects and an explanation of its ultimate fate (cf. 2 Kgs 17.16; 18.12). But since Judah also 'walked in the customs which Israel had introduced' (2 Kgs 17.19), the debacle at Sinai–Horeb could serve as a paradigm of Israel's spiritual failure in general, confirmed by the fall of Jerusalem and ensuing exile. The remarkable fact that, in spite of prophetic denunciations of social injustice, the D historian attributes political disaster to cultic infidelity to the exclusion of other considerations, may be taken as confirmation of the paradigmatic character of the Golden Calf incident.

According to the parallel account in Deuteronomy, the aberrant cult at Sinai–Horeb was only one in a series of acts of religious infidelity beginning with the exodus from Egypt (Deut. 9.7-8). In this version the smashing of the tablets, indicating the breaking of the covenant agreement (9.17), was followed by another forty-day fast of Moses and his intercession for Aaron and the other delinquents (9.18, 25-29). This in its turn led to the re-issue of the decalogue (10.1-5). At this point, however, the version in Deuteronomy diverges from Exodus 32–34 since it continues with the command to continue on to Canaan (Deut. 10.10-11) omitting the remaking of the covenant (cf. Exod. 34.10, 27). The difference is evidently due to the desire to bring the Deuteronomic law into direct association with entry into the land, a move which has been understood to have been dictated either by the expectation of political independence from Assyria in the last decades of the Kingdom of Judah or the setting up of a new commonwealth after the return from exile, or quite possibly both. In any event, the issuance of the Deuteronomic law represents a quite distinctively identifiable moment in the religious history of Israel: 'These are the words (i.e., stipulations) of the covenant which YHWH commanded Moses to make with the Israelites in the land of Moab in addition to the covenant which he made with them at Horeb' (Deut. 28.69).

4. If, then, the Deuteronomic version of the event as I have reconstructed it inscribes a religious interpretation of Israel's history as a history of failure, does it also prescribe what is to be done in the future? Has the collective experience of failure and moral incapacity made any difference? The rewriting of the same moral code in the Sinai–Horeb story suggests, at first sight, a negative answer to this last question. Moral obligation is still basic, apparently in the same way. The description of the second covenant in Deuteronomy, with its heavy emphasis on the oath (*'ālâ*, + Deut. 29.11, 13, 18-20) and the curse (*qᵉlālâ*, Deut. 29.26), suggests even more strongly that the relationship with YHWH is contingent on moral performance consisting in conformity to written norms and laws. But if we look more closely at passages in Deuteronomy, the Deuteronomistic History and D additions to prophetic books which reflect the experience of exile we will find reason to believe that the experience of failure has made a difference.

I note, first, some indications of a certain broadening of the idea of moral obligation understood as adhesion to divinely revealed and imposed norms and rules. Speaking with the experience of exile in mind, the D homilist assures his readers that those who seek God with total dedication ('With all your heart and soul') will be rewarded by finding him:

> From there (i.e., the place of exile) you will seek YHWH your God and you will find him if you search after him with all you heart and soul (Deut. 4.29).

> When you search for me you will find me; if you seek me with all your heart, I will let you find me...and I will restore your fortunes and gather you from all the nations... (Jer. 29.13-14).

Similar in character are the 'seek passages' in Amos (5.4-5, 6-7, 14-15), arguably of Deuteronomic origin from the time of the Babylonian exile, which link the seeking after YHWH with the attainment of true life (cf. Deut. 30.6). Seeking is also associated with the idea of returning to YHWH (Deut. 4.30; 30.2, 10), a biblical anticipation of Buber's 'true turning' (*tᵉšûbâ*), meaning a change in direction, a re-orientation of one's life. So, while it does not seem that the Deuteronomists had learned any radically new lessons from the experience of religious failure and political collapse, we can detect the beginning of a process in which law observance, a straightforward rules morality, is being recontextualized and broadened in scope.

There is another side to this which has to do with the competence to observe the revealed laws. The Deuteronomists obviously continued to believe in the moral capacity of those who entered the covenant community to observe its laws, and therefore continued to stress accountability, but the limitations of this capacity are coming increasingly into view (Deut. 5.29). We hear, for example, of the need for God to circumcise the heart of the believer (Deut. 30.6; cf. 10.16). This is one of a curious set of metaphoric applications of circumcision to other anatomical features including the lips (Exod. 6.12, 30) and the ears (Jer. 6.10). The point seems to be that by some mysterious action of God the mind of the individual will be sensitized resulting in a 'turning', a re-orientation of one's life. Interiority is, however, more clearly indicated in the contrast, expressed or implied, between stone tablets and the 'tablets of the heart'. One thinks in this connection of the new covenant of Jer. 31.31-34, one of about twenty sayings in the so-called Book of Consolation (Jer. 30–31). The origin of this passage has long been a matter of dispute. It does not seem to be foreign to Jeremiah's thinking insofar as we can reconstruct it. It agrees with the strong sense of moral incapacity expressed in sayings generally taken to be authentic—about the inability of the leopard to change its spots (13.23) and the desperate sickness of the human heart (17.9-10). But the new covenant passage also has close affinity with Deuteronomy. The latter does not speak of a new covenant, but it emphasizes the distinctiveness of the Moab covenant vis-à-vis the one made at Horeb (Deut. 28.69). It also speaks of the law in the heart, the law internalized (Deut. 6.6; 11.18; 30.14), and assigns great importance to religious instruction which, according to Jer. 31.34, will not be needed in the future ('no longer shall each one teach neighbor or brother').

In due course the new covenant text would assume great importance for the Qumran community (CD 6.19; 8.21; 19.33; 20.12) and of course for early Christianity (Lk. 22.20; 1 Cor. 11.15; Heb. 6.6–9.28). But if we read it without reference to these later appropriations, it conveys a strong sense of what is rather muted in Deuteronomy, namely, that individual and collective moral impotence calls for a different degree or kind of initiative from God if the relationship is to have any future at all. But the author of Jer. 31.31-34 does not seem to be clear as to how the new covenantal relationship is to be socially embodied. It will be different from the old, the law will still be basic, but it will be fully internalized in such a way that instruction, the entire legal tradition on which Deuteronomy is so insistent, will no longer be necessary—a potentially dangerous idea, one would think, and an invitation to antinomian enthusiasm. We will now go on to ask whether any alternatives to this rather utopian vision were on offer and, in particular, whether one may be found in the much-maligned Priestly source (P), specifically in the section of the P narrative dealing with the Sinai event.

5. The idea that a radical inner change, a kind of spiritual heart transplant, is necessary in order to assure conformity with a divinely revealed law is not confined to the Jeremiah text just discussed. It is, in fact, quite possible that the text in question draws on the promise of a renewal of heart and spirit in Ezekiel, the outcome of which will be to enable conformity with the divine law (Ezek. 11.20; 36.26-27). Few Old Testament scholars doubt a connection of some kind between Ezekiel and the P material in the Pentateuch, though no one is quite sure how the relationship is to be explained. It is certainly oversimplified to read P as a systematization of the teaching of Ezekiel. It may be nearer the mark to read both as expressing the same *Weltanschauung* in different literary forms and with different emphases. With respect to covenant, at any rate, the similarities are pronounced. For Ezekiel as for P the covenant is perpetual (*bᵉrît 'ôlām*, Ezek. 16.60; 37.26), is activated by God's memory (Ezek. 16.60), and is put into effect through the place, instruments and acts of worship (Ezek. 37.26-28).

With this we return to the P version of the Sinai event and what I take to be its most remarkable characteristic, namely, the severing of the contractual bond which of course was a standard feature of covenant according to the D school. The difference is expressed, as we have seen, in the designation 'perpetual covenant' (*bᵉrît 'ôlām*), and for the same reason a covenant according to P is not 'cut' (*krt*), a metaphoric usage implying bilaterality, but granted (*ntn*) or established (*hqym*). This kind of covenant remains in force regardless of the behavior of the human partner. In other words, no obligations are laid on Israel on the observance of which the covenant relationship depends. In the Abrahamic covenant (Gen. 17), according to P the only one made with Israel, circumcision is the sign of the covenant, not a necessary condition for the fulfillment of the attached promises. It is a necessary condition for membership in the community constituted by the covenant, but that is a quite different matter. Likewise in the covenant with postdiluvian humanity, the so-called Noachide laws are issued prior to the announcement of the covenant and therefore cannot be considered as obligations on the fulfillment of which the existence of the covenant rests (Gen. 9.1-17).

In his *Theologie des Alten Testaments* Walther Eichrodt made the point that since, according to P, the one covenant with Israel is antecedent to the revelation of the ceremonial law and the setting up of the instruments of worship, the implementation of the latter was not considered to be a human performance by which the covenant becomes effective, but rather Israel's way of appropriating the covenant offered to them through Abraham.[17] On this view, therefore, the purpose of the covenant is not to provide a theological basis for moral obligation but to create a community united in worship. In this purpose, according to P, Sinai represents a decisive stage but not an absolute beginning. Prior to Sinai only those religious institutions independent of the priesthood were established beginning with circumcision (Gen. 17.9-14), then Passover (Exod. 12.1-28, 43-51), and finally sabbath (Exod. 31.12-17; 35.1-3). The process, therefore, begins with the covenant with Israel. The historical and social counterpart to this schematic arrangement was no doubt the observance of these three practices as emblematic of identity by the Jewish ethnic minority in Neo-Babylonian and Achemenid Mesopotamia before the re-establishment of temple worship and sacrifice in the late sixth century BCE. The extraordinary importance of sabbath and its practical synonymity with covenant (Exod. 31.16-17) are amply in evidence in texts from the Persian period (e.g., Isa. 56.1-8 and Neh. 13.15-22) and in the occurrence, for the first time, of the name Shabbetai in Ezra–Nehemiah and the Elephantine papyri.

6. I have taken the view that the Sinai–Horeb episode presents paradigmatically the religious history of Israel viewed from the other side of disaster. The basic interpretative principle informing that history is one of moral obligation arising out of a formalized relationship, which relationship was not in the event sustained. As in the breakdown of a marital relationship—the analogy was, of course, familiar to the biblical writers—the need was felt to assign blame, and when disaster overcame Judah in the sixth century BCE many were quick to do so.[18] The issue then, inevitably, concerned the possibility

---

17. W. Eichrodt, *Theologie des Alten Testaments*, I (Göttingen: Vandenhoeck & Ruprecht, 5th edn, 1957), pp. 23-24.

18. E.g. Jer. 31.29; 44.18; Ezek. 18.2, 25-29.

of a future and whether anything could be salvaged from the experience of moral incapacity and failure. At first sight the Deuteronomist answer seems to be more of the same, new tablets but the same message, but we have noted signs of a greater appreciation for human neediness and a rather broader basis for understanding moral obligation. Taken by itself, the Priestly history does not reproduce the making–breaking–remaking pattern noted earlier. It replaces the sin of Aaron by that of two of his sons (Lev. 10.1-7) followed immediately, it seems, by a ritual of atonement (Lev. 16.1). The removal of the contractual element from covenant in the Priestly source does not, needless to say, diminish the importance of moral performance, the observance of norms and rules, but it does put them on a quite different basis. The resulting juxtaposition in the same Scripture of two irreconcilably different views of moral obligation may, one suspects, have interesting consequences for a Jewish or Christian ethic which takes the biblical texts seriously.

FROM FAITHFUL PROPHET TO VILLAIN:
OBSERVATIONS ON THE TRADITION HISTORY OF THE BALAAM STORY

John Van Seters

The figure of Balaam, son of Beor, is one of the most enigmatic of the biblical tradition. His origins are obscure. Is he summoned by the Moabite king from the neighboring region of Ammon or the more distant Mesopotamia? And how is it that he is a prophet of Yahweh? The discovery of the Deir 'Alla texts containing a seer of the same name, who is associated with non-Israelite deities and who appears to be of much more recent date than is suggested by the biblical tradition, has only made the puzzle all the greater. His origins remain obscure and his place in the biblical tradition even more curious.

Balaam has also attracted the attention of George Coats,[1] and so it is a fitting tribute to him and to our long-standing friendship that I offer this study. It is the apparent ambivalence of the biblical tradition towards Balaam that interested Coats and that he tried to address, and this will be the primary focus of my study as well.

In a recent publication, *The Life of Moses*, I have presented my literary-critical analysis of the Balaam narrative and I will assume the details of my analysis for the purposes of the present discussion.[2] Let me merely summarize by saying that, apart from the episode of the talking ass in Num. 22.22-35, some additions to the fourth oracle, and a few glosses, I regard the rest of Numbers 22–24 as a unified composition of the Yahwist. In J's story, Balaam is presented as the completely faithful prophet of Yahweh who blesses the people of Israel in spite of every effort by Balak, the king of Moab, to persuade him to

---

1. G.W. Coats, 'Balaam: Sinner or Saint', *BR* 18 (1973), pp. 21-29. Reprinted in G.W. Coats (ed.), *Saga, Legend, Tale, Novella, Fable: Narrative Genres in Old Testament Literature* (JSOTSup, 34; Sheffield: JSOT Press, 1985), pp. 56-62.

2. J. Van Seters, *The Life of Moses: The Yahwist as Historian in Exodus-Numbers* (Louisville, KY: Westminster/John Knox, 1994), pp. 405-35.

do otherwise. It is the talking ass story within the present narrative that has given Balaam a bad name.

In my book, mentioned earlier, I have also argued that J is later than the DtrH and that the account of the conquest of Transjordan under Moses in Deuteronomy 1–3 is the original version.[3] It contains the sequence:

1. the departure from Horeb in order to conquer the land from the south (1.6-8),
2. the appointment of the administrators and judges in anticipation of the conquest (1.9-18),
3. the spy story and initial defeat (1.19-46),
4. the period of delay (40 years) in the wilderness (2.1, 14),
5. the march through Edom and Moab (2.2-23),
6. the defeat of Sihon and Og (2.24–3.11),
7. the distribution of the land to the Eastern tribes (3.12-20),
8. and the assignment of Joshua as Moses' replacement (3.21-22),
9. Moses' plea to enter the land denied and final preparations for invasion (3.23-28).

Every one of these items is consistently focused on the theme of the conquest of the land after the departure from Horeb.

J has taken over this scheme with some modification of the individual items, and has inserted into it several new episodes to radically change the character of the whole.[4] Three new stories are added after the spy story in Numbers 13–14: 1) the rebellion of Dathan and Abiram in Numbers 16; 2) the bronze serpent story in Num. 21.4-9; and 3) the story of Balaam in Numbers 22–24. The Balaam story, therefore, along with the other two stories, is post-Dtr in its composition.

My primary concern in this paper, however, is with those texts that refer to the Balaam tradition outside of the narrative in Numbers 22–24.[5] Two attitudes are expressed towards Balaam, one positive and

3. Van Seters, *Life of Moses,* pp. 363-65.

4. The last two items dealing with Joshua's commissioning and Moses' death are taken up by J in Deuteronomy itself (Deut. 31.14-15, 23; 34.1b-3, 4, 6b, 7b-8, 10-12).

5. For the major recent studies see W. Gross, *Bileam, Literar-und formkritische Untersuchung der Prosa in Num 22-23* (SANT, 38; Munich: Kösel, 1974); H. Rouillard, *La péricope de Balaam (Nombres 22-24): La prose et les 'oracles'* (Ebib,

one negative, and some have put forward the view that they reflect two different traditions about the prophet. I do not think that this is warranted by the extant references to the prophet. They are all easily explained as arising from the one J story. Let us look at them. George Coats, in his article 'Balaam: Sinner or Saint?', notes these two contrasting attitudes towards Balaam but focuses almost entirely on the 'saintliness' of Balaam in Numbers 22–24.[6] He too regards the ass story as secondary.[7] Yet he does not come to terms with the origin of the negative tradition or its relationship to the positive presentation. It is this question that I will try to address.

Within Numbers, there is the vilification of Balaam in P, in Num. 31.8, 16, in which Balaam is made responsible for the defection of the Israelites regarding their affair with the Midianite women (cf. Num. 25). In v. 8 Balaam is mentioned as slain along with the five kings of Midian, and in v. 16 he is regarded as the one who gave counsel to the Midianites that led to the treachery at Peor. But nothing is said about him in Numbers 25, the initial account of the Baal Peor episode, and his vilification looks entirely secondary and incidental to the main narrative. Balaam's connection with Midian is also made stronger by the addition of references to Midian in Numbers 22, very likely by the same hand. There is nothing in Num. 31.8 and 16 that suggests an independent tradition about Balaam. His identity is entirely assumed and the remarks would be meaningless without the prior story of the famous seer whom kings are accustomed to consult in order to defeat Israel. P's negative view of Balaam is in sharp contrast to the presentation in J of Balaam as a faithful prophet, and it is these two contrasting perspectives that set the parameters for the discussion of the tradition-history about Balaam. This reference to Balaam's death with the Midianites is mentioned again in the P text of Josh. 13.22, where he is given the derogatory title of 'soothsayer' (הקוסם).

Outside of Numbers three texts call for comparison with J. That of Mic. 6.5 seems to correspond directly to the J story and be dependent

---

4; Paris: J. Gabalda, 1985); S. Timm, *Moab zwischen den Machten: Studien zu historischen Denkmalern und Texten* (Ägypten und Aptes Testament, 17; Wiesbaden: O. Harrassowitz, 1989), pp. 97-157.

6.   See note 1 above.

7.   Coats, *Saga*, p. 56. See also Gross, *Bileam*, pp. 331-69; Rouillard, *La péricope*, pp. 115-20; *idem*, 'L'anesse de Balaam', *RB* 87 (1980), pp. 5-37, 211-41; Timm, *Moab*, pp. 148-49.

upon it. It states, 'My people, remember well how Balak, king of Moab, plotted, and how Balaam son of Beor answered him.' Balaam is here treated in a positive fashion as the faithful prophet so that the negative view of him has not yet come into play. Deut. 23.4-6, however, has become quite negative. It contains the injunction:

> The Ammonite and the Moabite shall not be included in the assembly of Yahweh, even their tenth generation will not be included in the assembly of Yahweh, not ever. Because they did not meet you with bread and with water on the way when you came out of Egypt and because he (they?) hired against you Balaam son of Beor from Pethor of Mesopotamia to curse you. Yahweh your God was not willing to heed Balaam so that Yahweh your God changed for you the curse into blessing because Yahweh your God loves you.

As noted above, within Deuteronomy's historical prologue in Deuteronomy 1–3, Balaam is entirely missing. If Deut. 23.4-6 belonged to the D corpus taken up by Dtr, then one could have expected some reference to Balaam in the appropriate spot in Deuteronomy 2–3, similar to where it now stands in Numbers. Since there is none, this suggests that the remark about Balaam in Deut. 23.4-6 is a very late addition and this is confirmed by its clear reference to the Second Temple situation dealing with foreign participation in Israel's worship. This is how the law is used in Neh. 13.2 where it is quoted verbatim. Both references clearly belong to this late Persian context.

In order to square this strong antagonism against the foreigner with J's story of Balaam as the faithful prophet who blesses rather than curses the people, the author of Deut. 23.4-6 gave a midrashic interpretation of the story in which Balaam actually did curse the people, but it was the deity who changed the words as they were uttered into blessing. There is no need to suppose that this rests upon some independent tradition. It is merely an attempt to reconcile P's negative remark about Balaam with J's account in Numbers 22–24.

The assessment of Josh. 24.9-10, however, is much more difficult.[8] The present text in MT reads as follows:

> Then Balak son of Zippor of Moab arose and fought with Israel. He sent and summoned Balaam son of Beor to curse them. But I was not willing

---

8. See especially the recent treatment by M. Anbar, *Josue et l'alliance de Sichem (Josue 24.1-28)* (Beiträge zur biblischen Exegese und Theologie, 25; Frankfurt am Main: Peter Lang, 1992).

> to heed Balaam. He did in fact bless you, and I delivered you from his hand.

This text as it stands is very confusing, which is a clear indication that it has been altered in some way. The possibility of alteration is widely recognized, but there is little agreement on how. First, the remark about Balak 'fighting' Israel does not correspond with any other tradition and it is out of place after the reference to the wars with the Amorites to the north of Moab in the previous verse. It is also directly contradicted by Judg. 11.25 which states explicitly that Balak did not 'fight' with Israel. The fact that Israel is referred to in the third person instead of the second makes the phrase וילחם בישראל suspect. The rest of v. 9 corresponds well with J's story.

The real problem, however, comes in v. 10. If we accept the first phrase, 'But I (Yahweh) was not willing to listen to Balaam', then how are we to understand the statement, 'and he (Balaam) did indeed bless you' (ויברך ברוך אתכם). To make sense of the text the Revised English Bible renders this, 'Instead of this he was constrained to bless you', making it correspond to the statement in Deut. 23.6. That is taking considerable liberties with the Hebrew text. If this is what was really intended, why did not the writer of Joshua just borrow the whole text of Deuteronomy as Neh. 13.2 does. Furthermore, the following phrase is also confusing: 'Thus I delivered you from his hand'. Whose hand? REB makes this clear by inserting Balak's name into the text, but with Balaam mentioned in the preceding sentence in a negative way this connection with Balak is obscured. The Greek, however, does not have any reference to Balaam in v. 10. Instead, it renders the first line: 'Yahweh (your God) was not willing to have you perish' (και ουκ ηθελησεν Κυριος ο θεος σου απολεσαι σε). If this is the sense of the original Hebrew, then the whole of v. 10 would be quite clear and consistent with the account in J. It would suggest that for obvious ideological reasons the text was partially modified in agreement with Deut. 23.6 by the introduction of the phrase 'to listen to Balaam' (לשמע לבלעם) in place of 'to let you perish' (לאבדך)[9]. This change in MT, however, was not enough because what Deut. 23.6 intends to say is that what Yahweh did not heed was Balaam's cursing, and that it was Yahweh that did the blessing. Thus the remark in Deut. 23.6 would

---

9. See Anbar, *Josue*, pp. 26, 38-39, for a comparison of the Greek and Hebrew texts.

hardly result in a text that would make Balaam the subject of the blessing.

Consequently, it would appear that the original version of Josh. 24.9-10 read:

> Then Balak son of Zippor, king of Moab, sent and invited Balaam son of Beor to curse you. But I was not willing to let you perish; therefore he blessed you. So I rescued you out of his (Balak's) hand.

This version is in full agreement with J's story in Numbers 22–24 before the addition of the talking ass story. I have elsewhere argued that Joshua 24 is from the hand of J and this analysis would support that view.[10]

Let us return to the remark about Balak in Judg. 11.25, which is given without any reference to Balaam. Jephthah, in his dispute with the king of Ammon over territory in Transjordan, cites the following historical precedent:

> Are you better than Balak son of Zippor, king of Moab? Did he ever contend with Israel; did he ever fight with them? While Israel dwelt in Heshbon and its villages, and in Aroer and its villages, and in all the cities that are on the banks of the Arnon, for three hundred years, why did you not recover them in that time?

It is, of course, natural to take this as a reference to Numbers 22–24, but is that the most likely possibility? In Numbers Balak is aggressive and that story would hardly suggest this type of argument. It is more likely that Balak simply represents the name of an early king of Moab who is thought to be contemporary with Israel's exodus from Egypt. It is possible that J took up this name for the early king from this source and instead of having him fight or threaten Israel as the Edomite king does (Num. 20.20), he resorts to hiring a seer to curse Israel.[11] At any rate, the remarks in Judg. 11.25 do not prove that Dtr in Judges knew of the Balaam story.

Where does this leave the story of the talking ass in Numbers 22? I believe that this too was a late addition, probably under the influence of the anti-foreign sentiment of the late Persian period, as reflected in

---

10. See 'Joshua 24 and the Problem of Tradition in the Old Testament', in W.B. Barrick and J.R. Spencer (eds.), *In the Shelter of Elyon: Essays in Honor of G.W. Ahlström* (JSOTSup, 31; Sheffield: JSOT Press, 1984), pp. 139-58.

11. I have also argued that J is dependent on this text in Judg. 11 for the account of the conquest of Sihon in Van Seters, *Life of Moses*, pp. 389-98.

Deuteronomy 23 and Nehemiah 13. It could have been the latest modification of the Balaam tradition.

Conclusion

The oldest biblical version of the Balaam tradition is the one by J in Numbers 22–24, including both prose and poems, and this version is already exilic in date. It was unknown to Dtr and is lacking in his prologue of Deuteronomy 1–3. It is the creation of J and owes very little to the Ammonite tradition about Balaam son of Beor. For all the discussion about the Deir 'Alla texts they contribute little to our understanding of the biblical Balaam tradition. The P writer, in supplementing J's work with his story about the Midianites in Numbers 31, included a reference to Balaam in order to vilify him. He has no new information of his own. The anti-foreign sentiment of the Persian period leads to further discrediting of Balaam in Deut. 23.4-6 and Neh. 13.2. The talking ass story is the final degradation of the faithful prophet into a buffoon who must be instructed by his own humble donkey.

THE MISSING VOICE

James L. Crenshaw

A paternal voice reverberates throughout the initial collection in the book of Proverbs—berating, warning, pleading, instructing, admonishing. The son, ever present as addressee, never assumes the position of respondent. His well-being occupies the thought from first to last, but not one utterance escapes his lips. At best, the father ventures into ventriloquism long enough to attribute an expression of regret to a son whose sexual appetite has led him into deep trouble (5.12-14).

Silence reigns throughout wisdom literature insofar as the son as speaker is concerned. That absence of a youthful voice occasions little surprise in folk wisdom, where the voice of experience expresses itself succinctly in an artful manner.[1] Instructions, however, differ in their concentration on the pedagogic situation, which naturally involves young boys.[2] One therefore expects interaction between teacher and

---

1. Two recent publications by Claus Westermann and Friedemann W. Golka have strengthened the understanding of early Israelite wisdom as the product of popular reflection, thus undermining the view that the proverbs were written by teachers for students in temple schools (*Wurzeln der Weisheit* [Göttingen: Vandenhoeck & Ruprecht, 1990] = ET, *Roots of Wisdom* [Louisville, KY: Westminster–John Knox, 1995] and *The Leopard's Spots* [Edinburgh: T. & T. Clark, 1993]). Westermann emphasizes the rural context reflected in the sayings, concentration on the family and small towns, comparing their language and interests to those of simple African tribes. Similarly, Golka draws on African proverbs to show that the same concerns in biblical sayings indicate a setting other than the royal court or school. The minimal role of politics, war, and cult points to ordinary people, as does the emphasis on the interaction between brothers, cousins, spouses, old people and youth. In using the absence of prayer in African proverbs to bolster his argument, Golka overlooks the fact that the composers of these African sayings would have been loath to poke fun at this act of piety.

2. The genre of instruction has a long history. The Instruction of Šuruppak and the several Egyptian instructions (e.g. Ptahhotep, Amenemopet, Ani) indicate that both advanced cultures, Mesopotamian and Egyptian, valued the transmission of

student in the extant instructions within canonical wisdom, Proverbs 1–9, 22.17–23.33 and 31.1-9. Instead, the student's voice is drowned out by the steady drone of a teacher bent on passing along what he has learned over the years.

In one instance the maternal voice vies with the dominant paternal tradition, advising her young prince in an equally authoritative manner (Prov. 31.1-9). The combination of rhetoric and passion gives her counsel exceptional power, as if her gender qualifies the queen mother for instruction in the dangers posed by women, perhaps also by strong drink that often accompanied an evening of sexual pleasure. Curiously, Lemuel's mother urges him to speak up—but not on his own behalf. She reminds her son of the royal obligation[3] to attend to the needs of marginalized subjects, those who cannot speak for themselves, the perishing, the poor and needy.[4]

A case has recently been made for enlarging the scope of advice placed in feminine mouths within the book of Proverbs. The memorable description of a young man being seduced to utter ruin (Prov. 7.6-23) and the accompanying urgent warning (Prov. 7.24-27) has

---

teachings from an authority figure to his probable successor. In this context a father advised his son about the responsibilities of office and endeavored to prepare him for successful performance of duties. Eventually, the giving of advice became the prerogative of professional teachers, but they retained the earlier language implying an address by a father to his son. Whereas, with a single exception, Egyptian instructions restrict the direct address 'my son' to the introductory section, Mesopotamian and biblical instructions regularly insert these references in the body of the instructions.

3.   L. Kalugila, *The Wise King* (ConBOT, 15; Lund: Gleerup, 1980) discusses royal ideology in the ancient world, the expectation that the king look after the rights of disenfranchised citizens of the community, particularly widows, orphans, and the needy (cf. also F.C. Fensham, 'Widow, Orphan and the Poor in the Ancient Near Eastern Legal and Wisdom Literature', *JNES* 21 [1962], pp. 129-39 and N. Lohfink, 'Poverty in the Laws of the Ancient Near East and of the Bible', *TS* 52 [1991], pp. 34-50). This idealization of kingship occurs in early legal material, for example, in the prologue to the Code of Hammurabi, as well as in wisdom literature, and may provide the roots of later messianic speculation in Israel.

4.   For discussion of Prov. 31.1-9, see my article entitled 'A Mother's Instruction to her Son (Prov. 31.1-9)', in J.L. Crenshaw, *Perspectives on the Hebrew Bible* (Macon, GA: Mercer University Press, 1988), pp. 9-22. Although this maternal instruction is unique in the Bible and the ancient Near East, the association of mothers with fathers in the book of Proverbs suggests that within the family both spouses shared the responsibility for teaching the young.

been attributed to a woman on the basis of virtual consistency in the Old Testament when depicting someone looking through a (latticed) window (the mother of Sisera in Judg. 5.28, Michal in 2 Sam. 6.16, and Jezebel in 2 Kgs 9.30; the exception—Abimelech in Gen. 26.8), as well as the positive attitude toward female sexual arousal.[5] Moreover, the advice to observe the ant as a caution against laziness (Prov. 6.6-11),[6] the numerical saying about the mystery of sex and its abuse (Prov. 30.18-20),[7] and the description of a good wife (Prov. 31.10-31)[8] have also been claimed for feminine teaching. (Similarly, the well-known poem about a time for everything in Eccl. 3.2-8 has been interpreted as one about desire, sex, and gender relations, possibly masculine love lyrics aimed at feminine recipients.)[9] Because women can be just as critical of other women as men can, overt attacks against women and even statements that appear to be androcentric may reflect feminine acquiescence when confronting masculine cultural values and perspectives.[10] As a check on such broadening of feminine authorship, Carole R. Fontaine writes, 'Certainly, if women had written many of the proverbs found in that book, we would expect to see far more about drunken, violent husbands, and less emphasis on the "nagging wife" as the sole scapegoat for domestic discord (cf. Prov. 21.9, 19; 25.24; 27.15).'[11]

Neither the book of Job nor Ecclesiastes permits students to become vocal, although Elihu belongs to the awkward stage between youth and

---

5. J. Miles, *God: A Biography* (New York: Vintage Books, 1995), pp. 298-99. On the saying about the mystery of sex and its problematic outcome, he writes, 'This is, as the saying goes, splitting the arrow, a bull's eye followed by another bull's eye, eloquence about the wonder of sexual love followed by superb bluntness about what it can sometimes become. There is no reason whatsoever why "my son" might not have seen both arrows shot by his mother' (p. 300).

6. Miles, *God: A Biography*, p. 300.

7. Miles, *God: A Biography*, p. 300.

8. A. Brenner, 'Some Observations on the Figurations of Woman in Wisdom Literature', in *idem* (ed.), *A Feminist Companion to Wisdom Literature* (Sheffield: Sheffield Academic Press, 1995), p. 54.

9. Brenner, 'Some Observations', pp. 60-61. Also in *On Gendering Texts: Female and Male Voices in the Hebrew Bible* (ed. A. Brenner and F. van Dijk-Hemmes; Leiden: Brill, 1993), pp. 133-53.

10. Brenner, 'Some Observations', pp. 53, 55-56.

11. 'The Social Roles of Women in the World of Wisdom', in Brenner (ed.), *A Feminist Companion to Wisdom Literature*, p. 38 .

adult. What he says thus falls into the category of a self-defensive pique characterized by excessive heat. Such lack of control over the passions identifies him as one who has not yet achieved wisdom.[12] The closest Qoheleth comes to letting a student express himself amounts to an existential sigh in the face of the aging process (cf. Sir. 38.22). Actually, the poignant denial of finding any pleasure in the darkening days of old age belongs to everyone, hence cannot be attributed to students at their tender age.[13]

Ben Sira's manner of expression gives the appearance of elevating students' voices to the same level as that of teachers, but the formula of debate, introduced by *'al tō'mar* ('do not say') actually disguises his own voice of instruction.[14] What follows the introductory formula consists of imagined speech, none of it very flattering to the supposed speakers. Such speeches resemble that of the fool in Ps. 14.1–53.1

12. The metaphor for a fool in Egypt, 'the heated man', stresses his inability to govern the passions, perhaps the most difficult battle confronting human beings, if the unusual observation is correct that one who conquers the passions is superior to the person who takes a city in battle (cf. Prov. 16.32). N. Shupak, *Where Can Wisdom be Found?* (OBO, 130; Göttingen: Vandenhoeck & Ruprecht, 1993), p. 339 argues that eight biblical expressions in Hebrew (the heated person, chambers of the belly, a well-constructed saying [*taḥbulôt*], one who weighs the heart, cool-tempered, slow to anger, short-tempered) from wisdom literature are similar to Egyptian expressions and indicate a linguistic relationship, either direct or indirect, between the biblical texts and Egyptian literature.

13. The actual audience for these biblical books has yet to be determined. Rainer Albertz's hypothesis of three different audiences for the book of Job—a selfish upper class, a compassionate upper class, and a lower class—does not necessarily follow from the different attitudes to the poor expressed in the book ('Der sozialgeschichtliche Hintergrund des Hiobbuches und der "Babylonischen Theodizee"', in J. Jeremias and L. Perlitt (eds.), *Die Botschaft und die Boten: Festschrift H.W. Wolff* [Neukirchen–Vluyn: Neukirchener Verlag, 1981], pp. 349-72). Likewise Qoheleth's actual attitude toward the marginalized citizens of his own day is more complex than Franz Crüsemann's theory suggests ('Die unveränderbare Welt. Überlegungen zur "Krisis der Weisheit" beim Prediger [Kohelet]', in W. Schottroff and W. Stegemann (eds.), *Der Gott der Kleinen Leute* [Munich: Chr. Kaiser Verlag, 1979], pp. 80-104 = ET, *The God of the Lowly* [Maryknoll, NY: Orbis Books, 1984]).

14. For analysis of the ancient formula of debate, see J.L. Crenshaw, 'The Problem of Theodicy in Sirach: On Human Bondage', *JBL* 94 (1975), pp. 47-64. Although Ben Sira formulates the challenge to traditional teaching, he probably imitates actual language among the youth who, for whatever reason, found ancestral views no longer sufficient for the new situation in a Hellenized culture.

who denies God's existence and those of prophetic opponents who conveniently vocalize objectionable views. The author of Wisdom of Solomon carries this unflattering strategy to new heights (1.16–2.20), but this hedonism is more widespread than mere student unrest.[15]

This cry on behalf of instant gratification recalls a powerfully seductive appeal in Prov. 1.11-14, the invitation to join a band of highway robbers in a scheme to get rich quickly at the expense of weak, vulnerable travelers. The attractiveness of this alternative to inaction awaiting a parental legacy many years in the future made this appeal particularly dangerous, especially when combined with an exaggerated sense of camaraderie and adventure.[16]

Imaginary speeches, attributed to unsavory characters, do exist, but not in any large number. The pitiable drunk described in Prov. 23.29-35 recalls physical abuse that made no lasting impression because of his drunken stupor and then vows to take another drink. An adulterer convinces himself that secrecy surrounds his lecherous conduct: 'Who can see me? Darkness surrounds me, the walls hide me, and no one sees me. Why should I worry? The Most High will not remember sins' (Sir. 23.18). Similarly, an adulteress persuades herself that her behavior is perfectly appropriate; after eating and wiping her mouth, she observes nonchalantly, 'I have done no wrong' (Prov. 30.20). A person bent on revenge vows to retaliate in exact measure as he had received evil (Prov. 24.29). According to Prov. 30.15-16, an insatiable crea-

15. The ideas being combatted in this section resemble those of Qoheleth to some degree, especially the emphasis on enjoying one's youth, the portion granted everyone, the role of chance, the finality of death, the extinction of one's name, the bleak character of reality, and the image of life as a shadow—but the concluding remarks about oppressing the weak have no parallel in Qoheleth's thoughts. Michael Kolarcik (*The Ambiguity of Death in the Book of Wisdom 1–6* [Rome: Editrice Pontificio Istituto Biblico, 1991], p. 163) argues that the author uses three distinct yet related perceptions of death: mortality, physical death as punishment, and ultimate death. In Kolarcik's view, the author thinks that evil results from refusing to accept limits implied in mortality and this injustice 'brings on the ultimate death in the apocalyptic judgment according to the scheme of the trial' (p. 179).

16. C.A. Newson ('Woman and the Discourse of Patriarchal Wisdom: A Study of Proverbs 1–9', in P.L. Day [ed.], *Gender and Difference in Ancient Israel* [Minneapolis: Fortress Press, 1989], pp. 142-60) notes the dominance of the father's voice in this section and recognizes the problem presented by the long delay in receiving an inheritance, which she thinks would have troubled impatient young men. Perhaps an even greater source for concern was the meager prospect of inherited property before real disposable income became the societal norm.

ture, often translated 'a leech', cries 'Give, give', in the same way that
Sheol, a barren womb, earth, and fire are never content to the point of
saying, 'Enough'. In Prov. 20.14 the endless posturing of buyer and
seller in an economy characterized by a lively process of bargaining
issues in a humorous imagined speech: 'Bad, bad', says the buyer, then
goes away and boasts.[17] Within the profound prayer recorded in Prov.
30.8-9 an imaginary speech lays bare the dangers lurking in the shadows
for persons in dire straits and for others rolling in wealth. The former, people of action, proceed to steal as a way out of poverty,
whereas the latter intellectualize their situation with a question, 'Who
is the Lord?'[18] In Prov. 31.29 a husband praises an exceptional wife,
who may recall personified wisdom.

The proverbial fool who thinks a bountiful supply of worldly goods
assures well-being also comes in for censure. The hollow boast, 'I have
found rest, and now I shall feast on my goods!' does not take into
account the unknown factor, the hour of death (Sir. 11.19).[19] The fool
considers everyone else an enemy, consuming his bread without grati-
tude (Sir. 20.16); he lacks the mental capacity to comprehend simple
narratives, sleepily asking about the point of a story (Sir. 22.10); or
he makes rash vows only to reconsider the action when it is too late
(Prov. 20.25).

All the more astonishing, therefore, is the lavish attention within
Proverbs 1–9 to imagined speeches by two rivals, wisdom and folly,

---

17. Not every instance of imagined speech in wisdom literature has been assessed
here. One could also cite Sir. 29.26-28, where a guest must listen while a host orders
him around and even removes him entirely from the premises to make room for
someone else. Other examples exist, but the ones noted here indicate the essential
character of such speech. On the question whether or not to consider these speeches
authentic, Moshe Greenberg's approach to prayer as literary fiction is applicable here
(*Biblical Prose Prayer* [Berkeley, CA: University of California Press, 1983]). Just as
prayer in the Bible is modeled on real prayers, so these imagined speeches reflect
views prevalent in the community.

18. The LXX offers an interesting variant that approximates the Hebrew text
orthographically (*me hora*, 'who sees me?'), but this notion of sinners thinking they
escape detection may result from its common use elsewhere, especially in the Psalter.
The Hebrew text has the more compelling sentiment, for it strikes at the essence of
deity, whereas the Greek text merely expresses skepticism about God's visibility,
and by extension, punishment of sin.

19. The well-known parable of the rich fool in Lk. 12.13-21 brings the same
teaching into the context of dominical sayings.

here personified in poetic fiction. Nothing in the first speech by wisdom (1.20-33) moves beyond similar personifications in prophetic literature—of the two kingdoms Israel and Judah, or of the city Zion/Jerusalem—and linguistic affinities support this relationship.[20] Here wisdom is depicted as one who combines prophetic and divine characteristics in the same manner prophets move from first person speech to third person when representing the deity before Israel. In Proverbs 8, however, the imagery incorporates extrabiblical concepts more at home in hymns celebrating the virtues of the Mesopotamian goddess Ishtar and in descriptions associated with the Egyptian goddess of order, Ma'at, and perhaps also with the goddess Isis. Decisive differences prevent a simple equation of wisdom with any of these figures,[21] and the most one can legitimately conclude is that the Israelite author of Prov. 8.22-31 probably knew about similar hymns honoring other deities, especially Ishtar and Ma'at.

The juxtaposition of wisdom and folly in Proverbs 9, never again attempted in extant sapiential literature, features two hostesses who issue invitations to banquets. Asymmetry characterizes the banquet fare, with wisdom promising meat as well as wine and bread.[22] Folly offers a simple meal of bread and water, but this ordinary staple, becomes a culinary feast precisely because of its furtive circumstances, appealing to the sense of adventure and to a desire to taste forbidden fruit. 'Stolen water is sweet, and bread eaten in secret is pleasant' (Prov. 9.17). One suspects that her words persisted long after

20. The language for pouring out one's thoughts, refusal to listen, stretching out the hand, laughing at calamity, calling on someone but to no avail, seeking but not finding, eating the fruit of one's deeds—all this fits well in prophetic discourse on behalf of Yahweh. The teacher in this description is surely modeled after a prophet.

21. The primary difference, that wisdom praises Yahweh, accords with her subject status, whereas both Isis and Ma'at are goddesses. Moreover, Ma'at never utters a hymn of self-praise. Nevertheless, the language that wisdom uses comes very close to divine self-praise, particularly in Deutero-Isaiah, for she appears as an authoritative figure in Yahweh's presence, one 'acquired' in the beginning. R.N. Whybray (*Proverbs* [NCB; Grand Rapids: Eerdmans, 1995], p. 121) thinks Prov. 8.22-31 'can be regarded as a kind of baroque development of the simple statement made in 3.19 that "The Lord by wisdom founded the earth"'.

22. L. Boström (*The God of the Sages* [ConBOT, 29; Stockholm: Almqvist & Wiksell, 1990], p. 56) raises the possibility that the figure of folly is primary, arising from the constant emphasis on seductive women, and that personified wisdom came later as a contrast and foil to folly.

the teacher's warning about the consequences of eating and drinking with her had faded from memory. More abiding, perhaps, than this warning is that projected on an imaginary victim of the strange woman in Prov. 5.11-14:

> ... and the end of your life you will groan, when your flesh and body are consumed, and you say, 'Oh, how I hated discipline, and my heart despised reproof! I did not listen to the voice of my teachers or incline my ear to my instructors. Now I am at the point of utter ruin in the public assembly'.[23]

Shame, resulting from loss of honor, is teamed up with odious physical disease, possibly sexually transmitted, to evoke a rare admission of inattention, the exact opposite of what teachers desired ('The mind of the intelligent appreciates proverbs, and an attentive ear is the desire of the wise', Sir. 3.20; cf. the motif of the hearing one in Egyptian wisdom, accentuated in the conclusion to the Instruction of Ptahhotep, and in Mesopotamian lore about sages—and exceptional divine kings like Marduk—with four ears, a way of emphasizing their capacity for hearing).

Extracanonical wisdom literature sets the precedent for silencing students under a barrage of authoritative counsel. Exceptions do occur, but their paucity only heightens the point. The Sumerian text, 'Schooldays', has a graduate of the *edubba* (academy or tablet house) reflect on his earlier days as a student when seemingly everything he did provoked harsh beatings from those in charge of various tasks. 'The Disputation between Enkimansi and Girnishag' reflects a rivalry between two accomplished scribes, and 'Colloquy between an *ugula* (monitor) and a Scribe' deals either with a graduate of the school or with an advanced student. An interesting feature of this text is the teacher's appeal to a time when he was a student, a phenomenon also present in Prov. 4.3-9. Here the Israelite instructor recalls an earlier period when his own father taught him. By using this fiction of speech from a bygone era, the teacher allows the teaching to span three generations. In this way, the continuity of the instruction comes to the fore. The text entitled 'A Scribe and his Perverse Son' consists of a dialogue between teacher and student, one in which the son demon-

---

23. The sole national reference in Proverbs ('in the midst of the congregation') has a hendiadys, *betôk qāhāl weʿēdāh*. The adulterer is disgraced but not utterly destroyed, for he confesses that he was almost (*kimeʿaṭ*) ruined in public.

strates his worth by repeating verbatim what his father has said to him.[24]

The only surviving Egyptian instruction that allows a student to vocalize his point of view concludes with a brief dialogue between Ani and his son Khonshotep. Recognizing the disparity between volition and action, the boy feels incapable of reaching the moral heights which his father has attained. Merely reciting classical texts does not serve as a magic stone, enabling him to live up to admittedly worthy goals. Believing that wisdom, like good wine, requires time to establish itself, Khonshotep concedes that sons are by nature inferior to their fathers (cf. Sir. 3.2). In his view, nature determines one's conduct, making an individualist rare. Papyrus Insinger makes the point telling-ly: 'Whoever raves with the crowd is not regarded as a fool'. The path of least resistance, conformity, prompts Khonshotep to urge his father to weaken the requirements—as a concession to persons of less discipline than that possessed by the demanding teacher. Khonshotep appeals to parental practice in adapting to the taste and ability of infants, implying that a similar laxness should be followed in education.[25]

Ani asserts paternal authority from the outset, warning his son of the ruinous consequences of such reasoning. For the father, education has no recognizable limits.[26] It consists in radically reorienting the status quo. The nature of wild beasts can be changed; wild bulls can be domesticated, fierce lions tamed, wild dogs, geese, and monkeys subdued. Even Nubians and Syrians can be taught to speak Egyptian. Having subjected himself to the rigorous curriculum of the sages and moved beyond knowledge to wisdom, Ani resists the suggestion that the demands are unrealistic. The analogy with human development per-suades him that adults ought to consume hearty fare, not a weakened substitute for pabulum.

The debate ends positively, Khonshotep raising a voice to heaven

24. S.N. Kramer, *The Sumerians* (Chicago: University of Chicago Press, 1963), pp. 237-48. Learning consisted primarily of repetition, not original thinking.

25. The Apostle Paul uses the same analogy in correspondence with the Christians at Corinth; he reminds them that as a concession to their spiritual immaturity he fed them with milk rather than solid food (1 Cor. 3.1-3).

26. G. von Rad, *Wisdom in Israel* (Nashville: Abingdon, 1972), pp. 97-110 and J.L. Crenshaw, 'Wisdom and the Sage: On Knowing and Not Knowing', in *Proceedings of the Eleventh World Congress of Jewish Studies*, Division A (Jerusalem: World Union of Jewish Studies, 1994), pp. 137-44.

for divine assistance[27] and Ani appealing to the iron will of teachers who mold reluctant students into paragons of virtue. In the skilled hands of a carpenter, neither a straight stick nor a crooked one retains its original shape. The message comes across clearly: resisting my teaching will ultimately fail. The only disturbing possibility concerns corruption, a perverting of the son's cognitive processes. That is why poignantly emotional language sometimes occurs: this real threat gives paternal teaching its urgency, for a single generation can bring to a halt the entire sapiential enterprise.[28]

The urgency of such appeals from teacher to student, father/mother to son, assumes new importance in light of the popular story of Ahiqar, the victim of, among other things, an ungrateful son whose perverse mind produced faithless deeds that brought shame on the father who had adopted Nadin and taught him the virtuous way, from which he soon departed.[29]

What do these imagined speeches from ancient teachers convey to modern interpreters? Their fictional character does not mask a central concern among those responsible for composing wisdom instructions, and in that sense, the speeches communicate authentic reality. By studying the sentiments attributed by Israelite prophets to the populace

27. The overtly religious character of Egyptian wisdom beginning with the Middle Kingdom has been well documented, although its explanation remains in doubt. Whether the result of a social crisis or not, this growing emphasis on piety persists from Ani onwards, finally eventuating in resignation to divine fate, a constant refrain in Papyrus Insinger. M. Lichtheim (*Maat in Egyptian Autobiographies and Related Studies* [OBO, 129; Göttingen: Vandenhoeck & Ruprecht, 1992], p. 99) challenges the view that in the New Kingdom piety completely replaced Ma'at. In *Late Egyptian Wisdom Literature in the International Context* (OBO, 52; Göttingen: Vandenhoeck & Ruprecht, 1983), p. 63, she rejects the idea that Egyptian wisdom underwent a crisis similar to that in Israel. S. Weeks (*Early Israelite Wisdom* [OTM; Oxford: Clarendon Press, 1994], pp. 57-73) combats the notion that Israelite wisdom originated as a secular phenomenon.

28. The importance of an unbroken chain of tradition surfaces in the rabbinic tractate, *Pirke Aboth*. A Christian parallel can be seen in the emphasis on the role of the twelve disciples and Paul's insistence on a place in this chain of tradition, one granted him by special revelation.

29. J.M. Lindenberger (*The Aramaic Proverbs of Ahiqar* [Baltimore, MD: Johns Hopkins University Press, 1983], p. 4) cites a typical reproach for Nadin's conduct: 'My son thou hast been like a man who saw his companion shivering from cold, and took a pitcher of water and threw it over him'. Imagined speech occurs in saying 109: 'Let not the rich man say, "In my riches I am glorious"'.

in general, one arrives at concepts that an Amos or an Isaiah wished to eradicate.[30] Similarly, the imagined speeches within wisdom literature give voice to ideas currently in vogue that the teachers considered a threat to their world view. Like the popular voice ridiculed in prophetic literature, this collective voice in wisdom literature serves as a negative example, introducing us to the inner world of the composers of these imagined speeches, their secret fears.

When later sages finally take the step toward providing positive exemplars, they attribute the ideas to themselves and eventually relate them to an erotic quest for knowledge.[31] An internalization of speech, creating a monologue,[32] comes to the fore in Qoheleth, surfaces occasionally in Sirach, and reaches its peak in the self-reflections of the unknown author of Wisdom of Solomon.[33] In the view of ancient sages, children should be seen but not heard.[34]

30. J.L. Crenshaw, *Prophetic Conflict* (BZAW, 124; Berlin: de Gruyter, 1971).

31. The fascination with erotic language in regard to wisdom cannot simply be explained as teachers' attempts to capture the interest of young boys. The endless quest for knowledge, the excitement over discovering new insights, the seductive lure and secretive hiding of truth—all this and more resembles an amorous adventure where lovers come together and bask in each other's arms. Every disclosure opens up new possibilities, and this excitement characterizes all genuine pursuit of the unknown. That excitement fills the paternal advice in Prov. 7.4 that his son address wisdom lovingly as 'my sister', the normal expression for a lover in the ancient world.

32. S. Denning Bolle, 'Wisdom in Akkadian Literature: Expression, Instruction, Dialogue' (PhD dissertation, University of California, Los Angeles, 1982) discusses the relationship between monologue and dialogue in Akkadian texts, using the perspective of Mikhail Bakhtin as a heuristic tool.

33. The literary fiction of Solomonic authorship permits the author of this late Hellenistic work to describe in great detail his successful courtship of wisdom and thus to serve as a model for everyone who values her.

34. The harsh treatment of children in the ancient world carried over into the schools of Mesopotamia and Egypt, as demonstrated by frequent references. A saying from Ahiqar compares whipping children to putting manure on gardens; in his view, the infliction of pain resulted in growth toward maturity, a theory that has been taken over by modern sports enthusiasts ('No pain, no gain').

THE FUTILE QUEST FOR THE HISTORICAL PROPHET

Gene M. Tucker

Is the quest for the historical prophet a futile quest? The provocative title of this paper poses a question that has taken on increasing signficance in recent years. It is a specific form of the broader question facing biblical studies: Are we in the middle of a shift from historical-critical methods to literary or other approaches?

I suppose, before we are finished here, the reader will expect a direct answer to the question posed in the title. I am prepared to give a more or less direct answer, provided I am allowed to define the key terms in the question. As the famous linguist said in the discourse with Alice: 'When I use a word it means what I choose it to mean'.

In any case, the discussion of this important issue may be advanced by proposing some definitions of the essential language of the debate. A great deal of disagreement on these issues has resulted from different definitions; that is to say, from distinct critical ideologies. So definitions are required if we are to have, as the diplomats say, a frank exchange of views.

We need not trouble ourselves with the verb and the nouns in our question. The verb simply poses the question and the word 'quest' serves to stress the importance of the discussion by recalling the old and new quest for the historical Jesus. The other noun, 'prophet', I presume, refers to any or all of the persons so-identified in the Hebrew Scriptures, either in the prophetic books or elsewhere, and not limited to those who are mentioned by name. But both adjectives, 'historical' and 'futile', require serious reflection and comment.

The most important term to define in order to respond to our question is 'historical'. If one works with a positivistic view, that historical inquiry can produce the 'real facts', 'the wie es eigentlich gewesen war' of von Ranke, then the answer is yes: The quest for the historical prophet is indeed a futile quest. I suspect that this is the definition of history that is presumed by much of the vigorously negative polemic these days against the search for the historical prophet. If one cannot know with 'scientific' certainty, then one cannot know anything historically. To a great extent, objections to such a search for the historical prophet are justified. Certain scholarly traditions have assumed, on the one hand, that it was possible to establish the 'real' historical facts and, on the other hand, that such facts would function as the measure for all biblical—and, for that matter, theological—interpretation. Such an understanding of the historical enterprise is no longer tenable. It is the very historical view of reality that has undermined this positivistic viewpoint, that the facts of the past can be recovered once and for all. History undercuts the scientific understanding of history, by relativizing all events and individuals, including historians. Moreover, modern literary and sociological inquiry has made explicit what already was implicit in the historical approach, that any interpretation takes place in particular 'interpretive communities'.[1]

But if, on the other hand, one views history as the critical reconstruction of the past, including the work of the historical imagination (e.g., Collingwood, *The Idea of History*), then the answer is no, the search for the historical prophet is not a futile search. The object of the historian's quest is not what happened, but what is the most likely reconstruction of what happened, based on the available evidence. Historians must always limit themselves to establishing the balance of probability, and seldom if ever can that be done beyond a reasonable doubt. To be sure, there are a great many instances in which there simply is insufficient evidence for a critical reconstruction. The question is whether or not that is the case with the prophets. For the moment I want to argue the more basic point that critical historical thinking—in the modern world—is both inevitable and possible.

We all engage in historical thinking every day, and often it is even a matter of life and death. One of the best models for this enterprise is the law court, in which the goal, day in and day out, is determining what happened in the past. This determination will go far deeper than establishing the 'facts', which are the evidence on which the alternative reconstructions are based. The facts will be used to determine such matters as motives—what was going on in human minds and hearts in the past. And then the meaning of the events so reconstructed—in this

---

1.   S. Fish, *Is There a Text in This Class? The Authority of Interpretative Communities* (Cambridge, MA: Harvard University Press, 1980), especially pp. 15-17, 167-73.

particular interpretive community, the law court—will be determined
in the light of the law—in the American court system as spelled out for
a jury by a judge. If the jury should determine that thus and so is what
happened, is it a crime, and if so, what kind? Trials proceed according
to due process, especially by defining the rules of evidence. The kinds
of evidence include eyewitness testimony, physical evidence, and
'circumstantial evidence', all of which is subject to cross-examination;
that is, its meaning—even of eyewitness testimony and physical
evidence—is never taken for granted. All that one can expect to reach
is a judgment 'beyond a reasonable doubt'. Reason is the fundamental
criterion and method. One will then arrive at a reconstruction of
events and even of motives, or at least one that is persuasive to a jury.

Another model for historical reconstruction, without the explicit
adversarial and rhetorical dimensions of the American law court, is the
fact-finding work of such agencies as the National Transportation
Safety Board (and all nations have similar agencies). When an airplane
crashes, teams of 'detectives'—analysts of various kinds—rush in to
collect and interpret all the available evidence—physical, eyewitness,
etc.—and to reconstruct what happened. They operate under the strict
rules of reason and logic, and usually are able to draw persuasive conclusions. Persuasive, that is, except to some parties with particular
interests in the results: pilots generally do not like to hear the conclusion 'pilot error', and parties to law suits over the crash certainly have
their vested interests. At their best, the National Transportation Safety
Board and similar agencies have only one interest: to establish the
facts—historical reality—in order to reduce the possibility of future
disasters.

There is perhaps an even more fundamental issue at stake in the
historical enterprise and its application to the Bible. Historical thinking represents a world view that has dominated Western scholarly
thought since the late nineteenth century—and the popular mind perhaps somewhat later. The late nineteenth-century clashes within biblical
scholarship and the church that resulted in heresy trials such as those
of W. Robertson Smith in Scotland and Charles A. Briggs in the
United States were but the most visible signs of a deep conflict between
a traditional theological view of reality—it claimed to be biblical—
and historical thinking that affirmed the organic unity of history and
relativized everything as subject to the vicissitudes of time and change.
In 1931, historian Carl L. Becker observed that to regard 'all things

in their historical setting appears, indeed, to be... [the] procedure of the modern mind. We do it without thinking, because we can scarcely think at all without doing it.'[2]

We—and I do not mean just biblical scholars—have learned that the Old Testament is an ancient oriental book, and it is hardly possible to unlearn that lesson. Virtually every Western reader of the Bible—from the most radical critic to the fundamentalist—proceeds on the basis of some kind of 'historical' reconstruction of the events it reports and the characters that populate its pages.

The other adjective in our question, 'futile', also calls for comment. I presume that its surface meaning concerns the viability of a *critical* historical reconstruction of individual prophetic figures. But behind the word 'futile' is another and deeper question: Is the search for the historical prophet worthwhile or important? If the quest is futile—that is, an impossible quest—then the question of its importance is moot, and no longer subject to evaluation. One must avoid where possible confusing statements of 'fact' with statements of 'value'. And, of course, one of the most powerful arguments for one's values or ideology is appeal to 'the facts', to reality. In the case of our topic, the issue of the viability of the quest should not be confused with the importance of the quest.

If the question becomes is the search for the historical prophet worthwhile, then my answer is even more complicated. Yes, it is, because in some form it is all but inevitable. Since everyone has some historical reconstruction of the prophets in their heads, it is important that such images be subjected to the *critical* historical imagination, that is, based on the best evidence and the most responsible interpretation of it. (The attentive reader will notice that here I have employed appeal to the 'facts', the way things are, to support a value judgment.)

But, having argued that historical reconstruction is both inevitable and important, I hasten to insist that it is, in my view, secondary to literary study, and in two senses. Secondary in that the historian can proceed only on the basis of the analysis of the texts, and secondary in terms of significance for the reader. After all, the text—and not the events of history—is what is most immediately before us.

Modern critical study has tended to take the first of these affirma-

2.   Cited by G. Wacker, 'The Demise of Biblical Civilization', in N.O. Hatch and M.A. Noll (eds.), *The Bible in America: Essays in Cultural History* (New York: Oxford University Press, 1982), p. 126.

tions for granted, but not necessarily the second: analysis of the literary evidence should precede historical conclusions. Source-critical inquiry from the nineteenth century to the present day has focused on the history of the literature, the establishment of its date and 'authorship'. But that was a means to an end. Literary analysis and literary history were for the purpose of writing a history of Israel, a history of Israelite religion, or a history of ideas. After all, Wellhausen's famous work was *A Prolegomena to the History of Ancient Israel*. The several pentateuchal documents had to be dated before they could be used to write history, mainly because the historian seeks testimony that is contemporary with the period under review and reconstruction.

It remains a valid premise of historical inquiry that any text gives the historian more information about the time of its own composition than it does about any prior periods, including the one it describes. Thus the Priestly Document provides insight into the views and possibly even the circumstances of its authors in the exilic or post-exilic period, and the most reliable historical testimony given by any prophetic book will be to the time of its final composition, in so far as that can be determined. All texts may be employed as evidence for the history of some period.

But at least two major problems are part of the heritage of source criticism. The historical difficulty was not its famous skepticism about the 'unauthentic' or secondary passages in the prophetic books. That is what got so many critics into trouble with the ecclesiastical establishments of the late nineteenth century. The problem was, rather, the confidence of the source critics that once they had eliminated the later additions they had before them the authentic *ipsissima verba* of the prophets.

A second problem was the tendency to confuse questions of fact and value judgments. If a text is not from, for example, Amos or Hosea, then it is of lesser value than texts determined to stem from the prophets themselves. In part that value judgment was parallel to Wellhausen's view that the older is better. But with regard to the prophets it also entailed a romantic notion of authority: the words of the great and inspired individual whom we know by name are more authoritative than those of later disciples or editors, and certainly to be taken more seriously than those later additions that turn from words of judgment to announcements of salvation.

Form criticism typically is understood as one of the historical-critical methods, and—with certain qualifications—that is a legitimate classification. The approach views texts in their horizons in antiquity, and its dominant concern at the outset was the history of the literature. Arguing that the written sources were the end of the literary development, Gunkel and others attempted to uncover the oral roots of the biblical documents.

But as a tool of historical reconstruction, the contributions of a form-critical approach are not so direct as those of source criticism or, for that matter, redaction criticism. First, the history of literature that Gunkel and other early form critics proposed was limited to relative chronology. That is, often on the basis of preconceptions about development from the simple to the more complex, one tradition or one form of a tradition was determined to be earlier than another. Second, with regard to the quest for the historical prophet, form criticism was not designed to arrive at the original words of the individual prophets in historical context. Form criticism is a literary-sociological approach. Its most fundamental presupposition, albeit one that is confirmed over and over again, is that human discourse is formed—if not determined—by institutional structures of societies. By 'institutions' are meant the various conventional practices and even ideologies of social groups. Thus genre can be related to *Sitz im Leben*, and it is possible in some cases to reconstruct situations from the form of the discourse, for example, liturgical practices from the form of hymns and prayers. So form criticism provides more insight into institutional, sociological factors than it does into specific historical events and persons as such.

But many practitioners in the early stages of this approach—and some in our generation—assumed that in the case of the prophets the road to the oral tradition leads more or less directly to the actual words as delivered by those prophets. Gunkel and others went even further, concluding that the form-critical questions enabled the scholar to distinguish between the words of the prophet and the words of God: the invective contained the prophet's evaluation of the situation and the threat was the word of God. But the evidence from the early prophetic books argues against the idea that the prophets themselves made such a distinction.[3]

Certainly Westermann, Wolff, and many others argue that in many

3.   G.M. Tucker, 'Prophetic Speech', *Int* 32 (1978), pp. 31-45. Reprinted in J.L. Mays and P.J. Achtemeier (eds.), *Interpreting the Prophets* (Philadelphia: Fortress Press, 1987), pp. 27-40.

cases one can use the evidence in the prophetic literature—including its genres and formulas—to reconstruct the original oral situation. Thus, like the source critics before them, they would answer our question in the negative. Since it is possible to reconstruct the words of the prophets, the quest for the historical prophet is not futile.

Many of those who have worked in the form-critical vineyard have fallen into the same pits dug by their predecessors. First, they have been too quick to move from literary to historical conclusions—from description of prophetic speech to 'Thus Amos the prophet actually said'— when sociological conclusions are more warranted. To be sure, form-critical work, along with traditio-historical and redaction-critical approaches, reveals some of the evidence of the literary history of individual books. Some critics have scoffed at the seven or so stages of growth that Wolff posits for the book of Amos. But certainly the history of composition is more—rather than less—complicated than that. The question—in so far as one is interested in the literature's history—is, rather, whether there is sufficient evidence to posit particular stages in that history. With regard to identifying the words of the original prophet and therefore finding the prophet behind the words, one must be particularly cautious. In most instances, the best one can do is speak of the earliest discernible traditions about the prophet and his words.

Second, some form-critical work has, like that of source criticism, confused statements of value with statements of fact. Often there has seemed to be a romantic bias that values the more ancient above the later traditions, and the oral above the written. Some early form critics wrote off editorial work as 'mere scribilization'. There is no reason in principle why the written should be devalued, and in fact, such judgments reveal more about the social and ideological location of the critic than they do about the texts or traditions.

The current situation with regard to our question is marked by diversity if not chaos. Consider some of the recent works on the book of Isaiah. The commentary by John D.W. Watts[4] is mainly historical, but it is also a literary approach in that he wants to analyze the final form of the book. Hayes and Irvine,[5] mainly on the basis of circular reasoning, an understanding of history as concerned with international politics,

---

4.   J.D.W. Watts, *Isaiah 1–33* (WBC, 24; Waco, TX: Word Books, 1985).
5.   J.H. Hayes and S.A. Irvine, *Isaiah the Eighth Century Prophet: His Times and his Preaching* (Nashville: Abingdon, 1987).

and a dubious view of the prophetic role, argue that all of Isaiah 1–34 was written by the prophet and composed in historical sequence. Oswalt's commentary[6] is a polemical book that rejects the history of criticism from the rise of the documentary approaches to authorship to the present day, and argues that the entire sixty-six chapters must stem from the original Isaiah of Jerusalem in the eighth century. This is done with many of the trappings of historical scholarship, and not without some solid insights here and there. Then there are continuations of the 'traditional' scholarly treatments of the history of the book's composition, such as those of Clements[7] and Wildberger.[8] Finally, there are newer non-historical approaches, such as that of Conrad,[9] which focuses upon the book and the reader rather than the book and its historical background.

In so far as there is chaos in this state of affairs it is not so much because of the rise of alternatives to historical criticism. Conrad, for example, gives a clear statement of the goals and the criteria of his fundamentally literary analysis. The problems lie, rather, in the more traditional historical area. It is no longer so clear what counts for evidence, and, in my view, a great many irresponsible claims are being advanced.

The historian must at every point assume the burden of proof. The evidence for any reconstruction must be presented and analyzed critically. The texts will need to be cross-examined and their testimony confirmed. One cannot take it for granted, for example, that the provenance of the prophet or of the texts in a prophetic book are established by the dates and circumstances presented in the book's superscription.[10] Those superscriptions themselves presume the existence of, if not the whole book that follows, at least a body of written tradition, and they come from third parties who look back on the

6. J.N. Oswalt, *The Book of Isaiah, Chapters 1–39* (NICOT; Grand Rapids: Eerdmans, 1986).

7. R.E. Clements, *Isaiah 1–39* (NCB; Grand Rapids: Eerdmans, 1980).

8. H. Wildberger, *Jesaja* (BKAT, 10; Neukirchen–Vluyn: Neukirchener Verlag, 1965–66).

9. E.W. Conrad, *Reading Isaiah* (Minneapolis: Fortress Press, 1991).

10. Cf. E. Ben Zvi, 'Isaiah 1,4-9, Isaiah, and the Events of 701 BCE in Judah: A Question of Premise and Evidence', *SJOT* 5 (1991), pp. 95-111; and G.M. Tucker, 'Prophetic Superscriptions and the Growth of a Canon', in G.W. Coats and B.O. Long (eds.), *Canon and Authority: Essays in Old Testament Religion and Theology* (Philadelphia: Fortress Press, 1977), pp. 56-70.

prophet and his times. They are themselves exercises in the historical imagination, and like all texts give us at least as much information about their own times as they do about the times they report.

But we are not left speechless about the events, persons and circumstances reported or cited in the biblical texts. Like any good historian, one moves from the known to the unknown, and draws conclusions carefully on the basis of evidence and reasonable argumentation. The critical-historical task is important because posing the historical questions is all but inevitable. Everyone who reads a prophetic book has an image of the history of that book, of its ancient horizon. Thus the critical quest for the historical prophets is important as a point of departure for assessing various images of what and who those prophets were. Moreover, like all historical inquiry, it is for the purpose of human self-understanding.

Is it possible or desirable to investigate a prophetic book in explicitly non-historical terms, to consider it fundamentally within a contemporary reader's horizon? Yes, by all means, for not every scholar needs to be a historian, and after all the text is more immediately available than is history. But, given our cultural and intellectual history, it is remarkably difficult to set aside what some two centuries of scholarship have taught us about the past.

Whether the historical, literary, sociological, ideological and other modes of inquiry can collaborate or live together in peace is yet another question. As in the more familiar conflict between historical criticism and traditional theology, significant moral issues are at stake. Moreover, the differences on moral issues—what is good and true— do not sort themselves out simply among methodological tribes: historians disagree radically on questions of value, as do literary critics. Still, up to a point there is room for division of labor, collaboration, and dialogue, provided scholars are clear about the goals and the evidence for their inquires.

Let me be clear about my own position on the question before us: I want to have my cake and eat it too. Given the understanding of the historical enterprise discussed here, the quest for the historical prophet is neither futile nor unimportant. Certainly we can know some things about many of the historical prophets, including even some (Second Isaiah) whose names we do not know. But even more important is the analysis of the literature in order to better understand both ancient and contemporary social structures.

ON THE TASK OF OLD TESTAMENT THEOLOGY*

Rolf P. Knierim

1. *Introduction*

This discussion will focus on a method for doing Old Testament theology. In order to see this focus in its proper perspective, I will first of all discuss what I perceive to be the necessary distinctions between the disciplines of biblical exegesis, biblical theology, and biblical hermeneutics. In the process of interpretation, these three disciplines are closely related. Nonetheless, they must be distinguished because each confronts us with a different set of problems.

We first of all need to understand the individual texts to be examined each on its own terms and in its own right; this is the process of exegesis. But since the Bible consists of many texts, small and large, we need to explain the meaning of each text in the light of all texts. This task presupposes but goes beyond exegesis. *Exegesis* explains what the texts themselves say. In contrast, *biblical theology* must explain what is not, at least not sufficiently, said by the texts of the Bible; namely the relationship among the different theologies of the texts. And *biblical hermeneutics* then needs to explain what the encounter between the world view of the Bible and our modern world view means for us today.

Each of these tasks is distinct. But since we cannot interpret the encounter of the biblical world view and our own world view without understanding each, the task of biblical theology is not only distinct from, but also precedes the task of biblical hermeneutics just as it

* This essay is dedicated to Professor George Coats, a scholar totally committed to Old Testament scholarship and a good personal friend, on the occasion of his retirement with heartfelt good wishes. The paper represents a slightly revised version of a lecture given at the Annual Meeting of the Korean Society of Old Testament Studies in Seoul on 21 May, 1994, and at the Annual Meeting of the Japanese Society of Old Testament Studies in Tokyo on 25 May, 1994.

follows the task of biblical exegesis. Hence, biblical interpretation moves from the exegesis of the texts to biblical theology and then to a biblical hermeneutic.

In light of my topic, I leave aside discussing the question of the relationship between ancient and modern world views. But I will elaborate on some specific issues that are important for the distinction between biblical exegesis and biblical theology. These issues concern first of all the task of exegesis.

The methods of exegesis are well known and do not need be reiterated at this point. I need only to highlight four aspects that are intrinsic to exegetical work because they are also intrinsic to the nature of the biblical texts.

First of all, the texts are not quarries of words or sentences but entities (*Ganzheiten*) within which all elements are related in hierarchical semantic systems. These text-systems must be explained holistically rather than solely, as is often done, verse by verse, sentence by sentence, or word by word. Without a holistic explanation of a text's overall system, the meaning of a text cannot be understood properly.

Secondly and in particular need of attention is the fact that in each text, its story or message and its concept, idea, or doctrine are indissolubly connected and interdependent. While a text's story or message is explicit in what it says, its concept is basically inexplicit, *infra*textual or *sub*textual, but nevertheless operative in the text. It is presupposed and only coincidentally signalled by a word or phrase in the text itself as, for example, in the phrase 'let my people go!' (e.g. Exod. 4.23). In this phrase, the possessive pronoun 'my' is vital and reveals the conceptual presupposition for the liberation theology of the story: Yahweh liberates the oppressed because they are Yahweh's own people. Yahweh does not liberate all people who are oppressed. There is a theology of liberation in this text, but this theology is based on and controlled by the theological concept of Israel's exclusive election. Where this concept is overlooked in exegesis, the story and its concept of liberation are not correctly understood. The *concept* of a text controls its story, while the story actualizes its concept or idea. Sometimes, of course, the concepts are expressed directly in particular nominal phrases, as in the statement 'God is gracious'.

The recognition of the concepts or ideas of the texts has nothing to do either with a withdrawal from the texts into a world of abstract ideas, or with an abstraction of the ideas from the texts. On the contrary, this recognition is exegetically indispensable because the ideas are the ideas of the texts themselves. Ideas and thoughts are just as real as stories in human history and existence, and the fact that they may be considered as abstract ideas does not mean that the idea of a text is abstract. There is no text without an idea. Both its idea as well as its story belong to the concreteness of a text. Both are to be exegeted together. In a text, both language and thought, or its story and its concept, belong together; and the emphasis on the need to interpret the text's thought and concept has nothing to do with removing thought and concept from language and story, or with replacing narrative by abstract concept. What is called for is the interpretation of the *conceptualized* narrative, not just narrative. It is in this sense that the focus on concept is understood in this paper. It is important, however, that we distinguish between the ideas of texts and the ideas of the biblical world views. Many texts share the same world view such as, for example, the dynamistic ontology (Klaus Koch's *Tatsphäredenken* or my own category of the concept of the holistic dynamic). While by and large sharing such a common world view, many texts nevertheless have different conceptual foci such as justice, judgment, liberation, forgiveness, election, corporateness, individuality, and so on. And while it is necessary for us to be aware of their common ancient world view, this awareness only interprets what is common among them but not yet those varying concepts that are directly operative in them. The exegesis of the individual texts must interpret their specific concepts, or these texts cannot be distinguished from each other.

Thirdly, the exegesis of texts includes each text's theology. The biblical texts are essentially theological in nature. Without this nature, they would not exist. Exegesis which fails to include a text's theology is not exegesis in its proper sense. The interpretation of the theology of the texts is not something done in addition to exegesis. We exegete each text's own inherent theology. We do not theologize the texts. Were the texts not theological, exegesis should not say more about them than what they are. Inasmuch as exegesis may be called theological exegesis, it may be so called because of the theological nature of the texts themselves, and not because of our interest in theology. Yet precisely because of that nature of the texts, the attribute 'theological' added to 'exegesis' is pleonastic and should be avoided.

Attention to the theology of the texts is especially important because the theological task starts already with exegesis and is not reserved for biblical theology. Biblical theology is not theological because it is a discipline distinct from exegesis but because it evolves from the results of the exegesis of the theological nature of the texts. Whereas the theological task is common to both disciplines, the two differ in that exegesis interprets the theologies of the texts while biblical theology interprets the relationship of these theologies.

Fourthly, exegesis not only describes the texts and their theologies. It includes in its descriptions the fact that the texts claim to be true, valid, and authoritative. The Bible does not understand itself as a lexicon of science, history, or sociology, but as a collection of books which may in any of these aspects refer to what it claims to be divine truth which is therefore valid and authoritative for the world and certainly its readers. We may use it for all sorts of purposes, but if we ignore this claim, we certainly ignore its own *raison d'être*.

Thus, we exegete the theologies and truth claims of the Pentateuch, the deuteronomistic and chronistic history works, of Job, each of the Psalms, the Proverbs, and so on, and of each of the prophets, just as we exegete the theologies and truth claims of the synoptic Gospels, of John, Paul, and the rest of the New Testament books. And the more we do careful exegesis, the more we learn that the Bible is a compendium: of many theological concepts and their stories; of theologies that sometimes agree, sometimes differ even as they complement each other, and sometimes disagree. Every good student of the Bible is familiar with this fact. This situation is not only true for the relationship of the two Testaments. It is also true for the various theologies within each Testament.

After we have done our exegetical work, we write books in which we describe each theology or selected theological aspects, juxtapose our descriptions in anthologies of theologies, each bound in one volume, and call such a volume an Old or New Testament theology.

It is clear, however, that a theology of the Old or New Testament, let alone a biblical theology in the singular form, must be more than a collection of juxtaposed theologies derived from exegesis, a collection analogous to the collection of the juxtaposed biblical books even where those juxtapositions rest to some extent on organizing principles such as the tripartite TaNaK, or the distinction between the Gospels, Luke's Acts, and the letters in the New Testament. A theology in the singular must do what neither the biblical writers nor those who canonized the Bible have done: It must *interpret the relationship of the various theologies in the Bible*. This task presupposes the totality of exegetical work. But it involves *more* than the sum total of exegesis. Indeed, it is not solved but generated by that sum total. It is a task *sui generis*. The sum total of exegesis shows the diversity and even the divisiveness of the theologies in the canon. It reflects the theological pluralism of the biblical canon and the pluralism of its truth claims.

2. *The Old Testament Defines its own Agenda*

In the Christian tradition, the reading of the Old Testament has in one way or another always been controlled by the theological criteria expressed in the New Testament. Whether these criteria contributed to keeping both Testaments together in the one Christian Bible, or whether they contributed to separating the theology of each Testament from that of the other, they were in either case the basis for the judgment of the Christian movement that the Old Testament, whatever it may mean for Christians and humanity, is fundamentally different from and less important than the New Testament. And in whatever sense one may want to speak of a *biblical* theology, the burden for such an advocacy lies always on the shoulders of Old Testament scholars.

Of course, for at least the last two hundred years all biblical scholars have asserted that the Old Testament must be afforded the right to speak on its own terms. It especially must not be forced to speak against what its exegesis reveals. Still, the validity or truth of such exegetical results has always been adjudicated by the Christian perspective. Whether you say with Bultmann that the Old Testament, precisely when exegeted correctly, reveals how Christians or humans must not believe, or with von Rad or any similar interpreter that the kerygmatic axis of the Old Testament's salvation history leads to Jesus Christ, the Old Testament is in either case exegetically said to be theologically irrelevant without the decisive Christian perspective. It must have the right to its own position, but only as long as it defines its position in response to the predetermined Christian agenda. This situation amounts to a double standard for the Old Testament's freedom, a standard, both unconditional and conditional, which has no integrity. Instead, what is necessary is an Old Testament theology in which the Old Testament itself may define its own agenda, vis-à-vis the New Testament rather than be dependent on it, a theology that would precisely for this reason also be of benefit for the Christian faith.

3. *The Old Testament is One*

The Old Testament is one not only because it is the first part of the bipartite Christian Bible but also because it is the only Bible of the Jewish people. Its oneness is especially constituted by the fact that it is the original compendium of ancient Israel's Yahweh religion. Take Yahweh out of it, and it collapses. The TaNaK represents ancient Israel's wisdom as reverence for and knowledge of God Yahweh.

The oneness of the Old Testament does not mean that its Yahweh wisdom is conceptually uniform and that everything in it has the same degree of validity. Just as it is a collection of many literary works, so it is also a collection of diverse theologies. Exegesis has long since established that Israel's Yahweh religion is theologically pluralistic. This pluralism became decisively established in the final juxtaposition of the theologies of the Yahweh religion at the same historical level during the late post-exilic period. The theological traditions put together in this period had emerged diachronically, in the course of Israel's historical process, and to a large extent separately. But once they were juxtaposed, the meaning of the traditions was no longer determined by the diachronic but by the synchronic order of their relationship. What had formerly had a certain meaning because of its distinct time, came to have a different meaning as it was placed side by side (i.e., synchronically) with traditions of earlier times. This synchronization of the traditions amounted to the canonization of theological diversity. For the heirs of the TaNaK or the Old Testament, be they Jewish or Christian, this pluralism is its inevitable legacy.

The Old Testament's theological diversity, like the New Testament's diversity, is inherently connected to the Old Testament's claim to truth and validity and, hence, with the quest for truth and validity in Old Testament theology. This quest amounts to more than merely describing the Old Testament's texts and their theological concepts. Also, it is something different from a type of interpretation based on a confessional stance. It must explain why and in what sense any of its theologies are true and should be affirmed or confessed as true. Only this kind of explanation qualifies the discipline as theology. Otherwise it represents a phenomenology, history, or sociology of Israel's religion, or our confession of truth regardless of what is said.

In the history of the discipline, one has for too long attempted to overcome the Old Testament's theological diversity by focusing on its unifying aspects, on the unity in diversity. Thus, one has emphasized that the Old Testament is Yahwistic, monotheistic, word of God, inspired, revealed, the religion of holiness, covenantal, of the believing community, and so on.

All of these aspects exist, whereby some represent unifying factors while others, such as the aspects of holiness, covenant or even— strictly speaking—word of God, do not, as we have learned. Decisive, however, is the fact that none of the evidently unifying factors solves the problem of the theological diversity within each of them. The Old Testament is monotheistic, but its monotheism is theologically diverse and even divisive. It is divinely inspired and revealed, but the contents and concepts of inspiration and revelation (including theophany and epiphany) are diverse. It is altogether the witness of the believing community, but the beliefs of this community are diverse and the community itself has always from its beginning been divided precisely because of its different beliefs.

The unifying aspects of these theologies belong to the Old Testament's oneness and must be interpreted in this respect. However, if we want to know in what sense the Old Testament is true and valid, even with respect to its unifying aspects, it is imperative that the discipline of Old Testament theology shift from its focus on the Old Testament's theological diversity. Rather than focus on unity in diversity, we must explain the diversity within the unity, indeed, the diversity within each unifying concept. This shift is basic, and amounts to a change in direction compared to the direction of many approaches during the last two centuries.

This approach is not completely new. Gabler proposed in 1787 that we should describe the biblical books, interpret each of their concepts, compare them and arrange the results of their comparison in a system of biblical theology in which the validity of each can be determined precisely in its relationship to the others. Gabler thought of a biblical theology conceived from the doctrine of salvation expressed in the New Testament alone. Yet his method remains valid, indeed the best, for an Old Testament theology on its own terms. This method accounts for the relativity of each theological concept in its relation to all others. While none is irrelevant, the degree of validity of each is discerned in its relation to all others.

The basic approach to Old Testament theology is guided by our need to identify the Old Testament's theological concepts individually, to compare them, and thus to arrive at an integrated theological value system of the Old Testament. In the following, I will give some examples.

No system of positive values can exist without its opposite, a system of anti-values. In Old Testament studies, the system of anti-values is basically established through Old Testament hamartiology, the doctrine of sin and guilt. The Old Testament speaks neither only of what is good nor only of what is evil, but of both as opposites. When it speaks of what is valid, it is always aware of what is destructive and, hence, invalid. Indeed, it essentially derives its judgments about evil from its knowledge of what is good. Evil is what is not good. The distinction between good and evil, even terminologically, is widespread and fundamental. For this reason, Old Testament hamartiology is an indispensable part of Old Testament theology, even though it is subservient to the positive side of Old Testament theology.

Within Old Testament hamartiology, both the diverse terminology and the many texts have one uniting feature: no matter how diverse, the aspects always point to what is destructive. And this also shows that all aspects are not equally destructive. Someone who steals is not a murderer. Someone who holds a grudge against his neighbour or covets his neighbour's property does not publicly slander or rob him. Someone who inadvertently causes damage does not commit a crime. The murder of a person by an individual is a severe crime, but it is not as severe as genocide or the destruction of the whole earth by humanity's all pervasive violence.

When we come to the theology of the positive concepts in the texts, we encounter concepts such as liberation, justice, blessing, mercy, goodness, holiness, peace, and so on. Each of these concepts is indicated by its own word field, and all word fields signal an already conceptualized understanding of the constructive side of reality.

It is clear that these words and the concepts they signal do not all mean the same thing. Each has a distinct meaning. These meanings, including where they overlap, are interpreted in commentaries, dictionaries, monographs and articles. But Old Testament theology must interpret the relationship of these concepts and discern their degrees of validity within this relationship.

For example, the semantic fields and concepts of liberation, or salvation, and justice and righteousness are related but not identical. When compared, liberation appears as an element of justice, namely, as liberation either from injustice suffered by others or from self-inflicted sin. Justice is distinct in that it involves more than liberation alone. Justice also means that the liberated are freed in order to do what is just. It is not only more inclusive than liberation, it also is the criterion for the truth of liberation because it is both the reason for and the purpose of liberation.

When applied to the story of the Pentateuch, the result of this distinction becomes painfully clear. Israel's liberation from Pharaoh's oppression is an act of justice. But Israel, at Yahweh's and Moses' command, is to subjugate or ban the free Canaanites. Those liberated from oppression are commanded to use their freedom for the oppression of others. The reason for Israel's transition from being the liberated to becoming the oppressors is well known: it is the theology of Israel's exclusive election for its possession of and multiplication in the Promised Land. Also clear, however, is that in this kind of liberation theology, the principle of indivisible justice is destroyed. Justice, especially God's justice, cannot mean both liberation and oppression at the same time. And other Old Testament traditions, especially in the wisdom traditions, disagree with this concept in the Pentateuch.

It is known that the Old Testament does not represent a religion of judgment compared to a religion of grace in the New Testament. It is also known that the concept of judgment, present everywhere and not only in the prophetic literature, is an inevitable element of the concept of justice. No justice can do without judgment. But judgment itself must be valid. And the criterion for its truth is not emotional, irrational, or based on the mood of a tyrant. Rather, the criterion for judgment is the rationality of justice to which even the freedom of God is bound. The Old Testament texts demonstrate this rationality very clearly.

Is there also a criterion for the truth of justice itself, even for the truth of its rationales? I have in mind many texts which in various ways speak about judgment on the one hand, and about mercy or pardon on the other hand. The relationship of these two concepts pervades the entire Old Testament and the history of Israel's theology. Where there is judgment, there is no forgiveness. And where there is mercy, pardon, or forgiveness, judgment is replaced. And just as judgement must be justifiable, so can mercy not be unjustifiable. The Yahweh of Hos. 11.1-9 is caught in the tension between the justice of judgment and the justice of mercy, and is forced to replace his just judgment by just mercy because mercy is the better justice. Why is it better? Because allowing his people to live is better than destroying them. Justice itself is relative. A similar conceptual dynamic is also found, among others, in the primeval history and in the Joseph novella.

The Old Testament speaks about peace (*šālôm*) and war, especially Yahweh's wars which are perceived to be just wars. And while it is obvious that the notion of war is in need of theological evaluation, it is also obvious that no war, not even Yahweh's just wars, has the same validity as the condition of peace. The fact that there is 'a time for war, and time for peace' (Eccl. 3.8) does not mean that the times of war are as good as the times of peace. The Old Testament theology of war is, at any rate, subject to the distinction between just and unjust war. Even so, no war is as just as peace; nor is war ever considered just when compared with peace. The theology of war is evaluated sufficiently only when compared to the theology of peace.

What is the relationship between justice and peace? This question is not only important today; its importance is also reflected in the Old Testament itself. The texts speak about both peace and justice. God fashions justice (Jer. 9.24) and also peace (Ps. 147.14). Humans are to seek both. The world is in good shape when 'righteousness and peace will kiss each other' (Ps. 85.11). But peace and justice are neither the same, nor do they always kiss each other. The two realities differ and often conflict. What is their relationship? Is peace a precondition for justice, so that justice depends on peace, and there can be no justice unless there is peace? Or is justice a precondition for peace because there can be no peace without justice? Is the theology of peace subordinate to or the criterion for the theology of justice, or are both related on the assumption that justice and peace rotate about each other in a bipolar tension and complementation?

The evidence seems to support the view that, at best, there may be false but no true peace where there is no justice, whereas there can be a degree of justice even where there is no peace. Justice appears to be the criterion for true peace, whereas peace is neither the criterion for justice nor does it necessarily create justice. But more important than my opinion is the need for us to clarify their relationship in the horizon of Old Testament theology.

Finally, in this series of examples which can be expanded almost *ad infinitum*, what is the relationship between justice, liberation, mercy, or peace on the one hand, and blessing (*běrākâ*) on the other? The importance of the reality of blessing, and the difference between blessing and liberation, has especially been emphasized in the work of Claus Westermann. Blessing is the perpetual presence of the goodness of life, or of life as goodness, for all living beings and in everything that belongs to their earthly welfare.

Rather than merely being the *fact* of life, blessing is what we call the *quality* of life, as good rather than bad life, or life without any quality at all. And it is a gift because we have not created life but are sustained by it. The reality of blessing does not only differ from the reality of liberation, it is also more fundamental than that reality. Whereas the event, or the events, of liberation presuppose conditions of oppression, fallenness, or sin, the goodness of blessing is the original condition of life. Whereas liberation may or may not be experienced by all and at all times, blessing is the basic experience of all at all times. Blessing can be absent, as in the case of hunger. Such absence amounts to the threat to, or loss of, created life itself. The absence of blessing, for example in the lack of food, represents an attack against the order of creation. And liberation from hunger amounts to the restoration of the blessing of food.

Blessing belongs to the theology of creation, whereas liberation belongs to the biblical soteriology which is connected with the theology of history fallen out of the order of creation. The theology of creation is not replaced by soteriology. Rather it is the reason for soteriology. Liberation is only necessary where the order of creation has been corrupted. The restoration of the old or the vision of the new creation is the reason for the need for and truth of salvation.

Finally, Genesis 1, important Psalms, the deity's speeches in Job, and other texts say that the created world is good, or very good. These qualifying judgments are themselves acts of justice. They confirm that the creation of the world out of chaos and its sustenance above chaos are acts of God's universal justice. It has been said that creation theology is soteriology. It is more appropriate to say that the Old Testament's creation theology represents the first, and fundamental, chapter in the theology of universal justice, whereas its soteriology represents that theology of justice which deals with the restoration of creation.

The comparison of the biblical concepts involves a heuristic process through which we can establish their relationship systematically. We can discern the place of each concept in a hierarchy of values and, hence, the degree of validity or truth of each concept in its relation to all others. This heuristic process is systematizing in nature, and its results amount to a systematic Old Testament theology in which the relationship of the concepts is the basis for the evaluation of all that is said and presupposed, and also for the evaluation of all other kinds of systematization such as, for instance, tradition history or sociology.

Thus far, all the concepts mentioned are qualitative in nature. However, the texts show that correlated to the qualitative aspect of each concept is also a quantitative aspect. Mercy, justice, blessing, liberation, and peace apply to individuals, to groups, to Israel, to humanity, and even to nature on earth and the cosmos. Each of these aspects is everywhere evident in the Old Testament. They range from the narrowest to the widest situations. Their varying boundaries indicate the Old Testament's differentiating awareness of reality. None of the qualities is important only for the world and not also for each individual and every quantity in between.

However, the problem arises of whether, for example, justice and liberation are considered valid for individuals regardless of, or because of, their validity for all. If they are true for all, they are therefore also true for each person. If they are only true for one person, justice and liberation are divided, and what is justice for one party is injustice for another. The widest boundary, which includes all equally, is the quantitative criterion for the validity of the positive qualities, just as the widest boundary is the quantitative criterion for the anti-value of the negative aspects in Old Testament hamartiology.

The most inclusive aspect is directly important theologically. If God's peace is only for me, such a god is only my God and not the God of all. This god is my idol. If God's peace is for all, it is therefore also for me, and God is the God for me because God is the God of all. God is the deity of the total world, or god is not God. The universality of God is the criterion for the truth of God's presence in each particular situation.

This criterion is critically important for the evaluation of those texts in the Old Testament in which Israel's election is not seen as functioning for God's universal justice equally for all but at the expense of the other nations, or in which even the creation is seen as serving the purpose of Israel's election. Nothing is said against anyone's election. But in a particularistic theology of election, Israel subjects the nations to the interest of its own benefit rather than serving God's universal goodness for the benefit of all nations. This theology of Yahwism represents the opposite of a theology according to which God works out the same justice for all. It amounts to a nationalistic religious idolatry.

The Old Testament does not simply speak about God. From its first to its last page, it speaks about the relationship between God and world. Its focus on this relationship lies at the heart of its understanding of reality. In this understanding, the deity is considered as the ground of the truth of the world's existence, and the world is therefore considered as created and sustained by, and dependent on, this ground. If the world, including especially the humans, remains in accord with this ground, it actualizes it in its existence. The actualization of the ground of the truth of existence is represented especially in human ethos.

When speaking of ethos theologically, we normally use words such as response or reaction to God's word or action. God acts and we *re*-act; God speaks and we *re*-spond. This language is questionable. It means that by *re*-sponding or *re*-acting, we do on our part something that God does not do. I know that the Old Testament itself very often says that humans responded to Yahweh's speeches. Even so, the problem is deeper. It is clear that when responding properly, the humans accept *what* God says or does. They then transmit this content into, or actualize it in, their own existence and, hence, carry on God's own work and word. Rather than doing what God does not do, they continue God's own work by actualizing it. The actualization of God's own work in the world is both the matrix of and the criterion for the Old Testament's ethos.

Finally, the Old Testament focuses overwhelmingly on the affairs of this existing and ongoing world. With this focus, it speaks about God's presence in the originally created world, whereas its passages about the new creation are not only minimal but also textured in the sense of the restoration of the depraved world to the shape of its original creation. All of this is clearly distinct from the New Testament. The New Testament considers the original creation from the vantage point of its replacement by the new creation and the expectation that this replacement is impending.

Thus far, the new creation—though considered as already arrived in Christ's resurrection—has not replaced the old creation. Regardless of when, or whether, this will happen, the millennia of the ongoing original creation teach us that we must pay attention to the presence of

God in this original creation as long as it lasts. They teach us that the corruption in, and even the fallenness of, the original creation are no longer sufficient reasons for a theology of the *absence* of God from the structures of this creation, whether original or fallen. Indeed, if God were not present also in these structures, the deity would not be the God of the total reality, both new and old.

Thus, we realize that the total Bible teaches us this: God is not present because God comes out of the future, but God comes out of the future as well as out of the past because God is always present. When we come to these fundamental theological realizations, we will have to realize that the Old Testament, with its focus on the ongoing presence of God in this ongoing creation, original or fallen, represents in its totality an independent and critical complement to the world view of the New Testament. This function constitutes the legitimacy of the Old Testament theology in its own right in a truly bipolar theology of the Christian Bible.*

---

*   I am indebted to Brenda Hahn and Mignon R. Jacobs for editorial assistance.

Scripture and the Formation of Christian Identity

Roy F. Melugin

An essay written in honor of George Coats is for me a special opportunity, for we have walked many roads together. He was my undergraduate room mate, my student colleague in the Perkins School of Theology and in graduate studies at Yale. He was best man at my wedding and I at his. Numerous times we shared a hotel room at the SBL Annual Meeting. And in our many conversations, we were partners in a mutual concern that biblical interpretation speak powerfully to the life of the church. It is in honor of this shared history that I take up the specific concerns of this essay.

This essay proceeds out of an increasing concern on my part about the decline of mainstream churches in the United States. The reasons for the decline are undoubtedly manifold. One of them, I suspect, is related to the secularization which has taken place in our society. More than twenty-five years of teaching undergraduate students has persuaded me that the biblical heritage is no longer a major shaping force in the mainstream of our culture. Because this matter is so very complex, I can scarcely offer here a quick-fix or even a long-term cure. I can at best hope to be able to help us reconsider the role of the Bible in the shaping of Christian life and perhaps to rethink the nature of biblical scholarship for facilitating the use of the Bible in the Christian community.

The problem with which I am concerned is in large measure a question of identity. A great many of my students, scholarly colleagues, and other friends, whether church-affiliated or not, do not derive their most basic images of personal identity from the church's biblical heritage. A student of mine once told me that he saw his body as a machine—something to be turned on and turned off to suit his convenience. How different this is from viewing one's body as a temple— a sacred space! Yet my student's image seems to be widely shared. And it is not difficult to see how quickly that kind of talk becomes language which profoundly shapes identity. Many of my Christian friends in the business world are molded by images such as the person who pulls himself or herself up by his or her own bootstraps—an image which is suggestive of the self-made person. And many of them believe profoundly in a myth of social contract, in which basically autonomous individuals join together to maximize their own individual interests. How different from seeing oneself as a child of God, as a member of a worldwide community of God's children for whose needs one is willing to give oneself in love! Yet these Christian friends seem unaware of the incompatibility between some of the images which form their identity and those of the Christian tradition.

One of the most important challenges facing the church, then, is the use of its traditions as a powerful force in the shaping of identity.[1] There is nothing to be gained by breast-beating about the loss of a supposed bygone age. But we should look for ways to reclaim our heritage and to explore how the Bible can be used to facilitate the formation of identity. I shall argue that strategies of biblical interpretation which seek to explain what a text meant to its earliest audiences cannot succeed as the primary way of using the Bible if one wants to employ it for the purpose of constructing self-identity. Treating the Bible primarily as a text to be explained and using the Bible to transform persons are somewhat different enterprises. The differences between explanation and transformation must be clearly understood if we intend to be effective in the use of Scripture for the purposes of personal transformation.

1. *Using Scripture as Explanation versus using Scripture for Transformation*

Most biblical scholars have been trained to treat the Bible primarily as an object to be studied. We have learned to explain what texts meant

---

1.   Brevard Childs criticizes James Sanders for his focus on identity-formation at the expense of other historical and theological forces at work in the shaping and use of the canon. Childs quite rightly understands that there is much more to be considered than questions about identity. I choose to focus here on identity-formation because I think that ordinary people in our society either use scripture or do not use scripture in their lives because it either shapes their personal identity or it does not. Unless scripture can be used to shape identity, it will largely be seen as irrelevant. See B.S. Childs, *Introduction to the Old Testament as Scripture* (Philadelphia: Fortress Press, 1979), pp. 56-57.

to the audiences in antiquity to whom they were directed. Or if our approach is synchronic in focus, our primary goal is likely to be that of explaining a meaning for the sake of achieving an excellent intellectual understanding of the text.

Using Scripture for the purpose of facilitating personal transformation is something different. We use Scripture to praise God or lament; we use Scripture to comfort; we use Scripture to call people to repentance; we use Scripture to strengthen our bond with God. Calling people to repentance is not the same as explaining how biblical texts depict repentance; comforting people is scarcely the same as explaining the biblical understanding of comfort; that is, strengthening one's relationship with God. Using the Bible *performatively* is not the same as explaining what the Bible meant (or means).

Using the Bible to transform personal identity can profitably make use of scholarly analyses of biblical texts. Nevertheless, treating the study of the Bible as an end in itself and using Scripture for transformation need to be clearly distinguished. The former is often disinterested, dispassionate, and detached from the self-understanding of the interpreter, whereas, in the latter, Scripture is a vehicle for the formation of the self and thus an extension of the self.

The distinction between explanatory and performative use of language is nothing new. It is well established in the philosophy of language. J.L. Austin and John Searle are particularly known for their ground-breaking work.[2] Their work shows that language is quite often used performatively rather than to explain. 'Stop the car!' asks someone to do something; it does not explain or represent reality. 'I pronounce you husband and wife' *creates* a marriage; it does not describe or explain the marriage. An assurance of pardon does not explain the nature of forgiveness; rather it *addresses* the sinner and proclaims that he or she is pardoned. Such a pronouncement *does* something to those to whom the assurance is proclaimed.[3] Or to cite another example, a benediction does not explain blessing but rather gives a blessing. It creates in the listener the power to act and to transform

---

2.   J.L. Austin, *How to Do Things with Words* (New York: Oxford University Press, 1962); J.R. Searle, *Speech Acts: An Essay in the Philosophy of Language* (Cambridge: Cambridge University Press, 1970). See also the essays in *Semeia* 41 (1988).

3.   J.H. Ware, Jr, *Not with Words of Wisdom: Performative Language and Liturgy* (Washington, DC: University Press of America, 1981), pp. 83-88.

the future.[4] So also is the language which we use to form identity primarily performative in character.

2. *The Activity of Shaping Identity*

One of the fundamental things we do with language is the formation of identity. Let me illustrate: my mother was a skilled storyteller, and through listening to her stories year after year my identity gradually took shape. Through stories recounting the founding of the United States I took on identity as an American. Through listening to Bible stories I was molded and shaped as a Christian. Explanations were not primary in the forming of my selfhood. It was the force of words which gave my life its shape.

George Lindbeck helps us understand how this comes about.[5] For Lindbeck, myths, narratives, and rituals are primary vehicles which 'structure human experience and understanding of the world'.[6] Although Lindbeck is primarily interested in the formation of religious understanding, much of what he says can apply to the formation of identity, whether the context is secular or religious. In Lindbeck's view, a human life is shaped by a cultural-linguistic tradition.[7] A cultural-linguistic tradition is a communally shared phenomenon which 'shapes the subjectivities of individuals rather than being primarily a manifestation of those subjectivities'.[8] We simply cannot have certain thoughts, sentiments, and perceptions of reality without learning the appropriate symbol systems.[9] Having an identity as a Christian involves learning the biblical story sufficiently well that one can interpret one's own life and one's world within the framework of that tradition. Being Jewish or Muslim or Buddhist would involve something analogous.

Lindbeck believes that classic works such as *Oedipus Rex* and *War and Peace* shape the imagination of the reader and become lenses through which the reader sees the world. Even more forcefully do the canonical texts of religious communities perform such a function. As

---

4. Ware, *Words of Wisdom*, p. 94.

5. G.A. Lindbeck, *The Nature of Doctrine: Religion and Theology in a Postliberal Age* (Philadelphia: Westminster, 1984).

6. Lindbeck, *Nature of Doctrine*, p. 32.

7. Lindbeck, *Nature of Doctrine,* chapter 2.

8. Lindbeck, *Nature of Doctrine*, p. 33.

9. Lindbeck, *Nature of Doctrine*, p. 34.

Lindbeck understands the power of such canonical texts in the communities in which they are revered, there is no world more real than the one which these texts create.[10] Thus, for Christians, scriptural language functions as the lens through which the totality of experience is viewed.

Walter Brueggemann also understands identity as the way in which we use traditions to imagine ourselves.[11] And the ways in which we imagine ourselves characteristically involve language used figuratively. Brueggmann rehearses, for example, the way the psalmist imagines the presence of God in the formation of the embryo: 'For it was you who formed my inward parts; you knit me together in my mother's womb' (Ps. 139.13).[12] The self as imagined here is a creature of God, the product of God's handiwork. Yet it is not an autonomous self who does the imagining.[13] Identity is a product of the cultural-linguistic traditions in which one 'lives'. These traditions are the home—the symbolic world—in which we live,[14] the lenses through which we can see ourselves and the world. These traditions come to us and shape us, often without our choosing to be shaped by them. But even when we can in some sense exercise choice about our identity, we do not do so as autonomous subjects. Certain traditions are already at work in our lives. And even in our 'choosing', we are at the same time 'grasped' by particular traditions, before reflection and choice take place.[15] Thus our acts of imagining of ourselves are not autonomous but rather communal. Our acts of self-imagining in some sense 'happen' to us, even though at the same time we do exercise some degree of choice about our self-identity.

The plurality of cultural-linguistic traditions in North America results in a multiplicity of competing symbol systems. Whether competition is intended or not, the fact that language exerts force upon its audience means that a diversity of communally sponsored

10. Lindbeck, *Nature of Doctrine*, pp. 116-17.

11. W. Brueggemann, *Texts under Negotiation: The Bible and Postmodern Imagination* (Minneapolis: Fortress Press, 1993).

12. Brueggemann, *The Bible and Postmodern Imagination*, pp. 30-31.

13. See P. Ricoeur, *Essays on Biblical Interpretation* (Philadelphia: Fortress Press, 1980), p. 97.

14. Ricoeur, *Biblical Interpretation*, p. 102.

15. P. Tillich, *Systematic Theology*, I (Chicago: University of Chicago Press, 1951), p. 111.

voices often work forcefully upon particular persons all at once. Indeed, the very presence of a diversity of symbol systems makes a degree of choice about identity possible. At the same time, some voices are heard more loudly than others, with the result that certain choices are more likely to be made than others. Secular voices appear to me to be generally more dominant, though the religious right rather effectively makes itself heard. If the mainstream church wants to be a more forceful voice, its biblical scholars should ask themselves whether the kinds of biblical interpretations we typically produce lend themselves to the enterprise of constructing personal identity. Most of the remainder of this essay attempts to address this question.

3. *The Bible and the Construction of Identity*

Biblical interpretation designed to facilitate the formation of identity is a kind of interpretation which is geared more to 'use' than to 'explanation'. To be sure, the interpretation itself probably will not actually be the use. But the interpretation should be devised in such a way that it lends itself readily for use in the shaping of identity.

Let me illustrate through the telling of a story: when God planted the Garden of Eden and formed *ha 'adam* from the dust of the ground, God took the inanimate glob of clay which he had shaped and blew into the human's lifeless nostrils the breath of life until it became a living thing. Then God, after determining that the human should not remain alone, set about to create a helper fit for him. So God created a series of animals in sequence and brought each one to the human to name. Then God put the human to sleep, opened him up, took out a rib, and made the rib into a woman. 'At last!' cried the man. 'Bone of my bone, flesh of my flesh...'

This narrative is a good story indeed. One can identify with the characters and with what happens. One can identify with the solitary human's need for a companion and with his appreciation of a female companion and the community of marriage (Gen. 2.24). Moreover, as the story goes on and the snake declares that they won't die from eating of the forbidden fruit because God wants to keep wisdom for himself by preventing Adam and Eve from becoming godlike (3.5), one can appreciate the woman's calculation—how desirable was the tree for food, how delightful to the eyes, and how desirable to eat and become wise. So the woman took fruit and ate and gave to her husband who also ate.

One can appreciate also their hiding when God came to walk in the garden. God called to the man, 'Where are you?' 'I heard your sound in the garden and I was afraid because I was naked.' 'Who told you that you were naked? Did you eat of the tree from which I commanded you not to eat?' 'The woman who you gave me, she gave to me from the tree and I ate.' And God said to the woman, 'What have you done?' 'The snake seduced me, and I ate.'

Let us examine what I have just done. First of all, I have told a story. In large measure I have *told* it rather than *explained* it. Even my explanations about what may happen to the hearer in the telling of the story are concerned with the potential use of the narrative for the shaping of identity. This is of the utmost importance. I have not abstracted from the story any concepts. I have developed no concept of God or of sin or of human nature or any other concept. I have simply told the story. I have told it in all its drama because I believe that in the telling of the tale one can enter into the story. Indeed, in the telling of the tale one can gain a symbolic world. One can understand oneself and one's fellow humans as creatures—made by God the way a potter shapes clay. And one's own life-sustaining breath might be seen, in the context of this symbolic world, as God's own breath blown into us humans. In such a symbolic world, one can see life as not one's own but as a gracious gift from God. Or the dilemma whether to obey God and leave the desirable fruit alone can become paradigmatic of a life of obedience. And in the narration of the hiding from God and the shifting of blame when God asks 'Where are you?' and 'What have you done?' one can see oneself and one's fellow humans. Indeed, the use of the Garden story to build a portion of one's self-identity would lead to an identity rather different from one in which humans are seen as autonomous.

A second important point to make is that I have *re*told the story. I included certain things and left others out. I emphasized certain things and de-emphasized others. And I retold in a certain style. I retold the story first of all because I am convinced that any interpretation is in some sense a retelling. No interpretation of a text, no matter how scholarly, reproduces its original meaning. Every reader brings so much to the interpretation of a text that the interpretation is in no small way the creation of the reader.[16] Moreover, use of a text to shape identity

16. S. Fish, *Is There a Text in This Class? The Authority of Interpretive Communities* (Cambridge, MA: Harvard University Press, 1980), pp. 12-14, 153.

locates the text in the life of its user rather than its producer. Indeed, openness to be personally addressed on the part of the user of the text involves openness to the work of the Holy Spirit in the activity both of interpretation and of performative use.

The work of the Spirit enlivens Scripture and its use, 'contemporizing' or 'incarnating' it in the world of its users. Without apology, then, I consciously retold the story of the Garden in a modern North American idiom, with peculiarities of dramatic retelling which seem to be operative in that culture. My somewhat colloquial style, my particular use of humor were designed for performative effect in my culture's modes of hearing. My choices of what to emphasize reflect my intent to touch on the great issues of society, for example, its belief in the self-made person, its refusal to accept limits for human actualization, its tendency to deny authority outside the individual person. In short, my aim was to prepare the 'user' to 'hear'.

So also with Coats. As far as I can see, his interpretation of the shame associated with nakedness as the loss of *interpersonal intimacy* is not explicitly stated in the story.[17] But his interpretation is not only plausible, but also 'usable', that is, capable of speaking powerfully to many in a society preoccupied with intimacy and its fragility. Though his interpretation should be judged a rereading, it is a good one for identity formation.

The supposition that my retelling of the Garden story facilitates personal participation on the part of the reader is insufficient by itself to nurture the formation of Christian identity. Although interpretation that enables personal participation in the biblical tradition is highly important, the identity which takes shape may not necessarily be Jewish or Christian. The identity-formation might be private and not connected to any particular religious community. We must observe, however, that the Garden story is part of a larger body of authoritative traditions which belong to well-established religious communities. This is a critical insight which entails at least the following: (a) that the individual story is part of a larger body of canonical traditions, (b) that this body is constitutive of or in some other way authoritative for certain religious communities, and (c) that a given religious community which has a text may employ it to promote a particular kind of identity which is appropriate to the religious

17. G.W. Coats, *Genesis: With an Introduction to Narrative Literature* (Grand Rapids: Eerdmans, 1983), pp. 43-54.

community in which it is to be used. I have especially in mind differences in uses of Scripture which might be important for Judaism and for Christianity.

a. The Garden story belongs to a larger narrative. This story about disobedience in the Garden and the curses placed upon the snake, the woman,[18] and the man follows a report of blessing pronounced upon the male and the female whom God created (Gen. 1.28).[19] Indeed, the Garden story is part of an unfolding drama of hybris, disobedience, and the resultant imposition of additional curses.[20]

The narrative continues with a dramatic act by God to bring blessing to the human race. God calls Abraham, promises that his offspring will become a great nation, promises to bless him, and promises that all the families of the earth will find blessing in him (Gen. 12.1-3). But Abraham has no child. Yet God promises that this aged man will have descendants as many as the stars of the sky (Gen. 15.5). And Abraham trusts God—an act of faith which is accounted to him as righteousness (Gen. 15.6). Still, how will the child of the promise be born? Not through Hagar (Gen. 16) but by Sarah (Gen. 17.16). And this man of faith falls on his face and laughs: 'Can a son be born to a man who is a hundred? Can Sarah, who is ninety, bear a son?' (Gen. 17.17). Sarah, too, laughs (Gen. 18.12). But God fulfills the promise; these two senior citizens have a son, whose name means 'he laughs'.

Then God commands Abraham to offer up this child for sacrifice (Gen. 22). Though the narrator says nothing explicit about Abraham's feelings about this command, the difficulty of carrying out God's command becomes evident in the wording of the command: 'Take your son, your only son whom you love... and offer him up as a burnt offering...' (v. 2). Abraham, however, voices no objection. An extensive chain of verbs depicts Abraham as responding immediately in faithfulness: He '*got up early* in the morning, *saddled* his ass, *took* two of his young men with him and Isaac his son, *cut* the wood for the burnt offering, *arose*, and *went* to the place of which God had told him'

---

18. But see P. Trible, *God and the Rhetoric of Sexuality* (Philadelphia: Fortress Press, 1978), p. 126.

19. See the discussion about the role of blessing in the succession of generations by C. Westermann, *Genesis 1–11: A Commentary* (trans. J.J. Scullion; Minneapolis: Augsburg, 1984), pp. 160-61.

20. C. Westermann, *The Promises to the Fathers: Studies on the Patriarchal Narratives* (trans. D.E. Green; Philadelphia: Fortress Press, 1980), pp. 50-56.

(v. 3), and he spoke not a word to anyone.[21] It was Isaac who first spoke: 'O my father, look, the fire and the wood, but where is the lamb for a burnt offering?' (v. 7). Said Abraham, 'God will find for himself the lamb for a burnt offering' (v. 8). Abraham knew not what offering God would supply; for all he knew it would be Isaac. So in utter faithfulness he bound Isaac upon the altar and took the knife to kill his son, to be stopped only by the messenger of Yahweh.

Faith as portrayed in the entire Abraham narrative depicts a complex journey indeed. It begins with trust in an almost-unbelievable promise. For an aged man who has not even one child to have faith in a promise of descendants as many as the stars in the sky is a momentous act of trust. Yet that same man falls on his face and laughs in disbelief. But he can also behave in complete faithfulness, as the journey to sacrifice his son makes evident. A faith-identity modeled on the Abraham narrative would understand the meaningfulness of praying, 'Lord, I believe; help thou my unbelief'. Could not such a narrative powerfully function to shape one's journey of faith? Could not a literary study which interprets the narrative in this way be an important source for the performative function of the text in the formation of someone's faith journey?

The curses of the story of the Garden, then, belong to the promise of blessing in Genesis 12, and the narrative of the disobedience of Adam and Eve belongs to the story of faith in Genesis 12–25. But there still is more: the story moves from Abraham and Isaac on to Jacob, and then to Joseph, and on to Moses, and then to Joshua, and to Judges, and to the narrative of the Israelite monarchy, which ends with the exile of Babylon. Yet the context is still larger: each biblical text is commonly used as a part of a canon of Scripture, whether the canon of the Jewish community or one of the canons employed in Christian communities.

b. The employment of Scripture in the shaping of identity characteristically involves the use of the Bible as authoritative for persons in religious communities. Scripture as a whole—the particular canon which is operative in a given community—may be said to be constitutive of the community in which it is used. These communities are constituted by Scripture in the sense that the existence, faith, and practice of these communities are rooted in and authorized by Scripture. My

---

21. C. Westermann, *Genesis 12–26: A Commentary* (trans. J.J. Scullion; Minneapolis: Augsburg, 1985), p. 358.

intent here is not to privilege the traditional Protestant principle of *sola scriptura*. Indeed, I take quite seriously the authority of post-biblical tradition in both Judaism and Christianity, and I recognize also the activity of the Spirit working with ecclesiastical authorities in the ongoing life of the community (though there is disagreement as to how post-biblical tradition and ecclesiastical judgments are to be weighed).[22] Scripture is foundational for these communities nonetheless; other authoritative traditions and decisions which guide communities' life and practice are generally seen as rooted in or at least consistent with Scripture.

Even though it is quite true that everything in a canon of Scripture has status as constitutive literature for the community in which it is used, differences in genre and diversity of usage mean that, in practice, constitution of a community's identity is not the only usage to which Scripture may be put. As James Ware has shown,[23] Scripture may be used to praise or lament; it may be employed to strengthen the bond between God and people (e.g., calls to repentance, renewing of covenants); it may be used to prescribe behavior (e.g., commands, exhortations); it may indeed be used in many ways—too numerous to catalogue here. Constitutive usage is but one of various potential functions of Scripture, important though it is.

How then can we identity a constitutive text? Not by its genre but by its use (though type may well be related to potential function). Constitutive texts, says Ware, are texts which are used to shape the basic identity of the community. Texts such as the following might be critical for the community's identity-formation: narratives which are foundational for the community's existence, for example, narratives of creation, of patriarchs, of Exodus from Egypt, of the making of the covenant and the giving of the law (basic to Jewish identity). Jesus Christ is so central to Christianity that the Gospels and some of the epistles are surely basic in the formation of the identity of the Christian community. Because usage is more fundamental than genre, a given text might be capable of functioning in more than one way, for example, both for bonding and for constitutive purposes, or both for

22. See S. Hauerwas, *Unleashing the Scripture: Freeing the Bible from Captivity to America* (Nashville: Abingdon, 1993), pp. 19-28.

23. J.H. Ware, Jr, 'Biblical Theology, Hermeneutics, and the World of God' (unpublished paper presented to the American Academy of Religion, Southwestern Division, meeting in Dallas, Texas, 18 March, 1994).

prescriptive and for constitutive purposes.

c.   How Scripture can be used to facilitate the formation of identity depends in no small measure on the particular religious community and its construal of Scripture. Let us consider, for example, possible uses of the near-sacrifice of Isaac in Genesis 22. Although perhaps few would sharply disagree with my reading of this story, many might come to see that more needs to be said. Yes, Abraham's faith is being tested; yes, Abraham answers immediately in response to God; yes, Abraham without delay does the necessary deeds of preparation; yes, Abraham trusts God to provide the sacrifice; yes, Abraham lays his son upon the altar and prepares to use the knife. That Abraham is portrayed as faithful almost no one would disagree. But what more may be said? Jews might well see in the faithful Abraham one who obeys God's command—a spiritual equivalent of one who observes torah faithfully. Christians might see instead one whose faith in God leads to willing sacrifice—a spiritual equivalent of one who loses self and bears the cross. In using the self-same story, Jews and Christians may build a different edifice. In using the self-same story, two different religious communities will encourage the formation of somewhat different ways of being in the world.

What then shall we say? That 'Tanakh' and 'Old Testament' are not the same? Or better put: are the tasks of interpreting 'Tanakh' and 'Old Testament' somewhat different?[24] I say yes. Not completely different, but still distinct. That Judaism and Christianity share a heritage is by no means insignificant. That both groups share a heritage should never be forgotten, or even placed on a distant shelf. But the fact remains that Christians have used their 'Old Testament' in ways that differ from Judaism's use of 'Tanakh'. The story which Christians tell is somewhat different from the story told by Jews. The story Christians tell finds its fulfillment in Jesus Christ, whereas Moses is more central to the story told in Judaism.

As essay by Walther Zimmerli is relevant in the discussion of these matters.[25] He argues that the language of promise was of great impor-

---

24. See essays in R. Brooks and J.J. Collins (eds.), *Hebrew Bible or Old Testament: Studying the Bible in Judaism and Christianity* (Notre Dame, IN: University of Notre Dame Press, 1990).

25. W. Zimmerli, 'Promise and Fulfillment' (trans. J. Wharton), in C. Westermann (ed.), *Essays on Old Testament Hermeneutics* (Richmond, VA: John Knox, 1963), pp. 89-122.

tance in the shaping of Judaism and Christianity. Promises, he contends, are not 'soothsaying words', that is, true or false. They are rather performative utterances which shape communities of faith over the course of history. They are constantly reinterpreted. Indeed, a promise once fulfilled may well retain its force as promise. The promise of the land, fulfilled in the early Israelite occupation in Canaan, became promise once again when Israel was exiled to Babylon. Again and again over the long history of the Jews in diaspora, the promise once fulfilled retained its force as promise.

The most original connotations of a promise and its subsequent interpretations are often not the same. Surely the biblical authors did not imagine the ways in which the promises they uttered would later be reinterpreted. Analogously, I did not anticipate at my wedding in 1958 how in 1994 I would interpret the promises made then. Are my present interpretations of the promises uttered then invalid because they do not 'mean' what they 'meant' when first they were spoken? Such restriction of meaning would violate the very nature of promise-making and construal of fulfillment.

In a recent book on Paul's use of Scripture, Richard B. Hays recognizes quite clearly the differences between original meanings and Paul's construal of meaning.[26] Paul sees Scripture, Hays contends, as a story of election and promise—a story in which the promises of God are said to be fulfilled in the crucified and risen messiah, Jesus. All God's past involvement with Israel as told in Scripture points to the time of fulfillment in the apocalyptic new age ushered in through Christ's death and resurrection.[27] Although the *distinction* between past and present is not obliterated, the *distance* between past and present is collapsed as the testimonies of the past are brought near to speak to the church in the present.[28] Scripture must therefore be construed in such a way that it speaks to Christian experience.

Paul's use of Scripture is normally not literal but figurative instead— to *prefigure* that Christian experience. In Galatians 3, for example, Paul argues that Scripture, '*fore*seeing that God justifies the Gentiles through faith, *pre*preached the gospel to Abraham', so that in him all

---

26. R.B. Hays, *Echoes of Scripture in the Letters of Paul* (New Haven: Yale University Press, 1989).

27. Hays, *Echoes*, p. 105.

28. Hays, *Echoes*, p. 177.

Gentiles would be blessed (Gal. 3.8, as translated by Hays).[29] It is Scripture *quasi-personified*, Hays argues, which speaks to Abraham—in its *pre*-proclaiming the gospel to Abraham—who is presented, not so much as a past historical figure, but rather as a character 'inscribed' in a story.[30] Moreover, Paul's view of the word to Abraham as pre-preaching is a retrospective reading rooted in the perception of the promise as fulfilled in the church.[31]

Paul rereads Scripture in such a way that those who live by faith are children of Abraham (Gal. 3.7). The Genesis text itself (Gen. 12.10-13) does not indicate that the Gentiles who receive blessing through Abraham are Abraham's children; it is Paul who reads Scripture this way. And in such a reading, Abraham becomes a figurative father of Gentiles who are justified by faith. Indeed, as Hays interprets, Paul's use of Scripture is again and again figurative. His typologies involve 'imaginative correlations', so that the church achieves its identity in relation to Israel's sacred story; but the 'full significance' of that biblical story becomes understood when read 'in relation to God's unfolding design for salvation of Gentiles in the Church'.[32]

Space forbids the full discussion which Hays's book so richly deserves. Whatever one thinks of some of the particulars of his argument, his proposal that Christians read Scripture as 'participants in the eschatological drama of salvation' suggests the need to reread Scripture figuratively as Christians locate their lives in its story.[33] Jesus Christ is paradigmatic for the story Christians tell. If one 'uses' the text rather than simply 'explaining' the text in order to locate one's life within the Christian biblical story, one is not held captive by the 'rules' of historical criticism. Nor is the scholar who wishes to aid and abet such use of Scripture fettered to such rules. Such a scholar may follow 'rules' of scholarly analysis which facilitate the use of the text in the shaping of personal identity. A scholar dedicated to such a task, though open to historical criticism when it can be used to further the scholar's theological purposes, must preserve the freedom to construct figurative readings of Old Testament texts to the end that people might use the text to locate their identity within the Christian story. This is why

29. Hays, *Echoes*, p. 105.
30. Hays, *Echoes*, p. 106.
31. Hays, *Echoes*, p. 107.
32. Hays, *Echoes*, pp. 100-101.
33. Hays, *Echoes*, pp. 185-86.

I did not hesitate above to portray the faithful Abraham as a prefiguration of the Christian who takes up the cross. Nor would I shrink, in reading Exodus 1–2, from construing the defenseless Israelites who could foil Pharaoh only by quietly copulating in their homes, the powerless midwives who had nothing but the power of their wits, and the impotent babe in the bulrushes who had no defense apart from a flimsy 'ark' (*teba*) as prefigurations of God's use of what is weak in the world to shame the strong (1 Cor. 1.27)—even as a prefiguration of Christ Jesus who did not grasp at equality with God, but took instead the form of a servant (Phil. 2.5-11).

4. *Performative Hermeneutics and the Role of the Scholar*

I argued above that use of Scripture for the purpose of shaping Christian identity has more to do with performative use of Scripture than with explanation of textual meaning. I further proposed that an important task for Christian biblical scholarship is to interpret the Bible in such a way that performative uses of Scripture might better be grounded in competent biblical interpretation. Yet I maintained that scholarly interpretation is not itself necessarily a performative activity of identity-formation.

How are such scholarly interpretations and performative uses of Scripture both different and interrelated? The scholar's task is one of critical reflection for the sake of bringing hermeneutical, exegetical, and theological insights to bear on performative use of Scripture, while the performative task is the actual use of the Bible in the shaping of identity. The two tasks are so closely interrelated that it may not always be easy to distinguish which is being done. For example, the retelling of stories earlier in this essay might seem to be homiletical and therefore performative in character. Yet such acts of storytelling may be built upon and guided by scholarly reflection about structure, plot, and the like, as well as by careful hermeneutical and theological choices as to how the story is to be retold.

Much of the scholarly task, as I conceptualize it, will seem familiar. An entire box full of tools of literary analysis—including approaches widely known among historical critics—are available to the scholar to be employed in a critical fashion. But because the ultimate goal of the interpretive task sketched out here is for performative use in the present, a hermeneutic limited to replication of the past would not adequately serve the particular purposes for which interpretation is undertaken.

Because the church can scarcely avoid sometimes reading its 'Old Testament' as typological literature in which the church's experience is somehow prefigured, what texts might be interpreted to 'mean' cannot be limited to what they originally 'meant'. Such re-readings need not be uncritical; theologically responsible biblical scholarship could contribute much by attempting to develop hermeneutical 'rules' appropriate for interpretation designed to facilitate Christian identity. Rereading under the guidance of the Spirit need not necessarily be considered a non-scholarly enterprise. On the contrary, responsible Christian hermeneutics and biblical interpretation is itself a manifestation of the work of the Spirit.

Alas, I must close with much insufficiently explained. In particular, what 'rules' for rereading need to be developed for the church in a post-modern world cannot yet be adequately articulated, for we are still halfway-fettered to the Enlightenment even as we move into a new cultural epoch. But as I myself try to carve out a path in the partial darkness, two things seem clear. First, that we can make sense of no text whatever apart from 'rules' of reading which we and our interpretive communities bring to the text; we can never read from some neutral stance untainted by ourselves and our reading communities. And, second, no text, used canonically, can properly be interpreted without concern for its present significance for the faith community. Although Christian Old Testament hermeneutics need not necessarily imitate Hays or even be enslaved to Paul, we must nonetheless struggle for responsible ways to read and use 'Old Testament' as Christian Scripture.

BIBLIOGRAPHY OF WORKS BY GEORGE WESLEY COATS, JR

Books

Rebellion in the Wilderness: The Murmuring Motif in the Wilderness Traditions of the Old Testament (Nashville and New York: Abingdon, 1968).

From Canaan to Egypt: Structural and Theological Context for the Joseph Story (Washington, DC: Catholic Biblical Association, 1976).

(ed. with Burke O. Long) *Canon and Authority: Essays in Old Testament Religion and Theology* (Philadelphia: Fortress Press, 1977).

Genesis (FOTL; Grand Rapids: Eerdmans, 1983).

(ed.) *Saga, Legend, Tale, Novella, Fable: Narrative Genres in Old Testament Literature* (JSOTSup, 35; Sheffield: JSOT Press, 1985).

Moses: Heroic Man, Man of God: The Moses Traditions in the Old Testament (JSOTSup, 57; Sheffield: JSOT Press, 1989).

Essays

'The King's Loyal Opposition: Obedience and Authority in the Moses Tradition', in G.W. Coats and B.O. Long (eds.), *Canon and Authority: Essays in Old Testament Religion and Theology* (Philadelphia: Fortress Press, 1977), pp. 91-109.

'Strife without Reconciliation: A Narrative Theme in the Jacob Traditions', in R. Albertz (ed.), *Werden und Wirken des Alten Testaments: Festschrift für Claus Westermann* (Göttingen: Vandenhoeck & Ruprecht, 1980), pp. 82-106.

'The Curse in God's Blessing: Structure and Theology in the Tradition, in J. Jeremias and L. Perlitt (eds.), *Die Botschaft und die Boten: Festschrift für Hans Walter Wolff* (Neukirchen–Vluyn: Neukirchener Verlag, 1981), pp. 31-41.

'Humility and Honor: A Moses Legend in Numbers 12', in D.J.A. Clines, D.M. Gunn and A.J. Hauser (eds.), *Art and Meaning: Rhetoric in Biblical Literature* (JSOTSup, 19; Sheffield: JSOT Press, 1982), pp. 91-107.

'Patterns and Directions for Old Testament Theology', in G.M. Tucker and D. Knight (eds.), *The Hebrew Bible and its Modern Interpreters* (Philadelphia: Fortress Press, 1985), pp. 239-62.

'Lot: A Foil in the Abraham Saga', in J.T. Butler, E.W. Conrad and B.C. Ottenberger (eds.), *Understanding the Word: Essays in Honor of Bernhard W. Anderson* (JSOTSup, 37; Sheffield: JSOT Press, 1985), pp. 113-32.

Articles

'The Traditio-Historical Character of the Reed Sea Motif', *VT* 17 (1967), pp. 253-65.

'Despoiling the Egyptians', *VT* 18 (1968), pp. 451-57.

'The Song of the Sea', *CBQ* 31 (1969), pp. 1-17.

'History and Revelation: The Reed Sea Event', *Lexington Theological Quarterly* 4 (1969), pp. 22-32.
'Self-Abasement and Insult Formulas', *JBL* 89 (1970), pp. 14-26.
'The Wilderness Itinerary', *CBQ* 34 (1972), pp. 135-52.
'A Structural Transition in Exodus', *VT* 22 (1972), pp. 129-42.
'Widow's Rights: A Crux in the Structure of Genesis 38', *CBQ* 34 (1972), pp. 461-66.
'To Divide or Not to Divide: Reflections on Methodology for Source Criticism', *Hebrew Abstracts* 13 (1972).
'An Exposition for the Wilderness Traditions', *VT* 22 (1972), pp. 288-95.
'Moses in Midian', *JBL* 92 (1973), pp. 3-10.
'The Joseph Story and Ancient Wisdom: A Reappraisal', *CBQ* 35 (1973), pp. 285-97.
'Abraham's Sacrifice of Faith: A Form-Critical Exegesis of Gen. 22', *Int* 27 (1973), pp. 389-400.
'Balaam: Saint or Sinner?', *BR* 18 (1973), pp. 21-29.
'Redactional Unity in Genesis 37–50', *JBL* 93 (1974), pp. 15-21.
'History and Theology in the Sea Tradition', *ST* 29 (1975), pp. 53-62.
'The Death of God: Power and Obedience in the Primeval History', *Int* 29 (1975), pp. 227-39.
'On Narrative Criticism', *Semeia* 3 (1975), pp. 137-41.
'On Divine and Human Causation: A Response to David R. Griffin, Relativism, Divine Causation, and Biblical Theology', *Encounter* 26 (1975).
'Death and Dying in Old Testament Tradition', *Lexington Theological Quarterly* 11 (1976), pp. 9-14.
'Conquest Traditions in the Wilderness Theme', *JBL* 95 (1976), pp. 177-90.
'Legendary Motifs in the Moses Death Reports', *CBQ* 39 (1977), pp. 34-44.
'The Yahwist as Theologian: A Critical Reflection', *JSOT* 3 (1977), pp. 28-32.
'Vocational Identity in Ancient Entertainment Circles', *Lexington Theological Quarterly* 13 (1978), pp. 39-47.
'Strife and Reconciliation: Themes of a Biblical Theology in the Book of Genesis', *Horizons* 2 (1980).
'Parable, Fable, and Anecdote: Storytelling in the Succession Narrative', *Int* 35 (1981), pp. 368-82.
'The Way of Obedience: Exegetical and Hermeneutical Perspectives on the Balaam Story', *Semeia* 24 (1982), pp. 53-79.
'Melanoia in Ancient Israel: Clues for Unity and Change', *Mid-stream* 23 (1984).
'Exposition for the Conquest Theme', *CBQ* 47 (1985), pp. 47-54.
'The Ark of the Covenant: A Probe into the History of Tradition', *HAR* 9 (1985), pp. 137-57.
'2 Sam. 12: An Exposition', *Int* 40 (1986), pp. 170-75.
'The Failure of the Hero: Moses as a Model for Ministry', *Asbury Theological Quarterly* 41 (1986), pp. 15-22.
'The Book of Joshua: Heroic Saga or Conquest Theme?', *JSOT* 38 (1987), pp. 15-32.
'Another Form-Critical Problem of the Hexateuch', *Semeia* 46 (1989), pp. 65-73.

INDEX OF AUTHORS

JOURNAL FOR THE STUDY OF THE OLD TESTAMENT
SUPPLEMENT SERIES